Reimagining Theology for Postcolonial Africa

© 2019 Jacob Kimathi Samuel

Published by Borderless Press
Phoenixville, Pennsylvania
www.borderlesspress.com
info@borderlesspress.com

Design by Melody Stanford Martin

All rights reserved. No part of this book may be reproduced or transmitted in any form or by any means, electronic or mechanical, including photocopy, recording, or any information storage and retrieval system, without prior permission from the publisher, except by a retriever who may quote brief passages in articles or reviews.

Although every precaution has been taken to verify the accuracy of the information contained herein, the author and publisher assume no responsibility for any errors or omissions. No liability is assumed for damages that may result from the use of information contained within.

ISBN-13: 978-1-7331221-0-8
ISBN-10: 1-7331221-0-9

First edition

Printed in the United States of America

Re-Imagining Theology for Postcolonial Africa

A CASE STUDY OF THE KENYAN AKŪRINŪ CHURCH

Jacob Kimathi Samuel

*To my wife Florence Mukwanyaga Kimathi,
our daughter, Neema Ntinyari Kimathi,
and our son Keith Karani Kimathi*

Contents

Foreword v
Acknowledgments vii
Abbreviations. xi

INTRODUCTION . . . . **xiii**
Aims of This Book xiii
Main Dialogue Partners xv
Significance of This Study xxi

**ONE. CONTINUITY OR DISCONTINUITY —
ANALYSIS OF EMMANUEL KATONGOLE AND
KWAME BEDIAKO'S THEOLOGY** 1
Understanding New Ecclesial Movements 2
Emmanuel Katongole's Vision of a New Social Imagination for Africa . . 6
The Lingering Western Legacy on Social Imagination in Africa 13
Katongole and A Reticent Activist Church 15
The Church as an Alternative Route in Gleaning for a
New African Social Imagination 18
The Role of Indigenous Cultures in Social Imagination 21

Kwame Bediako's Search for African Christian Identity 25
Kwame H. Bediako's Search for African Christian Identity........... 32
The Primal Factor in African Religious Heritage 37
The Translatability of the Gospel 43
A Theological Framework for Understanding Culture 47
Conclusion 53

TWO. THE EMERGENCE AND GROWTH OF
AKŨRINŨ CHURCH MOVEMENT 57

Early Portuguese Travelers and Explorers to the
East Coast of Africa 57

The Coming of Modern Protestant Missions to the
East Coast of Africa 59

The Movement of Gospel from the East Coast of Africa
to the Interior of East Africa..................................... 62

The Growth of African Indigenous Churches (AICs) 64

    Indigenous Christianity in Western Kenya...................... 65

    Indigenous Christianity in Central Kenya...................... 66

The Socio-Cultural Background of the
Emergence of the Akũrinũ Church............................... 69

An Introduction to the Agĩkũyũ People 71

    The Cosmology of the Agĩkũyũ people 72

    The Traditional Culture of Agĩkũyũ people 74

    The Religion of the Agĩkũyũ people 74

    The God of Agĩkũyũ... 75

    Sacrifices in Agĩkũyũ Religion 78

    Priesthood in Agĩkũyũ Traditional Culture..................... 80

    The Tribal Organization or Political Life of the Agĩkũyũ 86

    The Traditional Education of the Agĩkũyũ People............... 89

    The Sexual Life of the Agĩkũyũ people......................... 92

European Inverted Hospitality.................................. 93

The Conflict Between the Agĩkũyũ and the Missionaries............98
The Birth of the Akũrinũ Church.................................103
Ecclesiology of the Akũrinũ Church..............................117
Akũrinũ Church Today..121
Conclusion..123

THREE. *AKŨRINŨ* VERNACULAR THEOLOGY: DATA ANALYSIS, FINDINGS, AND DISCUSSIONS..........127

Factors That Led to the Birth of the Akũrinũ Church.............128
The Major Teachings of the Akũrinũ Church.......................131
    Akũrinũ Pneumatology..131
    Akũrinũ Music and Worship (Liturgy).........................137
    Akũrinũ Teaching and the Ministry of the Word...............140
    Spiritual and Literal Interpretation of the Bible...........141
    Millennial or Eschatological Preaching and Living...........146
    Healing in the Akũrinũ Church...............................148
    The Basis of Faith Healing in the Akũrinũ Churches..........153
    The Role of the Bible in Healing............................155
    The Healing Procedure in the Akũrinũ Churches...............156
        Akũrinũ Childbirth and Baby Dedication..................159
        Akũrinũ Baptism and Its Origin..........................161
Akũrinũ Vernacular Theology as an Encounter of the Gospel with the Culture in the Formation of a New Community...........163
    The Akũrinũ New Church Community............................165
    Akũrinũ Church Organizational Structure.....................167
    The Akũrinũ Church Courtship and Marriage Procedures........171
    Akũrinũ Esteem for a Holy Wedding...........................173
    Circumcision Ritual Among the Akũrinũ.......................174
    Taboo Observance and Practices in the Akũrinũ Church........177
The Possible Sources of the Akũrinũ Vernacular Theology.........186

The Socio-Political and Socio-Economic Encounter of the
Agĩkũyũ and the European Colonialist and Missionaries. 190

The Church Tradition from the Interaction of the Akũrinũ
Founders and the Historical or Missionary Church 200

Conclusion 201

FOUR. AKŨRINŨ VERNACULAR THEOLOGY AND IT'S CONTRIBUTION TO GLOBAL THEOLOGY 203

Africans' Unique Spirituality. 203

A Shared Approach to Theological Reflection 206

Developing Culturally-Based Morality 211

Development of Authentic Ecclesiologies 219

Conclusion 221

FIVE. Conclusion and Recommendations 223

Theology of Culture 225

Integrative Value of Culture 228

The Functions of Culture 231

Reflexivity in Human Cultures, the Roadmap from
Contextualization to Contextual Theologies 234

Recommendations 241

Conclusion 243

Bibliography. 247

Index 255

Foreword

Borderless Press is a knowledge Activist charitable publishing organization. We operate with an understanding that knowledge production, distribution, and consumption have, for the longest time, privileged the Minority World (Europe and USA) scholars and writers at the expense of the Majority World (Africa, Asia, and Latin America). Consequently, our pubclications are works primarily written by Majority World scholars and knowledge activists. Like all academic publishers, we are committed to rigorous peer-review processes, celebrating scholarship that makes important contributions to academic discourse. Beyond this tradition, we seek to decolonize knowledge production and distribution through equality, creativity, and justice. This focus guides us not only in manuscript selection, but also in the ways we approach our work and organizational structures. Our authors:

- Choose the language in which they seek to write and publish their book and
- Collaborate with us on all publishing decisions

Most of our books are published through generous financial donations. Postcolonial Networks (PN) and Borderless Press (BP) would like to thank our donors for making it possible for us to publish our books. For this book, please join me to offer special thanks to Dr. Joe Duggan, founder of PN and BP for sponsoring its publication

Thank you for supporting our work and the work of our authors. All inquiries should be addressed to Dr. R.S. Wafula at drwafula@borderless-press.com.

Acknowledgments

This manuscript is the product of many years of research and writing. First, I thank God who saved me early, at the age of 7, and has led my life in a unique way, opening doors for me to study at the highest level of education. Many times, I felt the sense of the guidance, the leading, and the provision of the Lord in writing this book. If only this work could leave behind a footprint to guide the next generation, is all I pray.

I also thank Profs. William Dyrness and James Nkansah-Obrempong who guided the earlier version of this work from scratch to the end during my doctoral years. Their patience and valuable suggestions are highly appreciated. The entire Africa International University (AIU) fraternity was part of this process. I would like to offer special thanks to the university scholarship office that sourced funds for my studies. In this regard, I would like to thank the Vivends, the Overseas Council, The Mylne Trust, and Nairobi Evangelical Graduate School of Theology (NEGST) who combined efforts and availed funds for my studies. The head of library, Dr. Mudave and the entire library team supported this work especially towards the homestretch by providing me with a laptop when I lost mine to carjackers. All my professors; Prof. William Dyrness, Dr. Grace Dyrness, Prof. Professor James Nkansah-Obrempong, Prof. Yusufu

Turaki, Prof. Veli-Matti Kaerkkaeinen, Prof. Paul Gifford, Prof. Bernard Boyo, Prof. David Fraser and many others not included in this list, yet were very vital in the making of this scholar, I truly salute you all. To my research assistant, Lilian Mugure Maina, you are a part of this work and may God keep you close to his heart always. My readers, Christine Ndolo and Everlyn Gitau; may God remember your passion and commitment. My classmates in the PhD Theology class of 2012, especially Josephine Munyao, with whom I determined to soldier on in the face of setbacks, you have all greatly added value to this work.

I thank my employer; Christ is the Answer Ministries (CITAM) whose office time was shared with my studies. My Bishop, Rev. Dr. David Oginde, my immediate supervisor Rev. Kennedy Kimiwye and all my pastoral colleagues, all who rejoiced at this work by cheering me on — may God bless you all. I particularly single out my colleague Rev. Dr. Thuo Mbuuru and Deputy Senior Pastor, CITAM-Valley Road, for introducing me to many Akũrinũ leaders and scholars, who have been valuable in providing the data that has informed the writing of this book.

To my mother Lillian Nkirote Mugambi: I always know that you pray for me and you believe in me. Your sacrifices have brought me this far. To my late father Samuel Mugambi: You died too soon to share this joy with me, but I always know that I have inherited resilience and good demeanor from you. To my siblings, Helen Gaceri, James Gichuru, Fredrick Muriungi, Jane Kathambi (late), and Robert Muchai and your families: You are all great assets in my life.

And finally, to my wife, Florence Kimathi: You have been a partner and a fellow sufferer in this journey. To my daughter Neema, you have admired this work and even accompanied me in some of my research trips. My son Keith you always understood even when I couldn't create time to play with you and pray for you before bedtime.

I would be remiss if I don't mention the sheer dedication of the Borderless Press team for the publication of this work. Without their efforts, this book would never have seen the light of day. My special thanks to Dr. RS Wafula, the publisher at Borderless Press for accepting my work for publication. Thanks to Dr. John Ndavula, the Acquisitions Editor who initially approved my work for publication. I appreciate Dr. Andrew Mbuvi, the Managing Editor who did a fantastic job guiding me through the intricacies of publication. My thanks to Melody Stanford, my gifted cover designer and production editor. She is the best in her class of work. Finally, I would like to thank Dr. Joe Duggan, the founder of Borderless Press for paying for the costs of publishing my work.

I may not have mentioned all who were instrumental to this journey. Yet God will richly bless you for any part, great or small that you have played in this process. All that I can say is, "I am because you are, and because you are, so I am" (John Mbiti).

Abbreviations

AICs — African Indigenous Churches. The 'I' has represented different things to different scholars such as Independent, Instituted, Initiated, and even International. These are basically churches that were started by Africans themselves as opposed to historical missionary churches.

AIU — Africa International University

ATR — African Tradition Religion

CITAM — Christ is The Answer Ministries

CMS — Church Mission Society

KCA — Kikuyu Central Association

KISA — Kikuyu Independent Schools Association

MCK — Methodist Church of Kenya

NEGST — Nairobi Evangelical Graduate School of Theology

AIU — African International University

NEMA — National Environment Management Authority

NT — New Testament

OT — Old Testament

OAIC — Organization for African Indigenous Churches

UoN — University of Nairobi

ACCS — African Christian Church Schools

ABC — African Brotherhood Church

RQs — Research Questions

GCACA — General Conference of the *Akũrinũ* Churches Assembly

INTRODUCTION

Aims of This Book

The *Akũrinũ* church is an indigenous church movement that offers many important cultural lessons for the larger Church. In spite of this, the *Akũrinũ* church has largely been shunned and ignored by many Kenyan Christians. With their distinct dress code of neatly arranged head gear on unkempt beards for men, and long white dresses often dotted with red crosses for women, many have erroneously called this church movement a sect or even a cult. This stereotyping has inhibited any substantial theological engagement from mainline churches and theologians. For that reason, this research is an attempt to explore the vernacular theology of the *Akũrinũ* church and the possible fresh contribution that such a theology can offer to the growing search for authentic African theology.

William Dyrness defines vernacular theology as "the theological framework, often formed intuitively by Christians seeking to respond faithfully to the challenges that their lives present to them. It is the kind of theology people commonly do as part of their everyday lives. Such a people's theology tends to respond to very specific and concrete issues."[1]

The nature of theology from the Majority-World church, unlike in the West, tends to be more mission oriented, that is, closer to the real-life situations of the people whose lives God has touched. Often, such a theology is oral and communicated directly to the people, so that the Biblical passage is related directly to the daily problems and challenges of the people.[2] This is the kind of theology that one would expect from the Akũrinũ church. Though the Akũrinũ theology is not found in theological treatises, yet, it exists. If theology is a reflection of people's beliefs about God's presence among them, then all people have a theology. It would be futile to say that Africans or any other people do not have a theology because they do not have it in a written text. Moreover, comparing a people's theology such as the Akũrinũ's with Western theology, or dismissing their theology simply because it cannot be articulated in the category of Western epistemology and idiom would be inaccurate. Dyrness explains that,

> Often it is said that this or that group "has no theology." Now if this is taken to mean that this community has written no theological treatise, or has no theologically trained spokespeople, then it may be accurate. But if it is meant to imply this community has no framework or systematic understanding of their faith, it is clearly false.[3]

Another fundamental fallacy — the reverse of the first fallacy — is to expect Western theology to meet Africa's theological needs. As this research will demonstrate, people develop their own theology that is congruent to their context — seeking to discover how God addresses

---

1. William Dyrness, *Invitation to Cross-Cultural Theology: Case Studies in Vernacular Theologies* (Grand Rapids, MI: Zondervan, 1992), 16.

2. Dyrness, *Cross-Cultural Theology*, 16.

3. Ibid., 31.

or fails to address their circumstance. The Western historical circumstances and those of Africans are different, and consequently, their way of theological reflection is expected to be different[4].

Consequently, Dyrness argues that Western theology is "a particular understanding of the Gospel, and therefore a discipline of theology, [that] has grown up in the West under the influence of Greek philosophy and our interaction with that philosophy."[5] In contrast, vernacular theology is the basic theology that is common to all believers. This kind of theology is gleaned in the Christian music and art, preaching, the devotional life, testimonies, Christian rituals, and day to day Christian sharing. In this book, I will seek to discover and critically assess the vernacular theology of Akũrinũ church. Specifically, I will be looking to explore Akũrinũ's worship, organization, and community life and especially as they relate to the residue of their Agĩkũyũ traditional culture.

Main Dialogue Partners

Broadly speaking, the two most discernable approaches to African theology have been the political and cultural implications of Christianity to Africans. Most of the other approaches are mainly an elaboration of these.[6] This book has referred to a number of theological frameworks for African Christian theology that have emerged in the last seventy years — which this research will refer to simply as African theology. My particular approach is the cultural implications of theology. John Parratt explains

---

4. Ibid., 18: "Western theology is itself a reflection of its Western cultural and historical setting, and thereby cannot possibly meet the needs of the vastly different settings of Third World [or better put, Majority-world] churches — though it certainly may contribute to theological reflection in those settings."

5. Dyrness, *Cross-Cultural Theology*, 18.

6. John Parratt, ed., *A Reader in African Christian Theology* (London: SPCK, 1997), 4: "The two chief concerns of theology in Africa are, therefore, on the one hand its relationship to political power, and on the other hand its relationship to African culture."

the following distinction: unlike the political approach to theology that seeks to relate the political power to theology, the cultural approach to theology's main concern is the relationship between the Christian faith and African culture and tradition.[7] This approach begins from the conviction that all cultures are God-given and are part of the natural revelation of God to humankind — though all are disordered by the fall to a greater or lesser extent. African culture, far from being 'pagan' or 'satanic', provides a genuine, even if limited, knowledge of God. It must be regarded as a preparation for the gospel (see Paul's speeches in Acts 14:15, 17 and 17: 22-31), though not salvific.[8]

Parrett further states that the aim of the cultural approach to theology, then, has been to examine traditional concepts sympathetically, and to show the insights gained from them to make biblical ideas more real to Africans' experience. This type of approach has commonly been called 'adoptionism' or 'adaptationism', (two terms that pre-date and stem from inculturation, a concept that largely grew from Vatican II and are fast fading from theological discourse), because it seeks to adapt traditional ideas in such a way that they may be helpful in illuminating the Christian faith[9].

The present research commences on the presumption that God is present in all cultures and, because of this, human beings can learn some wisdom from culture and hopefully hear God's voice. God is in the business of establishing God's kingdom over all human habitation. Therefore, a gospel message mediated through the structures of culture is more likely to make a permanent imprint on people because it touches on every aspect of life and involves majority of people within their life context by transforming their worldview.

---

7. Ibid.
8. Ibid.
9. Ibid., 7.

The exploration in the present study has been done in dialogue with two leading contemporary voices in the theology of culture, Kwame Bediako and Emmanuel Katongole. Their dealing with the question of culture, how it aids or hinders a new social imagination in Africa, will prepare the background for the discussion of the Akũrinũ Church vernacular theology, as an example of how people's social imagination, grounded on their cultural worldview, gives them tools that aid them in understanding and meeting their socio-economic and socio-political needs within their socio-cultural contexts. Kwame Bediako from Ghana brings the protestant voice to this work while Emmanuel Katongole from Uganda, is a voice from a Roman Catholic tradition. The dialogue centers on Bediako's search for the African Christian identity, and Katongole's search for a new social imagination for Africa.

Needless to say, Katongole and Bediako deal with the issue of culture differently. In his book, *The Sacrifices of Africa: A Political Theology for Africa*, a study focusing on socio-political development, Katongole does not see much value in African pre-colonial cultures as a viable means of social change, suggesting that the church is the best option for a new vision of social change in Africa.[10] On his part, Kwame Bediako, in his seminal work *Christianity in Africa: A Renewal of a Non-Christian Religion*, focusing on religio-political issues, sees culture as a vital springboard for social transformation.[11]

Katongole argues that the problem of Africa is in her failure to have a different social imagination than that of nation-state that replaced the colonial imperialism. As I shall demonstrate in this study, Katongole traces this failure to the colonial project of destroying Africa's social

---

10. Emmanuel Katongole, *The Sacrifices of Africa: A Political Theology for Africa* (Grand Rapids, Michigan: William B. Eerdmans Publishing Company, 2011).

11. Kwame Bediako, *Christianity in Africa: A Renewal of a Non-Christian Religion* (Maryknoll: Orbis, 1995).

imagination in their civilizing project.[12] This alienation of Africa from her social history is of significance in developing contextual theologies. The missionary enterprise, like its metropolitan imperial governments, alienated Africa from her vast wealth of cultural wisdom when it found nothing of importance in her religious heritage as a building block or a dialogue partner in the evangelization of Africa. For example, the missionaries did not care to explore the deep religious consciousness and the pervasive preoccupation of the Africa with her ubiquitous spirits. John Mbiti's observation that Africans are notoriously religious is not a cliché.[13] Wherever an African is found so is his religion.

Upon considering the history that colonial Africa bequeathed the African nation-states, Katongole wants to replace the troubled history with a Christian one. He does not see any value, and therefore the need to recover the African traditional way of life disrupted by the encounter with the colonial administration and Western Christianity. Yet he remains somewhat vague on the kind of church that this social imagination would produce.

On his part, Bediako, decrying the same misrepresentation of the African cultures by the West, demonstrates that the question of identity remains important to Africa. The question of identity simply put is, "how can one be a Christian and an African at the same time?" This remains a legitimate question to which the main thrust of African Christian scholarship has argued that conversion to Christianity must be coupled with

---

12. Katongole, *Sacrifices of Africa*, 66. Referencing Basil Davison (*Black Man's Burden* [London: James Currey, 1994]), Katongole intimates — "The politics of suppression of the local history by the colonial regime can be traced to the colonial project whose moral justification was grounded on projecting Africa as a continent without history until the European's presence in Africa. This not only meant that Africa's history begun with the European's 'discovery' of various places, rivers, lakes, and peoples, it also assumed that Africans had no previous experience in social existence that could serve as helpful starting point in what was seen as the civilizing project of Colonialism."

13. John Mbiti, *African Religion and Philosophy* (New York: Prager, 1971), 1

cultural continuity. To the extent that this looking back to appraise culture gives meaning and hence identity to Africans, Bediako is important.

The theology of our two dialogue partners is developed in the next chapter. Their approach to the question of culture is important to our argument. The question of culture as determinative of people's socio-economic development has often been neglected in the main development discourse in Africa, while the Western theology, the theology that has grounded the mainstream Christianity in Africa, has often minimized its importance. Rather than ignoring or minimizing it, the Akũrinũ church vernacular theology has found a fertile ground in traditional culture from which this church movement has developed a unique ecclesiology that neither ignores culture, nor lifts it above the biblical teaching.

In this study, I have argued that the Akũrinũ church is a telling case study that challenges the erroneous western ideology that saw bankruptcy in African traditional way of life, by pointing to the values that are inherent in African cultural wisdom. The Akũrinũ believers are at home in their culture. They believe that God can speak to them without requiring them to be adopt European or other non-kikuyu cultures. They believe that the missionary God was not opposed to the God they have always worshipped.

The research has analyzed the Agĩkũyũ pre-colonial traditional culture to discover the cultural milieu that underlay the religious background in which the Akũrinũ theology evolved, and the possible contribution this background may have made to the Akũrinũ theology. In this analysis the historical inquiry of the first fifteen years of the Akũrinũ church movement, around 1927-1942, and its contemporary history will be critical. The anthropological studies by Jomo Kenyatta and other pioneer African authors are critical in recovering the Agĩkũyũ traditional culture. Ngũgĩ wa Thiong'o, among others, is valuable to the Agĩkũyũ cultural exegesis, while other African authors such as Chinua Achebe draw parallels to the other African cultures. The Agĩkũyũ pre-colonial cultural milieu, a general study of the AICs, with a specific focus on the Akũrinũ Church, has therefore formed the basis of the literature review for the research. The Akũrinũ church is a cultural movement that will not only help us to gain an insight into the entry of the gospel into a generally traditional culture, but also show how the ensuing contextual theology from such a movement can contribute to the global theological conversation. Such a reading of theology seeks to see God's activity in a cultural movement, as well as underscoring the fact that God has moved in culture and among all people, and that all people are capable of grasping the revelation of God within their cultural reality. If God has been revealed to the Akũrinũ, as I have sought to demonstrate through this research, and the Akũrinũ church has something to offer to the world about God, then it implies that indigenous groups offer no barrier or handicap to such revelation. Perhaps there is no greater fact and factor that appraises human dignity than knowing that God is, and has always been at work among humans, without the authentication of outsiders.

This study will demonstrate that the Akũrinũ church is an ecclesial cultural movement that has resisted displacement from their culture, in order to experience the Christian faith. The movement is a microcosm of how Christianity can be received within a people's lived culture. The Akũrinũ founders, the Arathi, were clear that the missionary faith was not entirely unfamiliar. They had confidence that their experience of faith was authentic and not different or opposed to the missionary experience of it. This is a classic example of a genuine encounter with the God of the gospel within a culture. This study hopes to bridge these gaps by presenting the Akũrinũ vernacular theology as an example of a model of an African theology from an African primal world view. The study will investigate whether the Akũrinũ vernacular theology presents a paradigm of a genuine encounter of the gospel with an African primal world view, an imperative approach in doing theology in a globalized world and explore its possible contribution to such a global theology.

Significance of This Study

The significance of this study is in its affirmation that any authentic theology develops out of peoples lived religious experience and imagination — not in a vacuum.[14] It is instructive that people respond to the theology that addresses their most important questions; ultimate questions of life embedded in culture — the level at which the gospel finds a home.[15] Unless the gospel addresses the level where values, core beliefs and belief systems are embedded, it fails to address the basic worldview of people, producing "schizophrenic Christians" who oscillate between faith and culture as need arises; a recipe for nominalism. It can be argued that to the extent that the missionaries ignored or underrated the African worldview, they produced this kind of anemic Christianity. It is sad to note that even today, whenever the gospel overlooks people's worldview or glosses over it, it produces the same effect.

Bediako says that whereas the venerable Nigerian theologian Bolaji Idowu was preoccupied with indigenization, and John Mbiti, the so-called "father of African theology" was more concerned with translatability, i.e., the capacity of the essential impulses of the Christian religion to be transmitted and assimilated into a different culture so that it has a dynamically equivalent response in the course of such transmission. Bediako references Ayayi Ayandele who formulated the idea of translatability when he said that evangelization is not simply the communication of foreign ideas to passive recipients who have to swallow every bit of the messenger's identity. Evangelization involves the process of assimilating the message making the recipient as important as the messenger.[16]

The theology that may result from this kind of engagement is important because it addresses the issues of the ontological being of a people.

---

14. Parrett, *African Christian Theology*, 23: "...theology emerges from, among other things, a historic community and people's experience."

15. Kwame Bediako, *Christianity in Africa: The Renewal of a Non-Western Religion:* Edinburgh, Scotland: Edinburgh University Press, 1995), 119.

16. Ibid., 118.

Imposed theology does not address people at the ontological level but instead, alienates them from the very course they are called to. The Western theology that came with the missionaries claimed universality. However, the missionaries who pioneered mission to Africa failed to exegete their own culture in which their imagined universalism was shaped. It is now common knowledge that Western theology has largely been influenced by Greek philosophies and the cultural development of the modernism. Dyrness demonstrates how;

> Two-hundred years ago this heritage coalesced in a cultural and intellectual movement called the Enlightenment, which celebrated reason, and the progress and perfectibility of human society. To defend themselves against atheism and agnosticism that threatened to take over this movement, Christians sought to define a 'reasonable Christianity' that reflected these challenges[17].

It is in this regard that;

> The preferred tools of theological inquiry for the West are reason, scientific methods, and other disciplines of social sciences, which sanction only that which can be thought and explained with precision and certainty with a maxim that — the knowledge gained must be first, and foremost, sure.[18]

It is this thinking that transmits theology in abstract nouns, borrowed originally from Greek philosophy, that has been the bane of Western theological methodologies. But outside the West, other communities, especially those of Africa where the primary method of storing information is the communal memory, abstract nouns are not used as the bastion of knowledge preservation. It would be wrong to dismiss the theology of such a community because it is not mediated in what others assume to

---

17. Dyrness, *Cross-Cultural Theology*, 18.
18. Ibid.

be the norm. It also is not difficult to see how in the Western approach myth and mystery are lost in the process. The early resistance of the gospel by Africans was a rejection of the European cultural garb in which the gospel was encased, together with the insult that African cultures suffered under the hands of the European missionaries.

Secondly, I address why people must develop a theology for themselves as they experience religion. This does not mean that theology develops in isolation. All cultures are dynamic especially as they interphase with other cultures. Theology develops out of the reflection on both the invading and the invaded culture. At this interim phase, a mixed religious understanding that is neither exactly the same as that which is being advocated by the missionary, nor the one experienced by the recipient cultures, develops. An outsider may erroneously describe this seeming mix as syncretism. The fact is that the recipients are receiving the new faith and placing it within known categories. The two cultures, the missionary and mission field, are gelling and forming a new synthesis. The missionary is calling the recipient community to worship. The community understands this as what they have always done. They respond by doing it within their own religious interpretation with its accompanying idioms and rituals.

As Bediako demonstrates, the extent to which a Christian community avails itself of and develops its heritage of Christian thought and tradition in the vernacular, is the extent to which it will be able to meet the challenge of showing the relevance and significance of Jesus. African theology needs to be in close contact with the vernacular apprehension of the Christian faith and its roots in the continuing realities of the traditional primal world-view[19]. The importance of this study has been to demonstrate that Akũrinũ vernacular or contextual theology largely builds on its roots in Africa primal imagination. Bediako accurately observes that African traditional religion is the authentic repository of African person-

---

19. Bediako, *Christianity in Africa*, 86.

ality[20]. This makes it imperative to study African traditional religions to understand African Christians.

Thirdly, the search for global theology is a growing pre-occupation of theologians whose patience on the presentation of Western theology as universal is running out. All contextual theologies can open new vistas into this dialogue. Instead of teaching other people our theology, a humbler approach is to seek to learn theology from them. Dyrness says that, "We cannot become a 'native', but we can converse with them, and they with us. The converse of this is that we can more accurately (and more modestly) begin to see ourselves, and our culture, as a case among cases."[21]

The energy spent on the whole project of contextualization, as usually understood, is fundamentally inadequate to address people's reception of the gospel from the primal religious consciousness. Contextualization in its basic definition, as I will argue, presupposes that there is a universal theology (often from the West) that needs to be contextualized in different cultural contexts. A better way of looking at this is to learn from insiders where multiple centers develop their own contextual theologies by reflecting on their primal traditions (not ignoring other traditions and the Bible). These contextual theologies then become a learning point for other Christians in other locations, all contributing to the global theology. An emergent movement like the *Akũrinũ*'s is a contribution to such a project if one considers, as I will demonstrate, that their starting point of theologizing, is their narrative or oral culture.

Some may object to such a study on the grounds that African traditional cultures and religions are dying out and being eclipsed by modern and Christian cultures. Kenyan theologian Zablon Nthamburi agrees with the fact that life in Africa has changed from its traditional practices due to

---

20. Ibid., 14.
21. Dyrness, *Cross-Cultural Theology*, 25.

civilization, Christianity and Islam.[22] Actually some religious and cultural practices have been rendered obsolete. However, Nthamburi asserts that there is a general realization that religion plays a great part in molding the community by organizing people to solve problems at the grassroots and even fostering unity.[23] Religion still plays an important role in the lives of the people. It helps people make important decisions that affect their lives, such as marriage, inheritance and choice of vocations.[24]

Nevertheless, this is not an uncritical rebuttal to the cultural assault on the African traditional cultures by the colonial and missionaries' value setting. Any critique of missionary work that does not recognize the gallant efforts and resilience, with which the missionaries undertook their mission to the benighted and tropical disease infested Africa, can only be borne out of arrogance and ignorance. However, equally true is that to ignore the history that attends to the general approach the missionaries took and some of the enduring effects their approach has had on the gospel reception in Africa is mere pretense which does not allow for any meaningful learning. So, this is neither an attempt to romanticize African traditional cultures nor to condemn the European missionary endeavor in Africa. As I argue, all cultures are victims of the fall of humanity into the original sin and Africans are not exempt. This work is instead an exploration and celebration of what God might be doing in a cultural movement such as the *Akũrinũ* church within its Gĩkũyũ context. Most significant for this study is the understanding that the most important theology for the ordinary Christian, as opposed to the trained theologians, is not the academic theology, but vernacular theology.[25] Elite or not, the ordinary Christian is concerned with practical and applicable

---

22. Zablon Nthamburi, *The African Church at the Crossroads: Strategy for Indigenization* (Kenya: Uzima Press, 1991), 12-15.

23. Ibid. 15.

24. Ibid.

25. Lamin Sanneh, *Translating the Message: The Missionary Impact on Culture* (Maryknoll, NY: Orbis, 2009).

theology; orthopraxis — right practice — for daily living rather than mere orthodoxy — right belief. It is my hope that the understanding of how the Akũrinũ theology has developed, will suggest ways in which academic theology can be bridged meaningfully to vernacular theology for any Christian community, including my own church denomination, in concrete ways.

Thus, utilizing anthropological, historical, and theological inquiry, I suggest an approach we are going to call "theo-anthropology" or "theological anthropology." This approach aims to study human beings both within their culture context, and at the intersection of culture and the gospel. It is my belief that God is at work in culture and that culture is partially a human effort to make sense of the created order. And so, it can even be argued then that culture is sacred to the extent that human life is sacred.

CHAPTER ONE

CONTINUITY OR DISCONTINUITY — ANALYSIS OF EMMANUEL KATONGOLE AND KWAME BEDIAKO'S THEOLOGY

In the *Akũrinũ* church in Kenya, music and dance play a very critical part in grounding the believers' (usually referred to as disciples) faith. The basic musical instrument is a drum. In a particular congregation, I counted more than ten traditional drums beaten by ten different people, including children, and all maintaining a very consistent and enthralling rhythm reminiscent of African traditional worship. The people of this small *Akũrinũ* church proclaimed to "hear the voice of God" through the songs.

In the five hours the service lasted, the congregants sung in the excess of sixty hymns — and this without referring to a hymn book. All were memorized. There was a relevant hymn for every aspect of the service. For example, before my research assistant and I would be allowed into the church building, we waited outside to be cleansed, a ritual they call *kũaraũra*, which simply means to seek permission to join in their fellowship. This ritual involves the pastor and his wife standing with us outside the church as we sang while the congregation inside echoed the hymns in a call and response style. This went on for a while, while I prayed for the community's welcome, otherwise our research would be in jeopardy. Eventually, to my joy and relief, the pastor announced that we were free to enter the service.

This incident highlights a different method of learning theology — the power of imagination in music and dance, in a distinctly indigenous African ecclesial movement; the Akũrinũ church. Put differently, how can we understand the Akũrinũ church, as distinctive expression of Christian theologizing that contributes to the universal church? Our theory is that a global theology recognizing the possibility of multiple expressions of Christian theologies, is pegged on God's original work of taking the gospel to "all peoples, nations, and communities" (cf. Matt 28:18 and Rev 14:6) and God's continued presence and interest in creation. This presence has animated such cultures and even guaranteed such communities a self-personhood that allowed them to not only embrace the gospel message but to also imbue it with distinct cultural elements that enrich its expression as part of global Christianity.

Understanding New Ecclesial Movements

One way to understand the insider and other emergent Christian movements is to examine the contextual or global theologies that emerge from such movement. In the study of the Akũrinũ, I infer for example, that perhaps the intuitive realization of faith that came to Joseph Ng'ang'a, its founder, in his drunkard stupor may say something of the idea of universal religious consciousness advocated by Fredrick Schleiermacher and furthered by Samuel Taylor Coleridge.[1] Together with Fredrick Denison

---

1. Friedrich Schleiermacher, *On Religion: Speeches to Its Cultured Despisers* (Rev. ed.: Philadelphia: Westminster/John Knox Press, 1994). "Frost at Midnight," in William Wordsworth and Samuel Taylor Coleridge, *Lyrical Ballads*, 1798.

Maurice, they greatly influenced Bishop Colenso and his great work of translation among the Zulu of South Africa, which I will analyze briefly.[2]

Willie Jennings reports that Bishop John Colenso came to Natal as a missionary-translator to an African people who had seen their ancient world collapse and reemerge fundamentally changed. The blacks of Natal were squeezed by Europeans in every side; the Portuguese who lived in the North East disrupted the people's life by drawing the natives into detrimental trading practices involving ivory, hides, maize, and slaves, which were instrumental to ecological destruction. The capitalistic operations of hunting and trading resulted in stimulation of tribal conflict, reconfiguration, and ultimately, the disruption and displacement of people. The British in the south-east and the Boers in the south-southwest created an appetite for land and laborers. With the arms they supplied to the Gradual Kola people, these tribal people descended on their fellow blacks killing and turning the populations to slaves for the settlers' labor force.[3]

The chiefs, tribes, and individuals were also being placed in the moral universe controlled by white opinion displayed in print media. The same happened in East Africa as I will mention in the next section. The morality of every African was determined by how much he supported white interests, accepted European culture, and yielded land, and life to European control.[4] The settlers and merchants had already begun to justify the narrative of their presence as salvific; bringing order to chaos and cultivation to the empty uninhabited lands. They attributed the chaos to the legacy of Zulu chief, Shaka Senzangakhona, and his terrorist behavior. All this amounted to what Colenso describes as displacement — from people's land and familiar culture.

---

2. Willie James Jennings, *The Christian Imagination: Theology and the Origins of Race* (New Haven: Yale, 2009).

3. Jennings, *Immagination*, 32.

4. Ibid.

Apparently, this is the same benevolent justification that the settlers gave for confiscating the land of the Agĩkũyũ of the central Kenya, namely, protecting the Agĩkũyũ from the Maasai raids, resulting in displacement with devastating consequences[5]. This unsolicited Euro-American benevolence continues today wherever there is political unrest in Africa such as the Democratic Republic of Congo. Ironically, unrest rarely surfaces where there are no natural resources. The biggest frustration with this meddling is not so much the Neo-colonial interests that precipitate such unrest, but the African despots who willingly kill their kin and kith for a cause that has great long-term repercussions. The European invasion of Natal resulted in the displacement of Africans, loss of land that turned many to squatters in their own homeland, and into laborers in now European owned land. Christian missionaries on the other hand were busy proselytizing Africans.

For his part though, Bishop Colenso as well as the colonial administration embodied by Shepstone, worked under the British vision of the colonial civilizing project in Africa.[6] This was a reading of African societies through the lenses of White paternalism. Nevertheless, Bishop Colenso somewhat challenged this when he invited his African informants, who were his language teachers, into his translation project. In so doing, he gained access to the African space in which his theological vision would encounter the thoughts and hopes, pain and the suffering of Africans.[7]

By encouraging his assistants, Magema Fuze, Ndiane Ngubane, and William Ngidi, to write and publish their work in isiZulu, Colenso led the way in Africans' self-articulation. He also granted his students access to a workbench of European discursive operations, the literary weapons of

---

5. C. Cagnolo, *The Akikuyu: Their Customs, Traditions and Folklore* (Nyeri, Kenya: The Mission Printing School, 1933).

6. Ibid.

7. Jennings, *Imagination*, 130.

warfare and defense, the tools of engaging in emancipatory politics, and the building blocks of nationalist existence.[8]

The genius of Bishop Colenso's translation project in Natal was in his folding of all humanity into righteousness, not damnation. Central to this universal affirmation, is the leveling of all people through their particular religious experience where divine righteousness enables religious ethnography; an ability to discern a theological sameness in all people. As Jonathan Draper notes, for Colenso "God has simply provided a righteousness to the human race in Christ, whether they knew it or not…All of us, Christian, Jews, heathen were dealt with by the creator God as righteous creatures, not only now, but 'from all eternity'. This was the reason for the universality of human religious experience, which impels people to live moral lives. This way of grasping the religious subject enables a benign, even generous posture toward different people."[9]

Colenso's approach suggests that all people operate in the moral and spiritual light they have been given, with punishment being calibrated by their moral failure or integrity, operating in their inherent righteousness. The Christian faith is the revelation of this very fact — that is of inherent righteousness — and the Zulu are a perfect example. In this way Colenso rewrites salvation history as the history of religious righteousness.

Colenso's theology draws a straight line from biblical Jews and gentiles (or heathen) to Christian settlers and Zulu (or heathen). What holds them all together is his vision in the fatherly love of the creator God who has sent light 'into their very heart'.[10] Their moral duty –white settler, Zulu, gentile, Jew — is to move toward the inward light that is also reflected in God's son. In this way Colenso rightly evaluated the Zulu religion for what it really was, as Jennings reports:

---

8. Ibid., 132.
9. Ibid., 143-144.
10. Jennings, *Imagination*, 145.

> It was Colenso who, among others, reversed the idea that the Zulu had no religion and no knowledge of God. He pressed the possibility that among the Zulus God was known and had been called *uNkulunkulu*, the great-great one, or *umvelinqangi*, the Supreme God. Indeed, Colenso's deep commitment to recognizing Zulu religious consciousness helped fuel Zulu cultural nationalism ... Colenso, believed in building Christian civilization on top of existing native logics, such practices as cattle or property exchange as part of arranged marriages.[11]

One may wonder how many other such logics and shades of beauty existed in the African traditional religions for the missionaries who thought of such possibilities. Jennings' universality of human religious experience, which impels people to live moral lives, should be the basis of the possibility of global or contextual theologies. Contextual theologies recognize such logic in emergent ecclesial movements like the *Akũrinũ* church. Such communities testify to God's movement in unique cultures, a movement that can open new vistas in learning God's work of redeeming creation.

Emmanuel Katongole's Vision of a New Social Imagination for Africa

Emmanuel Katongole is a professor at Notre Dame in South Bend, Indiana, USA, and a Roman Catholic priest from Uganda. He says that the way Africa was steeped into modernity by colonialism required a reorganization of the society. He demonstrates how, for example, King Leopold's rubber economy in Congo required the reorganization of the Congo society under new rational modalities that ensured efficient ad-

---

11. Ibid.

ministration and economic production.[12] In the process, large areas of forest were cleared, villages were resettled, quotas were assigned, compliance was recorded, and slackers were punished.[13] In this reorganization Africans were displaced from their land and made to fit into modernity and late capitalist economic arrangements. The current socio-economic challenges in Africa can be traced back to this invasion and interruption.[14]

On this continued negative impact on the African cultures by the invading colonial economic system, Hannah Kinoti, rightly observes that the current moral crisis experienced in Africa all begun with the African encounter with the colonialist.[15] She says that, "colonialism was an encounter of Africans and Europeans on unequal terms and it set in motion upheavals in practically every African institution."[16] Kinoti further states that because of this encounter with missionaries, the government official, the European farmer, the Indian trader, and the newspaper, there was a change for good or evil. The missionaries condemned African religion and morality. The colonial officials subdued the people to servitude, the European planters displaced them from their land and turned them into laborers, the Indian traders made profit out of the newly introduced wants which soon became needs, and the news on the newspaper fed them with images of atrocities of the First World War.[17]

Kinoti further decries the sudden introduction of the capitalist monetary based economic system and the social differentiation that came with it. According to Kinoti, before the Europeans came, the Africans

---

12. Ibid.

13. Ibid.

14. For further reading on the impact of colonial cultural invasion on African culture you can read Hannah Kinoti's "Morality is Vital to Economic and Social Development," in George Kinoti and Peter Kimuyu, eds., A *Vision for a Bright Africa: Facing the Challenges of Development* (African Institute for Scientific Research and Development: Kampala: Uganda, 1997).

15. Ibid., 257.

16. Ibid.

17. Ibid., 257.

practiced barter trade, which essentially meant exchanging what you do not need for what you need. She observes how a capitalist economic system on the other hand introduced competition in the society which she says meant that the more you have, the more you can afford; the more you can afford, the more you can accumulate things and the more things you can have, the richer you are. But to have more meant to take advantage of others either by swindling them or failing to compensate them adequately for their labor by transferring this surplus labor to your benefit.

Capitalism had both negative and positive effects in Africa. Gustavo Gutierrez, whose point of departure in doing theology is the social condition of man, has rightly observed that the capitalist economy creates a center of a few wealthy nations, and a periphery of poverty for the majority.[18] The resultant unfair competition and the class differentiation have brought problems to every sector. In the public service, the wage difference is astronomical. Unfortunately, the same is true of the government, private sector, Non-Governmental Organizations (NGOs), and even the church. Those in top-level management earn astronomical salaries and perks, while policy makers often enact laws that shield them from any accountability. Those in the lower cadre's content themselves with nothing or the bare minimum, yet the basic human needs for shelter, food, clothing, and education of children are arguably the same for all people whether rich or poor.

All means, from corruption to tribalism and nepotism, sexual favors, and even witchcraft, are employed in an effort to climb up the ladder in the job market. Those who have no hope of climbing to the top result to grassroots corruption; The government driver sells spare parts from government vehicles while the cleaner and the tea girl carry away beverages, stationeries, toiletries and virtually anything they can lay their hands on. Those who feel sidelined in the upward mobility are so

---

18. Gustavo Gutiérrez, A *Theology of Liberation* (London: SCM Press, 1974).

demoralized that they either put in less than their full potential in their job or run parallel personal business enterprises to which they are more committed than their jobs. This net effect was the general trend in many parts of Africa wherever the colonizers were at war or at work.[19]

As in all human systems, capitalism has been misused and is in dire need of redemption. Groody says that the problem of today's global economy is not capitalism per see, rather the abuses and excesses that flow from capitalism. A good example of this is the wage disparities between the chief executive officers of corporate organizations and their workers, with some earning up to 411 times more than that of the average worker.[20] Capitalism therefore needs to be infused with godly values to work for the good of humankind.

Kinoti concludes her argument by calling for the rehabilitation of the African culture, which she says had attained an "internal balance" or equilibrium before the invasion of the colonial powers. The internal balance was a system of values that Africans had developed over the centuries. This system maintained a balance between needs and the means of satisfying them, a balance between individual aspirations and collective aspirations, and a balance between the technical and ethical.[21] For a better appreciation of the African cultures, a course that Katongole does not take, I will turn to Kwame Bediako a little later.

Katongole whose approach is socio-political, in particular a search for Christian social ethics, says that the current socio-political challenges that face the nation-states in Africa can be traced to this truncated history — a history of displacement. On account of this, he advises that in solving the problem of African politics, we must look not at strategies,

---

19. Katongole. *Sacrifices of Africa*, 45.

20. Daniel, G.Groody, *Globalization, Spirituality, and Justice* (Maryknoll, New York: Orbis Books: 2007), 17.

21. Cf. George Kinoti and Peter Kimuyu, eds., *Vision for a Bright Africa: Facing the Challenges of Development.* (African Institute for Scientific Research and Development. Kampala: Uganda, 1997).

but the stories that have shaped the present state of politics because we are how we imagine ourselves, and how others imagine us. Who we are, and who we are cable of becoming, depends very much on the stories we tell, listen to, and live by.²²

The stories are important to Katongole because they constitute social memory which is not necessarily written but can be found in the culture of the people e.g. songs, poetry, and fiction, beside official texts. Katongole says that the European invasion of Africa suppressed the local history:

> The politics of suppression of the local history by the colonial regime can be traced to the colonial project whose moral justification was grounded on projecting Africa as a continent without history until the European's presence in Africa. This not only meant that Africa's history begun with the European's 'discovery' of various places, rivers, lakes, and peoples. It also assumed that Africans had no previous experience in social existence that could serve as helpful starting point in what was seen as the civilizing project of Colonialism.²³

In this arrangement, which Katongole argues has remained unchallenged to date, all such local history was devalued as folklore, animism, paganism, and barbarism, which was seen as both distracting and hard to absorb into the colonial project. The wealth of Africa's ethnic cultures, for instance, came to be branded as tribalism and as such retrogressive.

Katongole and Bediako deal with the issue of culture differently. Katongole, whose focus is on socio-political as noted in the introduction, does not see much value of African pre-colonial cultures as a viable means of social change. He sees the problem of Africa as her failure to have a different social imagination, other than that of nation-state; a

---

22. Katongole, *Sacrifices of Africa*, 11.

23. Katongole, *Sacrifices of Africa*, 66, quoting Basil Davison, *Black Man's Burden* (London: James Currey, 1994).

failure that he attributes to the colonial project of destroying Africa's social imagination through invasion, interruption, and suppression. He doesn't see the rehabilitation of this culture as useful in social re-imagination. Instead, he proposes to replace the troubled history with a Christian one. He does not see any value, and therefore need to recover the African traditional way of life that was disrupted by the encounter with the colonial administration and their project of civilizing Africa, and the Western Christianity. He is keen to say that the two are incompatible.

In this approach Katongole says that the Church is the most uniquely situated community for the task of the social re-imagination in Africa.[24] However, Katongole comes short of showing how this can be achieved. Whereas he asserts that the Church is uniquely situated to lead in social re-imagination for Africa, he is not concrete on what kind of a church. He only notes that the Church must see her mandate going beyond the narrow category of the salvation of the soul, and the activism that trails governments' blunders (both socio-political and religio-political), to being a movement whose basic mandate is to establish the Kingdom of God and work for the ascendency of Christ over all spheres of life as Lord.

In this thinking Katongole gives three examples of how a different social imagination might look like. All the three examples are efforts that point to what good can come out of Africa. Angelina Atyam leads her community of Northern Uganda to interrupt the terror of Kony and the Lord's Resistance Army (LRA) through forgiveness and reconciliation. Instead of revenge, which Katongole likens to storing acid in a metallic container that eats up the container, Angelina calls our attention to how unconditional forgiveness can break the cycle of revenge and hate. On his part, Bishop Paride Taban and his Kuron peace community in the remote, extreme North of South Sudan demonstrates how people of different ethnic backgrounds can co-exist together in a new *ecclesial* community. This is the same approach that Marguerite Barankitse takes

---

24. Ibid.

when she creates Maison home for the destitute children — ravaged by war in Burundi. Truly the three examples are a pointer to the possibilities that Africa is capable of. However, one cannot help seeing the challenges of this approach.

The three examples succeed in creating ecclesial communities. They are like peace islands that one has to leave where they are in order to enter. Sadly, this kind of leaven cannot ferment the whole dough. In the end Katongole, perpetuates the same old formula of alienating Africa from her culture in the name of helping her. Besides, the three examples are efforts driven by individuals. The three examples therefore fall short of a cultural movement. Sadly, the three approaches are borne out of a crisis, casting doubt as to whether they can be replicated in a real-life situation.

Katongole sees nothing of value in the African culture in re-imagining the future. This is seen clearly in his critique of the umuofia community in Chinua Achebe's *Things Fall Apart*, to which he has devoted a full chapter. Katongole states that the invading colonial administration was not different from the African traditional one that had perpetuated a culture of fear. One wonders what difference it would bring to confront the fear in umuofia's culture with the Christian faith, rather than vanquish the whole culture which had many other good sides to it.

Katongole is right in arguing that African needs a new social imagination, and that her current woes have something to do with the destruction of her culture. The ruthless and sudden severance of the African past remains the single-most important obstacle to any genuine and authentic progress in Africa. It is so demeaning to this day to observe how Africa has no confidence in her institutions. African governments continue to photocopy constitutions from their Western counterparts despite the obvious fact they cannot work in the African context. Even in the shopping malls, you only need to label an item 'made from' some country out there, and customers will line up. In the job interview, including in your Curriculum Vitae (CV) that you have studied in Europe or America will give you an automatic head start. The brain drain to the West is uncalled for. Africans are not trooping to the West because their brains are needed there more than they are needed in Africa, but because to have gone out of Africa is itself a social status.

Yet Katongole is mistaken in not seeing ways that much of the good he is looking for is rooted in traditional culture. Consequently, Katongole looks forward but with a perspective not rooted in any particular cultural situation. Even though he calls for an understanding of the narrative that pre-dates the colonial incursion and the nation-states, he does not look back to this history as a resource for a future but as a kind of catharsis. In this way Katongole therefore sees Christianity as a way of life extracted away from culture.

The Lingering Western Legacy on Social Imagination in Africa

The encounter of the colonial imperial government and the missionaries with the Africans altered the African social imagination for better or for worse and continues to do so. Katongole observes aptly the current social state of Africa with this statement;

> If Churches and coffins represent two dominant cultural realities in Africa, they also represent the predicament of a continent suspended between hope and despair. They capture the hope and pain, the beauty and tragedy, the dreams and the frustrations of a continent that is at once overwhelming Christian and at the same time politically, economically, and socially distressed.[25]

---

25. Katongole, *Sacrifices of Africa*, 29.

Mugambi concurs with Katongole when he tacitly paints the reality of the African social state; Africa is faced with a food deficit, it is the hungriest continent in the world, it is faced with debt crisis.... It is the most indebted continent; it has the highest level of illiteracy in the world, and half of the world's refugees are Africans.[26]

The picture can even be painted gloomier when you consider that there are more of HIV and Aids cases in Africa in than any other continent. Furthermore, since independence in the 1950 through 1960s for most African countries, there have been more coup d'états in Africa than elsewhere. Diseases such as Malaria continue to devastate entire population in conjunction with a host of other new diseases that are major killers. Besides, Africa suffers from political ineptitude, negative ethnicity, nepotism, witchcraft and backwardness, child soldiers, child labor and abuse, high illiterate levels, corruption; the list is endless. And all this is happening in an overwhelming Christian continent. As Mugambi wonders:

> How can such a contradiction be explained? Is this religiosity authentic and genuine, or is it just superstitious arising from despair? How could it be that the people who continue to call upon God most reverently are the ones God seems to neglect most vehemently? Could it be that "the Gospel has reached many people in Africa as very bad news"?. [27]

Katongole challenges this social imagination in Africa by suggesting that probing it must be the first order of business for Christian social ethics in Africa.[28]

But how did Africa come to this state of affairs? And how is such an image to be changed? Katongole blames the nation-state, which he claims

---

26. J. N. K. Mugambi, *Christian Theology and Social Reconstruction* (Nairobi, Kenya: Acton, 2003), 160.

27. Ibid., 40, 140.

28. Katongole, *Sacrifices of Africa*, 29.

operates from an empire mentality, and which succeeded the colonial administration, for the woes of the independent Africa. Katongole says that nation-states, like super powers, are built on a vision of power as domination and invincibility. Accordingly, it would seem like the greatest desire of nations is to be the most successful or the most advanced, which means even small nations, are born with the soul of empire. But one may want to ask on whose shoulder is the empire mentality predicated? On whose blood does the empire sail?

The empire mentality that the colonial regime bequeathed to Africa remains so prevalent and must be interrupted with a different social imagination that is more sensitive to people's felt needs, and able to organize the society to meet them. Our observation is that by creating in her membership 'sensitivity' to the African way of life, the Akũrinũ church has created a community with reduced exploitation and a more horizontal pecking order, rather than a hierarchical one, and hence a marked effort to care for one another. The organizing factor in Akũrinũ church can be attributed to the African view of reality.

Katongole and A Reticent Activist Church

Katongole maintains that the current interventions of Christian theological and social reflection paradigms in the African mainstream church, namely deeper evangelism — the spiritual paradigm (often among the evangelical churches), development and relief — the pastoral paradigm, as well as mediation, advocacy, and reconciliation — the political paradigm, etc., are all based on prescriptive haste, lacking in a deeper search for the real cause of the problems facing Africa.[29] Among these churches, donor money and NGO craze are rife. Yet, one can't help but see that the desired transformation is seldom seen, at least not at a rate com-

---

29. Katongole, *Sacrifices of Africa*, 33–40.

mensurate with money raised from the West and poured into the South. Clearly, there is a disconnect somewhere. All the three interventions are based on the premise that Christianity is a religion and therefore distinct from politics — a dualism. Such an understanding leads to the disappearance of the Christianity as a social and political body and consequently, renders it impotent in determining social change.[30]

From this understanding, Katongole says the first problem that the church will face in her effort to form any significant social imagination is a result of seeing her role as confined primarily to the religious realm, and therefore not fully at home with the concerns of social, material, and political complexities of Africa.[31] Secondly, to the extent that the Church feels uneasy in these processes — social, material and political — it follows that she will be ambivalent and shy. She will not be at home with the complexities of African life. Consequently, she will also not be proactive in imagining new frames of reference (namely ideas, and visions of human flourishing), but only concerning herself in influencing.[32]

Katongole says that the current Church in Africa is either reticent, shying from being involved in the socio-political realm and confining herself in the spiritual realm, or involved in activism (the Church acting as an NGO). He says that the Church, especially in rural Africa, where the power of the nation-state is felt least, seems to be waiting for the political actors to set the pace before she can react with activism. His observations are right, with one addition. Many will observe and be grateful that the mainstream churches have from time to time chided the government and managed to offer occasional mediatory roles in many political wrangles in Africa. This is true whether in Kenya's second liberation, South African black theology, Catholics Bishops in the Democratic Republic of Congo (DRC), or even in the Sudanese crisis where the

---

30. Ibid.
31. Ibid.
32. Ibid., 43.

clergy was on the forefront in the talks that led to the independence of Southern Sudan ending over two decades of bloody civil war and human displacement. But again, one wishes this would not always be reactionary, waiting to respond only when things go wrong. Effort in seeking a more determinative social vision, from the start should be in the African church's agenda always.

Katongole's observation can also be said to be true of the ever-growing Neo-Charismatic movements, many of which draw their charter from their counterparts in North America with a sharp focus on wealth and wellness gospel.[33] Sadly, when the Church is confined to her religious corner and activism, or enriching the clergy at the expense of gullible poor enthusiasts, the result as Katongole observes is that she becomes a tool in the hands of the politics of the day, co-opted into the schemes of the politicians or held captive to the whims of its often selfish leaders.[34] He goes on to say that the Church in Africa acts from the Western concept, that Christianity as a religion is not a social vision, but only becomes socially relevant when it contributes to the social and material processes that are determined, and controlled by the sphere of politics.[35] Katongole adds that this assumption must be set aside if Christianity is to recover her social vision.

This narrow vision of the Church is one of the unfortunate legacies that the European missionary legacy bequeathed African Christianity. In this regard, Katongole laments that the Roman Catholic church (and this can be said of the other mainstream Churches as well), was used in the Rwanda genocide, taking sides in stereotyping one community against the other with Churches becoming centers of massacre;

> Since the dominant discourse and practice of the Christian social responsibility in Rwanda succeeded in securely lock-

---

33. Kantongole, *Sacrifices of Africa*, 50.
34. Ibid.
35. Ibid.

ing the self-understanding and mission of the church within the dominant political vision of a "tribalized" society, when it came to the final showdown, the Church simply performed the story so well that being a Christian made no difference.[36]

Again, this is a lingering legacy of the colonial church where she took sides with the colonial government, and today taking sides or being mum when she should speak on behalf of the poor to the nation-state governments, in subjugating the Africans and confiscating their land. On the whole, the missionary churches advanced the mission of the colonialist. It was the same scenario — turning a blind eye when it came to slave trade earlier, the current Neo-colonialism, and geo-political agendas.

The *Akũrinũ* demonstrate a different way of doing church; away from activism and reticence. Though many *Akũrinũ* believers are poor, they harbor little class difference. They help each other in dealing with socio-political and socio-economic issues that face their members by forming a close knit and caring community based on their African tradition of being a brother's keeper.

The Church as an Alternative Route in Gleaning for a New African Social Imagination

It is this background of a nation-state mentality and reticent church that convinces Katongole that the problem of Africa lies in a wrong social imagination. He blames first the colonial administration that disrupted the Africans former life, and secondly the nation-state that took over from the colonial administration, and now a reticent and activist church, for the woes of the independent Africa. Maintaining the African kings and presidents together with all other governments' dignitaries with their empire lifestyles today, is a constant pain and burden on the taxpayers.

---

36. Ibid., 48.

The challenge then for Africa should not have been simply to achieve sovereignty in order to determine her own destiny (and actually all countries in Africa are sovereign states), but rather to interrupt the imperial vision of power as domination with a different account of power. Thus, creating a different vision of society and politics where the African would be truly free to determine their social, political, and economic destiny. Katongole's observations here are worth noting. But he also understands the difficulty in changing the mindset of the nation-state mentality. It is for this reason that he turns to the church as a more viable alternative to model his vision of a new social imagination.

It is in this thinking that Katongole says that daring to invent the future in Africa requires a certain kind of a church. One that is able to live out a practical theology of relocation. This relocation is from top to bottom, from the city to the village, from the center to the periphery. Katongole says that the practical face of this relocation flies in the face of conventional wisdom, which assumes that the way to effect social change in Africa is from locations of power like IMF, the World Bank, big cities, and developed countries. There is a tendency to believe that these places of power provide not only the right reading of what the problems of Africa are, but also the right theories of economics and politics, and the right prognosis of what Africa needs in order to end poverty, eradicate tribalism or fight corruption. To this end, we are treated to one grand theory after another — incredible and magnificent promises of salvation for Africa through civilization, modernization, nation-building, globalization, privatization, a new world order etc.

But these centers of power only seem to benefit the elite club and not majority of the poor and needy. Relocation, on the other hand, points to forms of Christian social engagement that, having learned to suspect these old formulas, ground their praxis in the local, concrete, and particular communities of neglected villages.[37] Here, as a protestant, I should

---

37. Katongole, *Sacrifices of Africa*, 137.

pause and salute the Roman Catholic Church (never mind that Katongole decries their activism and reticence and rightly so). Whereas many of my Pentecostal fellow ministers are enmeshed in their near-sighted vision of amassing wealth, acquiring the latest gadgets of prestige in the shortest time possible and with shedding the least sweat, many Catholic fathers will be found in the remotest corners of Africa, at home with the poorest of the poor in their pains and joys.

As I noted earlier, before the colonial interruption, the African traditional cultures had developed traditional institutions that ensured life's preservation and the dignity of all people, a fact that Katongole ignores. For example, I have cited elsewhere in this research how the *Agĩkũyũ* land tenure system was seen as the best option to emancipate the poor. Other institutions can be added. They include the polygamy, adoption, wife inheritance (not the current shell of what it was meant to be), kinship ties, age-sets, etc. They ensured that everyone belonged and that there was no extreme destitution. Although some of these institutions may seem outdated in a globalized age, they still hold the basis of cohesion in the society, and every attempt must be made to make their underlying principle the backbone of morality and development. The *Akũrinũ* church is tapping into a history that predated the nation-state and even colonialism, in addressing this problem of cultural dislocation.

Consequently, Katongole neither shows an example of how the church can achieve this envisioned social imagination nor gives an example of a church that has done this. Our argument, on the other hand, is that by using some of the traditional institutions that are rife in the African psyche, the *Akũrinũ* church has developed an ecclesiological approach that has produced a community that minds the welfare of one another. There is a lot of solidarity among the *Akũrinũ* of central Kenya and similar churches i.e. the *Roho* churches of western Kenya. The members regard each other as brothers and will no pass each other without exchanging pleasantries.

Chapter one

The Role of Indigenous Cultures in Social Imagination

Perhaps one of the questions that Katongole does not answer is the importance of indigenous cultures. We need to contend with the fact that the epic battle that Africa faces today is a cultural one. The Majority-World, especially Africa, has lost the capacity to believe in herself. As Archbishop Desmond Tutu tells us:

> The worst crime that can be laid at the door of the white man (who, it must be said, has done many a worthwhile and praiseworthy thing for which we are always thankful) is not our economy, social and political exploitation, however reprehensible that might be — no it is that his policy succeeded in filling most of us with a self-disgust and self-hatred. This has been the worst violent form of colonialism, our mental and spiritual enslavement where we have suffered from what can only be called a religious or spiritual schizophrenia.[38]

Because of this cultural bankruptcy, Africa has lost her capacity to set her own development agenda that is not tied to expensive strings-attached loans and grants from the West.

Katongole does not see the need for Majority-World governments to safeguard indigenous cultures from the hegemony of the West, and the subsequent erosion of traditional values, structures, and institutions that support life. Here I note that whereas other countries like Japan and China have developed while retaining their indigenous cultures and languages, African countries have foreign languages for their national and official languages all in the name of being globally competitive. Their indigenous cultures are viewed has an impediment to the modern economy. Again, where many countries in the orient have safeguarded their media from the West, Africa is admonished to liberalize her media waves. Currently, foreign aid is tied to neoliberal laws including the injurious

---

38. Desmond M. Tutu, "Black Theology/African Theology — Soul Mates or Antagonists?" in Wilmore S. Gayraud and James H. Cone, eds., *Black Theology: A Documentary History, 1966 -1979*. (Maryknoll, New York: Orbis Books, 1979), 484.

women's reproductive health rights that aim at legalizing abortion, and those on same-sex unions, that distort the family order.

The *Akŭrinŭ* church is able to chart a new vision for her members because she is alive to the African enchanted worldview, one that though ignored by Katongole, mainstream churches, Bretton hood institutions, and the NGOs in their development agenda for Africa, arises to prevent such efforts. Melba Maggy reminds us that the work of the cross is a reminder that social action, by the church and we can add other development initiatives, is a confrontation with powers both in cosmic and social dimensions, and because of this such powers must be named before any social transformation can take place. We must know what demonic powers are entrenched in our social systems; mammon, injustice, indiscipline, subhuman forces such as colonialism, market dominance, multinational debt or undue concentration on spiritual spectacles under which the evil hides its sinister plots, and deodorizes its filth.[39] There must be an actual transfer of power where the lordship of Jesus takes place in all the areas of the life of a believer and not make the people we are seeking to transform into a middle class pursuing the American dream.[40]

Maggay, however, adds an important and often easily missed dimension to social transformation, one that escapes the eye of Katongole. She says that both the popular development programs and social action often fail to appreciate and consequently discern very subtle dimensions of power encounter in a culture that impedes development. The most discernable ones in Africa include wife inheritance (which traditionally had a good value but currently greatly abused), witchcraft, early marriage of girls, and asymmetrical power in gender roles, besides others.

---

39. Melba Padilla Maggay, *Transforming Society* (Eugene, OR: Wipf and Stock Publishers, 1996), 78.

40. Ibid.

Often many good projects are abandoned because such strongholds (often under the radar) stand in the way unchallenged.[41]

Unlike Katongole's missionary church, the Akũrinũ church is alive to the fact that there are such cosmic powers that need to be confronted and subdued to the Lordship of Christ. This they have come to by appreciating the enchanted African worldview, an approach that cannot be observed in the same measure among the mainstream churches. On this, Paul Gifford reminds us that the traditional missionary approach, which has been continued in the historical churches, was either to denounce the African worldview as superstitious, or merely to stay silent, hoping it would disappear on its own.

According to Gifford, the failure to address this worldview gave rise to what he calls 'the dual allegiance' phenomenon, where mainline Christians would attend church on Sunday, only to turn to diviners during the week. He argues that churches which by contrast have unashamedly built their Christianity on precisely this enchanted worldview have a considerable appeal, at least in certain circumstances. Such churches revolve around culture in a very different way from that of mainline or mission churches. The later may officially profess a conscious project of inculturation, but many AICs build on culture in a far more unconscious and natural way.[42]

Gifford says that the enchanted religious imagination remains powerful in Kenya, and those viewing the world in this way, and any Christianity that simply ignores or actively dismisses it as superstition leaves most of life un-catered for. Likewise, if practices like circumcision or wife-inheritance are deemed essential to a community's way of life, any form of Christianity that condemns or repudiates them has lessened its appeal. By contrast, the Christianity that celebrates the enchanted reli-

---

41. Ibid.
42. Paul Gifford, *Christianity, Politics and Public Life in Kenya* (London: Hurst and Company, 2009) 87.

gious imagination by finding spiritual causes for misfortune, and which rejoices in and celebrates traditional practices, exerts great appeal. Celebrating the enchanted worldview and cultural traditions constitute precisely the appeal of most of the AICs.[43]

For our argument I suggest that a new social imagination for Africa will be achieved by the church that is alive to the great wealth of cultural capital in African traditional culture, and is able to confront every aspect of this culture with the gospel aided by a government that is able to create an environment that allows for human flourishing. In particular, the government should safeguard the socio-cultural values and heritage of her people from the hegemonic western cultures that threaten to flatten local cultures, whose value has proved useful for many generations. In this regard, children must not be made to feel ashamed of, and even despise and undermine their mother tongue, i.e. their primary language of socialization — an enduring colonial legacy in many African countries in the 21st C.

The Church in Africa is best placed to link culturally based values and biblical teaching so that both can ground a development agenda that is sensitive to the African ethos and telos, taking advantage of the existing African cultural institutions. Such a development agenda may prove far less expensive. Among the *Kikuyu* for example, land was seen as basic for emancipation. However, not everyone could afford the luxury of land, especially after the colonial invasion. But the *Kikuyu* had a land tenure system that defined the relationship between the rich and the poor where the poor attached themselves to a rich landlord as tenants-at-will (*ahoi*), immigrants (*athami*), or voluntary servants (*ndungata*) with the hope of improving their lot enough to buy their own land. If the landowner wanted to sell his land, he would give these tenants the first priority. It was seen as the best method to emancipate oneself. The tenant-at-will institution was killed when land was taken by force by colonial settlers

---

43. Ibid., 90.

and by the capitalism, individualism, and materialism that was introduced by the European civilization.[44] Thankfully the Akũrinũ church unlike the mainstream Church is sensitive to such culturally based solutions to the socio-economic needs of her members and has continued to apply them to various degrees to empower them.

This research seeks to demonstrate how the Akũrinũ church in a small way is showing a different kind of social imagination. The Akũrinũ church is an African church trying to solve African problems using culturally sensitive African worldview, the resources of the Bible, and the Spirit of God. The Akũrinũ churches alongside other spiritual churches support their members in such events as marriages, funerals, and other crisis points in the society. By being alive to the importance of these aspects of traditional culture, they apply their sense of Christian fellowship more radically to recreate the traditional African clan solidarity in Christian terms.[45]

Kwame Bediako's Search for African Christian Identity

The late Kwame Bediako was a doyen of theology and culture from Ghana, West Africa. He looked to the future while looking over his shoulder to suggest a future that is based on the past. The Akũrinũ church is an example of a church movement that has built her theology on the religious consciousness of the past, the African primal religious worldview.

Kwame Bediako and other theologians such as Andrew Walls and Lamin Sanneh have amply called attention to the phenomenal growth of

---

44. For further reading on the impact of colonial cultural invasion on African culture you can read this in, George Kinoti, "Morality is Vital to Economic and Social Development" by Hannah Kinoti in George Kinoti and Peter Kimuyu, eds., A *Vision for a Bright Africa: Facing the Challenges of Development* (Kampala: Uganda: African Institute for Scientific Research and Development. 1997).

45. Bediako, *Christianity in Africa*, 67.

Christianity in the global South. This has seen its epicenter tilt steadily South with the unequivocal move of its center of gravity moving specifically to Africa.[46] Bediako observes that;

> Though the origins of the phenomenal presence of Christianity on the African soil coincided with an intensified impact of the West on African life, one is compelled to recognize that the waning of the Western dominance has not produced any general diminution in the influence of Christianity on the continent. On the contrary, the Christian Churches of Africa, whether they be of missionary origin or the fruit of solely indigenous African initiative, whatever their varying fortunes in their diverse socio-political contexts, remain important religious and social institutions in their own right which cannot be ignored.[47]

Once introduced to Africa, Christianity took on a power of its own. Christianity was instantly at home. At home because Christianity was in North Africa for a long time before it was eclipsed by Islam, and presently because its spiritual core resonates with traditional African religious values.

This unprecedented growth should elicit some interest in the study of the theologies of the global South — the theology of the majority. In appraising the African primal religions, Bediako notes that;

> The way the African seek spiritual help today (from praying for or dedicating a new house, for fertility, to success in examination etc.) all shows that far from obliterating the African primal view of things, in its essentially unified and "spiritual" nature and replacing it with a two-tier modern Western view compromising sacred and secular dimensions, the Christian faith has reinforced the African view. Even though African Christian communities were generally

---

46. Bediako, *Christianity in Africa*, 126.
47. Ibid., 3.

the earliest to be exposed to Western education through missionary enterprise, African Christians have not, on the whole, any significant secularization of their outlook. New knowledge in science and technology has been embraced, but it has not displaced the basic view that the whole universe in which human existence takes place is fundamentally spiritual. The African experience here points to the African insistence that technology has to be without materialism. God is an inner necessity for humankind.[48]

Bediako maintains that what the gospel has done to the African Christian is to affirm a spirituality that was there already, even if it has also pruned off some of its features, and sharpened its focus, this time, upon Christ. Accordingly;

> It is hardly surprising that the Christologies that have emerged in African theology so far are predominantly 'pneumatic' presenting Christ who is a living power in the realm of the Spirit. African Christological titles such 'Eldest Brother' (H. Sawyerr), 'Ancestor', 'Great Ancestor' (J. S. Pobee, C. Nyamiti, K. Bediako), are neither from below, nor strictly 'from above'; rather they are indicative of the way the primal imagination grasps the reality of Christ in terms in which all life is essentially conceived — as spiritual.[49]

For Bediako, the search for Christian identity in Africa remains elusive. Yet, however elusive, African primal imagination provides the structure and the epistemology upon which real and authentic Christianity in Africa will of necessity need to rest. Bediako notes that African theologians such as John Mbiti have through serious intellectual engagement, succeeded in Christianizing the African past, not a mean achievement at any

---

48. Ibid., 192.
49. Ibid.

rate. What remains is Africanizing the Christian experience.[50] Bediako surmises this of the 'African Theology';

> We are now able to conclude quite firmly that we cannot understand the fortunes of Christianity in Africa if we ignore the impact of the continent's primal religious background.[51]

To this, Bediako adds;

> The primal religions of the continent have thus been a significant factor in the immense Christian presence in Africa. While this cannot be taken to mean that there has not been any 'paradigm-shift' in African religious consciousness, it does confirm that the African apprehension of the Christian faith has substantial roots in the continent's primal traditions at the specific level of religious consciousness. At least we can say that if it did not have the primal religions as its sub-stratum, the story of Christianity in Africa at the closure of the present century [referring to 20th C], would be very different.[52]

Referring to the Edinburg Conference of 1910, Bediako can confidently say; at the beginning of the western missionary enterprise, the question was, "can the animist be converted? Today the question is — can the West be converted?."[53]

Consequently, as Katongole demonstrates, the colonial and neocolonial preoccupation with 'tribalism' reflects a specific attitude according to which Africa's social history, instead of being viewed as a resource providing the building blocks for any modernizing projects, has been viewed as a 'problem', which needs to be overcome.[54]

---

50. Ibid.
51. Ibid.
52. Ibid.
53. Ibid.,193.
54. Katongole, *Sacrifices of Africa*, 67.

This alienation of Africa from her social history is of significance in developing contextual theologies. The missionary enterprise, like its metropolitan imperial governments, alienated Africa from her vast wealth of cultural wisdom when it found nothing in her religious heritage to use as a building block on which to anchor Christianity. For example, the missionaries did not care to explore the deep religious consciousness and the pervasive preoccupation of Africans with her ubiquitous spirits. Mbiti's observation that Africans are notoriously religious is not a cliché — whenever an African was found, so was his religion.

Bediako concurs with Katongole on the failure of Africa. He says that the failure of Africa is a failure to appreciate her culture with its religious consciousness and thus use it to imagine. Again, like Katongole, he traces the failure to colonial project of denying any value of the African culture. The missionary Christianity, which was undifferentiated from the colonial government, followed the same script of reading bankruptcy on African culture on any social imagination. But where Katongole sees no value for African cultures for a new social imagination, Bediako appraises African culture.

It is in this thinking that Bediako says that the challenge to Christianity in African life, in terms of its cultural and intellectual relevance, becomes a challenge to demonstrate its spiritual credentials for what they are, and to show how efficacious these spiritual credentials are at providing a unified world of meaning to meet African needs.[55] Bediako concludes that "Africa Traditional Religion (ATR) has been a serious preparation for the Gospel in Africa and forms the major religious substratum for the idiom and existential experiences of Christianity in African life."[56]

Bediako also informs us that "the primal religions of Africa and elsewhere in the world have entered upon a new career in Christian scholarship." On this he says;

---

55. Bediako, *Christianity in Africa*, 81.
56. Ibid., 82.

> Not only have we learnt to understand the primal religious traditions as the background of the Christian profession of the vast majority of all Christians of all generations and all nations in the twentieth centuries of Christian history, and therefore as the most fertile ground for Christian conversions, but also this peculiar historical connection between the primal religions of the world and Christianity may have implications for understanding possible affinities between them.[57]

Bediako then draws this conclusion, "the impact of such insights is far reaching in the shaping of the mind of the new African theology."[58] Speculating on what kind of African theology that may emerge, Bediako says that this theology would seek an African idiom.

He draws from the fact that a number of writings that came up between 1979 and 1984 on Christology, all referred to Christ as an *ancestor* based on the vernacular reading of the Bible which took seriously the African religious apprehension of Christ in the African worldview, and answering to the challenge of showing the relevance of faith in Christ at the root of African existence and humanity.[59]

Remarkably Bediako also points to what he calls relevant theology in the context of Christianity in African life and at the living roots of the Church. He says,

> It seems that the new African theology will have to attempt what the writer of the Epistle of Hebrews did; that is, to make room, within an inherited body of tradition, for new ideas, for new realities which, though seemingly entering from outside, come in to fulfill aspirations within the tradi-

---

57. Andrew F. Walls, "Africa and Christian identity," *Mission Focus*, Vol. 6/7 (1978) 83.
58. Bediako, *Christianity in Africa*, 83.
59. Ibid., 82.

tion, and then to alter quite significantly the basis of self-understanding within that tradition.[60]

Bediako welcomes the gospel that the missionary brought to Africa, what he describes as, "new ideas and realities seemingly entering from the outside."[61] But he is against the universalization of western theology that calls for contextualization of the gospel in Africa. African scholars should ask themselves: Why should ideas of theology come from outside to Africa? While missionaries are indispensable wherever the gospel has not reached, the propagation of the gospel does not mean that people's theology must also be foreign.

The history of contextualization is long. But the bottom line, and in the most simplistic way, contextualization as it is usually understood, assumes that there is a 'universal theology' (from the West) that needs to be contextualized to Africa, and for any other place for that matter. Understood as such, it is our belief that contextualization would bring the same alienation of African cultures and further compound the search for identity. This is because contextualization too often uses the idiom and epistemology of the 'contextualizer' and invites the recipient to judge what is being contextualized in his religious category. The 'contexualizer' comes in as an informer and an expert — not a learner.

Our argument is that instead of contextualization, we need to move on to global theologies or grassroot theologies whereby theologies from multiple centers contribute to the growing search for global theology. The Majority World Church influence on the universal Church has been to bring a broader understanding of her role as a witness to the Word of God among men; the effect of this is to cause her to adopt a humbler, servant posture among the people it encounters, rather than the stance of crusader or inquisitor.[62]

---

60. Ibid., 84.
61. Ibid.
62. Bediako, *Christianity in Africa*, 153.

In this important work, Bediako demonstrates that the question of identity remains important to Africa. Simply put, identity asks how one can be a Christian and African at the same time. This remains a legitimate question in which the main thrust of African Christian scholarship has argued that conversion to Christianity must be coupled with cultural continuity. To the extent that this looking back to appraise culture to aid in giving meaning and hence identity to Africans, Bediako is important. However, identity should not be an end in itself. Rather, it should be the launching pad upon which to undertake life. Armed with the confidence that Africans are whole human beings, they should move on unapologetically to creatively explore and exploit reality. It is in this regard that Africans must seek both socio-economic and socio-political developments that are true and reflective of their cultural heritage.

Kwame H. Bediako's Search for African Christian Identity

Whereas Katongole finds little value in the African traditional culture as a starting point for social imagination in Africa, Bediako whose focus is religio-political, has greater sympathy. Bediako argues that by moving and functioning more intensely within the African traditional worldview of their members and applying the Christian understandings which they gain from the vernacular Scriptures, some of the African Independent Churches (AICs) arrive at solutions which tend more clearly towards a christian direction while remaining African. On the other hand, the historical churches, because they present 'Christian' solutions which have not been thought through from a standpoint of the persisting traditional world-view of their members, prove in the end, less helpful.[63]

---

63. Bediako, *Christianity in Africa*, 68.

Accordingly, the phenomena of 'living in two worlds' half-traditional and half-Christian, and not belonging to either, can be said to be more characteristic of members of the historical churches than those of spiritual churches. While the latter appear to be attempting to work out their salvation in Christ within the traditional religions, the former, on the whole, are failing to do so. Bediako concludes that because of this many of the members of the AICs or spiritual churches are ex-Roman Catholics, ex-Methodists, ex-Presbyterians, ex-Anglicans.[64] By this, Bediako means that these believers have migrated to the AICs which they deem more apt to enter and understand their world-view.

Interestingly, African Christianity has often been described as being shallow — a mile wide and an inch deep! This may be attributable to the way Christianity was introduced to Africa. Missionary Christianity did not confront the African world-view since she did not recognize the African tradition religions. Bediako observes, quoting Williamson's observation on Akan tradition,

> If Christianity failed to take serious account of the traditional beliefs held about 'gods and lords many', ancestors and spirits and other spiritual agencies and their impact on human life, then it also failed to meet the Akan in his personally experienced religious needs. Looked at from this perspective, the missionary activity never amounted to a serious encounter, and the Christian communities that have resulted have not really known how to relate to their traditional culture in terms other than that of denunciation of separateness. Dialogue has been distinctively absent.[65]

Bediako further says that the missionary enterprise of the 19th century did not see in African traditional religion and culture, a partner for dia-

---

64. Ibid., 68.
65. Bediako, *Christianity in Africa*, 68

logue the way in which it viewed Buddhism and philosophical Hinduism in Asia.

The 1910 World Missionary Conference in Edinburgh concluded that African traditional religions, which it loudly described as animism, probably contained no preparation for Christianity. When more positive appreciation gained currency, it was too late. The mission Churches were already in place, marked generally by their separateness from their cultures, rather than their involvement in them. The Christian tradition as historically received through the missionary enterprise has on the whole been unable to sympathize with or relate to the spiritual realities of the traditional world-view. It is not so much a case of unwillingness to relate to these realities, but of not having learned to do so.[66]

It is on this account that Bediako says that the flowering of the African theology of the early post-independent period by the most eminent writers, Bolaji Idowu of Nigeria, Harry Sawyerr of Liberia, and John Mbiti of Kenya, focused more on giving a positive interpretation of the African religious past than the missionary assessment had done. In so doing, they demonstrated the continuity of the religious past with the Christian present. This theology was an effort towards indigenization of Christianity by Christianizing the African past rather than contextualization or inculturalization.[67] This Christianization of the past was a search for African Christian identity that had suffered under the hands of the missionaries. The same people who had enslaved Africans for decades came to repent and restituted by repatriating the slaves in the 19th century, a period that coincided with colonialism by the same people.[68] One can say the enslavement of Africans continued in the colonial era only this time; Africans were slaves in their own countries.

---

66. Ibid., 69.
67. Ibid., 76.
68. Ibid., 80.

Another way that Bediako sees the value of African culture is in the use of African vernacular languages in understanding the Christian faith. Bediako argues that it is only through vernacular that a genuine and lasting theological dialogue with culture can take place. This is more so if we consider that majority of Christians in Africa speak vernacular and read the Bible in vernacular. The value of making the Scripture in African vernacular languages a major focus and point of reference is that African theological methods, interests, and goals will then be shaped and controlled by the genuine needs of Christianity in African life.

Unfortunately, missionary schools and those of independent Africa have not encouraged the development and use of vernacular especially in early childhood education. This is rather interesting because the missionaries made gallant efforts in translating the vernacular Bible. It is only in Africa where speaking in mother-tongue is made a serious crime for school going children. Kenyan novelist Ngũgĩ wa Thiong'o describes how school going pupils were punished for speaking their mother tongue. They had to run around with a metal disc hanging on their necks with the inscription, "I am a fool."[69]

Bediako says the challenge to Christianity in the African life, in terms of its cultural and intellectual relevance, becomes a challenge to Christianity to demonstrate its spiritual credentials for what they are and to show how these provide a unified world of meaning to meet African needs.[70] Bediako also informs us that, "the primal religions of Africa and elsewhere in the world have entered upon a new career in Christian scholarship." Quoting Andrew Walls, Bediako says;

---

69. The scholar and novelist Ngugi wa Thiong'o, in his many fictional and non-fictional writings, among them *Decolonizing the Mind* and *The River Between* (Nairobi, Kenya: Heinemann, 1981) remains a classic reference for the clash of cultures that occurred between colonial education and Christianity on one, and the Kikuyu traditional cultures on the other. In particular, the requirement for school going children to denounce their mother tongue for English was a harsh judgment on the traditional cultures that paved the way for easy colonization of the mind.

70. Bediako, *Christianity in Africa*, 81.

> Not only have we learnt to understand the primal religious traditions as the background of the Christian profession of the vast majority of all Christians of all generations and all nations in the twenty centuries of Christian history, and therefore as the most fertile ground for Christian conversions, but also this peculiar historical connection between the primal religions of the world and Christianity may have implications for understanding possible affinities between them.[71]

On this, Bediako says, "The impact of such insights is far reaching in the shaping of the mind of the new African theology."[72] As I demonstrated earlier in chapter one, both Katongole and Bediako work within the framework of contextualization. Bediako believes we are in a new era in contextualization evidenced by the many ecumenical bodies in Africa such as the Ecumenical Association of the Third World Theologians (EATWOT). He says that both Black theologies in South Africa and Liberation theology in Latin America all seek to contextualize the Christian faith.[73]

On our part we have argued that contextualization, crucial as it is in the current theological discussion, is inadequate to explain the marked growth of Christianity in the global South and the emergence of many ecclesial groups that have mushroomed. This seriously begs for hermeneutical humility on the part of the West where Africa is concerned. What is the real fuel for this growth? This is why I argue that instead of contextualization we need to move on to global or contextual theologies where theologies from multiple centers contribute to the growing search for global theology. There is need to study these ecclesial groups in their theological context.

It is our belief that the efforts of contextualization will further complicate the African search for Christian identity because it seeks to ac-

---

71. Ibid., 83.
72. Ibid., 86.
73. Ibid.

commodate the missionary Christian faith in African culture, rather than confront the culture. Contextualization does not adequately address the African religious experience. Instead it just seems interested in finding its equivalence in the African setting thereby making theologizing in Africa a superficial and non-engaging exercise.

It is in this argument that we see the Akũrinũ church as an example of a cultural movement that not only helps us to gain an insight of the entrance of the gospel unmediated (away from contextualization) to a culture, but also how such a theology can contribute to the growing search of global theology. Such a reading of theology not only help us to see God's activity in a cultural movement but also underscores the fact that God has moved in culture and in all people and that all people are capable of grasping the revelation of God within their cultural reality. If God has revealed himself to Akũrinũ as I will seek to demonstrate through this research, and if the Akũrinũ church has something unique to contribute to the world about God, then I will affirm the fact that all people are at par before God. I do not know of a greater fact and factor that appraises human dignity than to know that God is and has always been at work among them without requiring them to be photocopies of other people to authenticate Gods' movement among them, to reiterate what I have said before.

The Primal Factor in African Religious Heritage

What might answer the source of the tremendous move of God in Africa in the face of what Bediako describes as diminishing fortunes of the colonial and missionary presence? In quoting Harold W. Turner extensively, Bediako has pointed out an affinity between Christianity and primal religion[74]. On the nature of the primal religion, Turner says that

---

74. Bediako, *Christianity in Africa*, 94-95.

the primal religions have a sense of kinship with nature, in which animals and plants, no less than human beings, have their own spiritual existence and place in the universe as interdependent parts of the whole.

Turner describes this "ecological aspect" as a profound religious attitude to man's natural setting. Perhaps this is what Ngũgĩ alludes to when he says that, "In the African customs everything could be explained in a spiritual sense. For example if one was sick, witchcraft was to blame. Everything in nature was a voice from God; the roaring thunder in the sky, the blinding lightning flash across the earth."[75]

Secondly there is a deep sense that man is finite, weak, impure or sinful and stands in need of power not his own. Turner says that this is the natural reaction of the creature hood of man before a holy God. He adds that such an assessment of the human condition can be drowned by technology and socio-political power. This has certainly happened in the post-Christian nations. There is enough fear that Africa is quickly developing in the same trend of Western technology. If technology and socio-political power produces same effect in all people, one may have a reason to fear for Africa and other primal worldviews.

This raises the need to engage post-modernism from the bedrock of primal world-view. In my estimation, one of the ways in which the West killed her primal worldview is by portraying it as incompatible with civilization. On this Bediako says that,

> A serious Christian theological interest in the European primal traditions and in the early forms of Christianity that emerged from the encounter with those traditions could provide a fresh approach to understand Christian identity in the West, as well as opening new possibilities for new Christian theological endeavor today. The primal world view may turn out to be not so alien to the West after all, even in a post-Enlightenment era.[76]

---

75. wa Thiong'o, *The River Between*, 56.

76. Bediako, *Christianity in Africa*, 261-262.

Bediako arrives at this conclusion by observing that;

> Some aspects of the post-modernist rejection of the Enlightenment in the West — the resurgence of the occult as well as the various 'quests' for spiritual experience wholeness, even if without explicit reference to God — bear the marks of a primal world-view. They are sufficient indicators that the primal world-view, suppressed rather than encountered, redeemed and integrated rises to haunt the future.[77]

Consequently, Bediako suggests that the viability of a Christian consciousness that retains its sense of the spiritual worldview of primal religions, and the theological encounter between the primal worldview and Christian faith evident in African Christianity — constitute an implicit challenge to the notion that humanity can be fully defined in post-Enlightenment terms.[78]

Thirdly, the primal worldview affirms the conviction that man is not alone in the universe for there is a spiritual world of powers or beings more powerful and ultimate than man himself. Again, this may evoke reverence and even worship of the transcendent. The gospel gives a clear focus as to the object of worship, and the means of this worship. Where the gospel is not known, the spiritual entities may evoke great fear.

Fourthly, this view believes that human beings can enter into a relationship with the benevolent spirit-world and so share in its powers and blessings while receiving from these transcendent helpers' protection from evil forces. This essentially becomes the basis of approaching God in prayer.

Fifthly, there is an acute sense of the reality of the afterlife, a conviction that explains the important place of ancestors or the "living dead" in many primal religions. A life in view of eternity is able to keep human beings in the right perspective as they journey through life. Lastly, there

---

77. Ibid., 262.
78. Ibid., 60-61.

is a conviction that humanity is in a sacramental universe where there is no sharp dichotomy between the physical and the spiritual. Accordingly, the physical acts as a vehicle for spiritual power, whilst the physical realm is held as patterned on the model of the spiritual world beyond.

Turner further demonstrates from this observation that primal religion can be used to understand other religions and also be applicable to Christian traditions. He points out that the spread of Christianity has been solely in the regions with primal religious consciousness. These include the Mediterranean world of the early Christian centuries, the tribal peoples of Northern and Western Europe, the primal societies of Africa, the Pacific, and parts of Asia.

Accordingly, there seems to be an affinity between the primal religions and Christianity that seems to say to the missionary, "this is what we have been waiting for."[79] This may explain the fertile ground on which Christianity in Africa has landed. And more fortunes could be realized if this primal worldview was exploited and made the basis of understanding Christian faith, an approach that the Akũrinũ church has taken full advantage of. The sad fact, unfortunately, is how from the period of renaissance, the West has sought to deny and denounce primal thinking, terming it as primitive and overtaken by the secularization process. In this process the West has lost any sense of mystery to which Christianity and every faith belong.

Regrettably, the world of the African primal religion has not been fully explored. Bediako notes that though African scholars such as Bolaji and Mbiti have been able to articulate the God of the primal religions of Africa as the God of the Bible, they have not been able to deal with the issues of divinities adequately. They wished them away instead.[80] This attitude of the pioneer African theologians was most probably predicated on the then pressing need to defend the ATR as monotheistic — it must be

---

79. Bediako, *Christianity in Africa*, 95.
80. Bediako, *Christianity in Africa*, 98.

noted that the West had long placed African polytheistic religions at the bottom of religious ladder behind Christianity, Judaism, and Islam.[81] Here again we see how the West sets a theological agenda for Africa to which African runs helter skater in self-defense, or in defense of their God.

On his part, Bediako says that the divinities are inherited, acquired and can be dropped when they cease to be useful. The ancestors are irreplaceable and are more difficult to deal with. He alludes to the fact that the divinities in the light of Christianity must be understood as the angels and saints. Bediako says that though the African theologians have been able to establish the continuity of monotheism, they have failed to account for the multiplicity of the transcendent by failing to articulate the reality of the divinities, and the contribution that it can make towards a fresh understanding of Christianity.

Our observations are that divinities are rife in the African primal worldview and cannot be ignored. The divinities must be dealt with because they dictate the affairs of many African Christians. Some demand to be placated, while others dictate certain actions especially during the rites of passage, and still others torment people almost holding their life at ransom. Again, as I have demonstrated that historical churches prefer to ignore the existence of the divinities which unfortunately being so real to believers, they move on to seek help on how to combat them even from the most unlikely places. The Bible treats these entities with seriousness and wants them to be brought under the Lordship of Christ. Paul says in Philippians 2: 9-11;

> *Therefore God exalted him to the highest place*
> *and gave him the name that is above every name,*
> *[10] that at the name of Jesus every knee should bow,*

---

81. Jennings, *Imagination*, 34.

> in heaven and on earth and under the earth,
> [11] and every tongue acknowledge that Jesus Christ is Lord,
> to the glory of God the Father.

It is not far-fetched to imagine that the whole preoccupation of the AICs with the pneumatic phenomena, a subject that the mainstream churches largely prefers to shun, is based on this being at home with the divinities.

Kagame-Mulango says that the African primal worldview is not dualistic like the Western worldview.[82] It has two vital centers, God and man, where the exaltation of man does not displace God. From this Bediako concludes; the primal religion is this-worldly, and that this-worldliness encompasses God and man in an abiding relationship with the divine destiny of humankind, the purpose and goal of the universe. Again, while the West is grappling with the ills of dichotomizing life, Africa coming from a primal worldview, views life as holistic with no serious divide between the sacred and the secular. It is our view that it is a tall order to repudiate the primal worldview and retain a holistic view of life at the same time.

The Kagame-Mulago conclusion that at the heart of the universe and religion is a divine-human relationship for the fulfillment of man's divine destiny, constitutes man's destiny, a real destiny that lies at the heart of the contribution which African theology, from the primal perspective, can make a fresh Christian account of the Transcendent. This insight signifies that in Christian terms, the revelation of God in Christ is the disclosure that God is abidingly involved in a relationship with man, and for man; God has never left man and never been far removed from man, Acts 17:27.

Bediako recalls Mbiti's ontology where God, spirits, man, animals, plants and inanimate creation, are in unity. In this ontology all things exist in unity so that to break up the unity is to destroy one or more of

---

82. Kagame-Mulago quoted in Bediako, *Christianity in Africa*, 101.

these modes of existence, and to destroy one is in effect to destroy all of them. Accordingly, in Jesus' incarnation, God becomes one with humankind so that man can become one with him.[83] Consequently the seeing of visions and dreams are transcendent happenings in the churches that are alive to the primal worldview.[84] Bediako says that the community that is open to the manifestations of the Transcendent come to participate in the Transcendent. Many AICs and in particular the Akũrinũ, are open to the Transcendent and many such manifestations are not uncommon. Unfortunately, the historical churches frown on such manifestation, thanks to cultural evolution from Protestant Reformation to date.

In dealing extensively with the issue of primal religion and primal imagination, Bediako opens a new dialogue for theological conversation. He notes that, "Primal religions generally conceive of religion as a system of power and living religiously as being in touch with the source and channels of power in the universe. On the other hand, Christian theology in the West seems, on the whole, to understand the Christian gospel as a system of ideas.[85] These understandings are a world apart.

The Translatability of the Gospel

Another way to understand the fortunes of Christianity in Africa is via the discourse of translatability. In this thinking Sennah shows how unlike Islam, Christianity has no single revealed language, a fact supported by historical experience where on the day of Pentecost the believers were heard praising God in their different mother tongues when the Spirit fell on them. [86]The translatability or universality of the gospel, and hence its ability to be incarnated in different cultural settings, can be said to be

---

83. Kagame-Mulago quoted in Bediako, *Christianity in Africa*, 102.
84. Ibid., 103
85. Ibid., 106.
86. Sanneh, *Translating*, 253.

actually the basis of the thriving and mushrooming of the gospel in Africa, and the basis on which to expect the flourishing of African theology, and for our case *Akũrinũ* vernacular theology. Sanneh goes to document how the translation of the Bible whether to the Slavs, among the Armenians or the Coptic Church all thrived when the Scriptures were translated into their native languages.[87]

In this cultural incarnation of the gospel, Bediako referencing Andrew Walls says that each incarnation has been different yet preserving certain elements that unite them all as sharing in a common reality. These elements include; the worship of the God of Israel, attribution of ultimate significance of Jesus Christ, a sense of belonging to a people of God extending beyond the local context and in the midst of whom God's activity is recognized, reading of the common Scriptures, and the sacramental use of bread, wine and water.[88] Bediako says that this translatability of the Christianity signifies its fundamental relevance and accessibility to persons in any culture within which the Christian faith is transmitted and assimilated.[89] Here Bediako argues that this character of Christianity is seen most clearly in the Christian view of Scripture and in incarnation of Jesus Christ, the God-man. Christianity rejects any esoteric language, unlike Islam, allowing the scriptures to be translated into any language.

In incarnation, we see the fullest of divine communication reaching beyond human word to human form. In this way, Bediako says that translatability may be said to be in-built into the nature of the Christian religion and capable of subverting any cultural possessiveness of the faith in the process of its transmission. For Bediako, the importance of the principle of translatability is that we can be able to appreciate the

---

87. Ibid., 257.

88. Andrew Walls, "Christian Tradition in Today's World," quoted in Bediako, *Christianity in Africa*, 109.

89. Bediako, *Christianity in Africa*, 109.

true character of continuing Christian witness and enhance the genuine development of new indigenous traditions of Christian thought.[90]

Bediako traces the thought of translatability from Mbiti's writing. Though he described the African church born of the missionary effort as one that had come of age evangelistically but not theologically, and as such a church without theology and consequently without theological concern, Mbiti was also able on the same breath to make a distinction between "Christianity" which 'results from the encounter of the gospel with any given local society' whereby it is always indigenous and cultural bound, on one hand, and the gospel, which is God-given, eternal and unchanging, on the other hand.[91]

It is in this effort of seeking identity for African Christianity that Mbiti called for translatability — the capacity of the essential impulses of the Christian religion to be transmitted and assimilated in a different culture so that these impulses create dynamically equivalent responses in the course of such a transmission. Bediako calls for indigeneity that is based on translatability. He recognizes that universality, translatability, incarnation, and indigeneity are all in a continuum.

Comparing two African theologians of note, Bolaji Idowu and John Mbiti, Bediako says that Idowu described African Independent Churches as syncretistic. Such thoughts live on in a number of prejudiced individuals who have been socialized to regard the West as best and anything else anywhere as second best[92]. John Mbiti on the other hand saw in AICs, an African Christian consciousness and experience, having its own integrity. In this thinking, the missionary endeavor becomes of secondary importance to God's project of revealing himself to all cultures in which case, missionaries did not bring God to Africa, but God brought

---

90. Ibid., 110.

91. John Mbiti, "Some African Concepts of Christology" in *Christ and the Younger Churches*, ed. G.F. Vicedom (London: SPCK, 1972), 51-62.

92. Bolaji Odulumere Idowu, *God in Yoruba Belief* (London: Longman, 1962), 211-12.

them so that Africans may worship Jesus Christ who fulfills the highest aspiration of the African religious quest.[93]

Whereas Idowu was preoccupied with indigenization, Mbiti was more concerned with translatability. It is in this aspect that indigenization becomes a blind path. Evangelization is not simply the communication of foreign ideas to passive recipients who have to swallow every bit whether or not they approve.[94] Africans received the missionary message in their own terms and understanding, informed by their own religious understanding embedded in their cultural wisdom and primal worldview. Sanneh's argument is that the reception of the Scriptures on the indigenous language allows for the reader to have a new sense of agency and initiative, apart from the missionary presence, what he calls, "an increasing awareness of Africans of the significance of their own mother tongue in the universal design of God."[95]

Bediako says that we need to appreciate that between the two processes at work in Christianity, i.e., historical transmission and indigenous assimilation, the more significant is the process of assimilation because it is within this process that the historical process itself becomes meaningful. Consequently, not what the Western missionaries did (or did not do), but what Africans did, and have done with the gospel, that has proved the most enduring element in the making of the Christian Africa in the 20th century.[96]

---

93. Bediako, *Christianity in Africa*, 118.

94. Ayayi and Ayandele, 'Writing African Church History', 68, quoted in Bediako, *Christianity in Africa*, 119.

95. Sanneh, *Translating*, 219.

96. L. Sanneh, 'The Horizontal and the Vertical in Mission: An African Perspective,' *International Bulletin of Missionary Research*, Vol.7 no.4, (1983), 166.

A Theological Framework for Understanding Culture

A theology of culture is critical in formulating contextual theologies that embody those cultures. As I have demonstrated above, contextual theologies and indeed all theologies reflect on the culture of a particular people, particularly their understanding and practice of religion. Richard J. Gehman says that, "All learning proceeds from the known to the unknown. What the person believes and knows forms the basis of further knowledge." [97] But the framework that I am proposing here is beyond the cognitive and the language level because cultural moorings are much deeper in any people. The framework for understanding contextual or global theologies envisioned in this research is based on two thoughts; the centrality of creation in God's past, present, and continued work in guiding and directing creation (or what we refer to as reflexivity) so that creation can ultimately glorify His name, and secondly, on what Jennings calls, "Intimacy" or "Joining."

The reflexivity of God, in man may be said to be the reason why Africans cultures retained some shades of beauty and grasped something of God, however vaguely, and in spite of the fall. Before the fall, Adam did not need a religious culture. He lived in the presence of God. He and his wife were naked or innocent before God. Religious culture became necessary when man was estranged and separated from God. Protestant Christianity has been rightly accused of picking the story of God from the New Testament as though the New Testament replaced or did away with the Old Testament. Although creation suffers the effect of the fall of the first Adam, the second Adam came to restore or better put, renew creation (what Dyrness calls re-creation). Despite the fall, God's reflexivity is discernable in all of creation.

---

97. Richard J. Gehman, *African Traditional Religion in Biblical Perspective* (Nairobi, Kenya: East Africa Educational Publishers Ltd, 2005).

The starting point in understanding contextual theology is to see the missionary work as a response to what God may be doing in culture. To this Dyrness says,

> The focus in missions should be less on what missionaries are doing, and more, in the first instance, on what God is doing, an observation that does not result from an abundance of piety, but from the simple fact that what we humans do is always a response and interaction with what God is doing.[98]

In this regard creation was not a contingent in God's work. It has a bigger role and implication.

Dyrness maintains that the continuing activity of God in culture, or reflexivity, is evident both in a general sense, God makes the rain to fall, adorns the lily, cares for the birds and takes delight in the creatures of the sea, and in a particular sense as God calls Abraham, delivers Israel from bondage in Egypt, and brings them into the good land (again as a secure place the Host has prepared as a home for Israel). Dyrness stresses in particular two aspects of this continuing work of God in the first Testament; the *acts* of God: creating, speaking, sustaining, delivering, and judging, when God often self-identifies as this active deliverer: "I am the God who brought you out of the land of Egypt, out of the house of slavery," Exodus 19: 2. Secondly, creation has a purpose and goal namely renewal and restoration of the creation (of which culture is part and parcel). Creation from the start has a particular direction.

The ongoing work of redemption inaugurated by the incarnation story presupposes the redemption (which Dyrness calls "renewal") of culture. Culture, one can construe, had a twin purpose; to enhance human agency, and ultimately to glorify the creator. Religious culture in all human cultures no matter how debased, was an attempt to seek something of the divine.

---

98. Dyrness, *Insider Jesus*, 10-11.

Though Adam and Eve had unique roles to play, they were to work alongside God in ordering and making sense of creation. God clearly gave both Adam and Eve a role in having dominion over all the creatures of the land, sky and sea and even naming the animals, Genesis 1 & 2. This renewal and restoration culminated in the incarnation story. Dyrness says that in Christ's incarnation, death, and resurrection, God's primary purpose was to renew His creation. To this he adds; "If God's primary work is creating and renewing, then it is possible—and in the biblical narrative necessary—to see Christ as the fulfillment of this primary work."[99] It is for this that Dyrness says: "if we are to understand what God is up to in creation and recreation, we need to hold together this primary work of renewal, and the special call to the human creativity to work together with God in this restoration, as this enabled by Christ and the Spirit." To this Dyrness adds:

> That though created order is deeply marred by human disobedience; this does not keep cultures from developing varieties of wisdom that bring glory to God. People are always making something out of the situation they find themselves in, and this often brings about good in a way God approves. He gives the example of how man has developed the ability to grow food and domesticate animals, or to discover healing remedies in certain plants. These are all things that Scripture says God delights in, even, seems eager to take credit for.[100]

To this I add that no culture has a monopoly neither is there one that is completely devoid of God's reflexivity.

Dyrness then points to what makes culture important for our study;

> The connection of religious faith and wise living has a deeper implication that I want to draw out. This deep connection

---

99. Dyrness, *Insider Jesus*, 39.
100. Ibid.

> between faith and wisdom implies that a significant part of every culture, one might say its heart and core, involves the religious practices that have developed in that place. The perennial human search for God animates culture. Religious practices reflect the human desire to respond to the gods or powers they encounter, and in this desire, they are also responding to the call of the biblical God. But note the implications of this: If it is true that religious traditions reflect a response, however incomplete (or even misguided) to God's call, they must be in some way capable of being taken up into God's project of renewing and restoring the earth.[101]

In this I deduce that there is great cultural wisdom embedded in the traditional cultures and all other cultures. It is our humble submission that more study be devoted to the African and other traditional cultures without discounting the modern cultures, in particular to discover God's continued work of grace that finds its fulfillment in Christ.

In addition to God's reflexivity in humans, the centrality of God's call to the nation of Israel — a call located in the context of Ancient Near East (ANE) culture from which Moses and the Israelites borrowed in trying to make sense of God — helps us understand contextual theologies. Melchizedeck, the Pharaoh who attempted to take Sarah from Abraham for a wife, Abimelech who attempted the same for Rebecca, Jethro — Moses' father-in-law, King Cyrus the Persian, and a host of others depict a culture that clearly shows that they knew something of the true God. Dyrness says that;

> Evidence for this lies in the fact that Israel's religious practices, like cultural practices, were not, in the first instance, unique in the ANE culture — priests, sacrifices and sacred spots were common to Israel and her neighbors. It is true that the law God gives to Moses, and that is laid out in the book of Leviticus and Deuteronomy, includes details of re-

---

[101] Dyrness, *Insider Jesus*, 39.

ligious practices—including food preparation and appropriate sacrifices, along with ethical precepts. God had a clear interest in all of this and demanded a specific obedience on the part of his people. But when one examines these practices carefully, even the ethical instructions (enshrined for example in the Ten Commandments), one finds that these frequently reflect widely shared practices and values in the Ancient Near East."[102]

It is in this argument that Dyrness conveys that:

> Religion must always be seen in terms of the cultures they indwell—the historical and social situation in which they have developed. Israel was no mythical but real. The Bible is careful to record the history of Israel in details that include her failure, as a history of God's dealing with real people. And as culture itself is an accumulation of human efforts and the resulting wisdom, creating spaces for medicine and science, and art and literature to flourish, so religion represents an accumulated wisdom about living in the world and endowing life with significance.[103]

Colenso's gallant translation efforts among the Nguni should be seen in this light. Jennings captures both Lamin Sanneh and Andrew Walls' reading of the historical benefits of the translation project.

To Sanneh, the translation project's unintended benefit was the formation of the black agency and cultural being.[104] Sanneh sees the translation process in the light of the historical Christianizing process through the idea of a universality of humanity that transcends Jewish particularity. Paul's writing captures this process where he understood his mission to the gentiles could not be isolated from Judaism. Paul understood that the center of Christianity was in the heart and the life of the believer

---

102. Dyrness, *Insider Jesus*, 45
103. Ibid.
104. Jennings, *Christian Imagination*, 155.

without the assumption of conformity to one cultural ideal.[105] To Walls, incarnation is translation. When God in Christ became man, divinity was translated to humanity as though humanity were a receptor language.

Unfortunately, both Sanneh and Walls fail to see the supersessionist's vision in the translation project that failed to recognize the eternal centrality of Israel to the redemptive story, and instead sought to replace her with the West. Read from this angle, where in their translation of the Bible they took the stance of a host and not the visitor, the Protestant's translation project reduced the Bible to a cultural Bible. Colenso's translation work among the Nguni can be read in the narrative of the protestant project of a cultural Bible expected to produce the same enlightenment effect in Africa as it had done in the West. In the translation project, the African theological commodification is complete where his voice (referring to the insights of William Ngidi, Bishop Colenso's African intellectual provocateur) only speaks to substantiate the white's presence. It confirms that the African is a white, or should be a white in the embryonic stage, who will eventually be a full-grown white when he is fully civilized. Thus, there is no possibility of a theological conversation partner (the African recipient) who would significantly affect the outcome of modes of life.[106]

Jennings sought to underscore that everlasting place of the Bible people through what he calls "Joining" or "Intimacy." The story of the gospel is the story of inviting all cultures to the space of Israel, "Joining" or "Intimacy" made possible by Christ; "Christians are, through Jesus Christ, brought into the history of Israel, which indeed is God's story." On this Jennings says;

> Translation not only leads to textual representation; equally important, it is an invitation to a process of concurrency,

---

[105]. Joseph Rouse, "Power Knowledge," in Cary Gutting , ed., *The Cambridge Companion to Foucault* (Cambridge: Cambridge University Press, 1994), 92-114.

[106]. Jennings, *Christian Imagination*, 154.

not simply linguistic, social, or cultural, but also theological. This process of concurrency describes the possibilities of cultural inner logistic being joined together, to the possibility of freedom in the transgression of boundaries. However, the Colenso-Ngidi collaboration displayed a lack of the initial bedrock of concurrency, the Gentile joined through the body of Jesus. The tragic effect of its absence is a Christian theology that is unable to enter fruitfully into the cultural inner logics of people.[107]

As one would expect, this is the theology that underwrites the missionary translation project. The missionary work seen best in the translation project, was a tragedy when it imagined an entrance of a God devoid of real history, of a God moving through time and history through God's people, Israel. In the end, it produced a theology that is provincial, locked in a false universalism, lacking patterns of communication and' intimacy' or 'joining' with the cultures that it seeks to reach.

Conclusion

In this chapter I have argued that Christianity has become a non-Christian religion with its nerve center in the Majority-World and specifically in Africa. This makes it imperative to regard the theologies that undergird such a growth as important. The Christian growth experienced in Africa and especially as embodied by the AICs (with their spectacular growth) raises an interest on the kind of theology that is coming from the global South. I have argued that this growth can be explained in at least two ways.

First, the primal religious imagination as inbuilt cultural factors in African tradition and religious cultures (a creation construct), placed religion at the highest premium. When this religious outlook to life was

---

107. Ibid., 154.

affirmed by the gospel as it was spread by missionaries and especially through the translation of the Bible to African languages, the Africans' spiritual quest was instantly satisfied. People felt that the Jesus of the gospel is what Africans' deep spirituality and spiritual hunger had always longed for. Primal religious understanding can and should arguably be located in creation wisdom through which though man fell, but God did not give up on him and instead through culture, however fallen, man continued to glean something of God as he tried to make sense of his creature hood.

The human religious search culminated in the incarnation of the God-man, Jesus Christ, who entered the realm of creation and thereby affirmed creation's sublime beauty in God's economy of redemption. Currently the creative work of God continues through the church as the community of believers being energized and empowered by the Holy Spirit, bringing creation to a position where it can submit to the Lordship of Jesus Christ, to the glory of God. In this ongoing work of the Holy Spirit, culture (as part of God's creation) is not contingent, but at the center of God's redemptive activity. In this reasoning creation should always then be the starting point in discerning God's work. All religions of the world therefore, as expressions of human culture, are in the forefront in seeking or rejecting God. Either way, God is at work in them. This then should invite all to look deeper and discern God's action in culture and enlist it for furthering the work of God. Consequently, contrary to Katongole's repudiation of Africa traditional cultures as a starting point for a more meaningful social imagination for Africa, I agree with Bediako and others like Mugambi that in a Christianity that is sensitive to the African sensibilities, embedded in these cultures, and therein lays the real potential for Africa Renaissance. Secondly, I have demonstrated that the gospel is translatable, that is, it is universal. While it cannot on one hand be held captive by any culture, it can on the other hand be received within all cultural diversity. In the tower of Babylon, many theologians only see a distributive judgment. But a better way of seeing this is to see the restorative justice of God whereby God did not want man rammed in one culture in his fallen state which held a potential for total apostasy. Instead, in distorting their language, God made it possible for sections of humanity to come to their senses and return to God. Religious diversity is therefore not a problem; at least not to God.

Although the gospel is likened to a beggar, by John Mbiti, seeking clothing in the cultures that it experiences in its wandering, which I would rather call its leavening journey, its real substance is never lost in the course of its transmission so that in the end the gospel is not the work of man or the efforts of men [read missionaries] but God who desires to reveal himself to all people. These two phenomena; the primal religions of Africa reflecting "reflexivity," and the universality or translatability of the gospel may have the cue for the proliferation of Christianity, especially among the AICs. It is this "reflexivity" in primal culture and the universality of the gospel that underpin our research — Akũrinũ vernacular theology.

Finally, I have argued that contextualization is inadequate to explain the proliferation of ecclesial movements especially in Africa. Instead, I call for migration from contextualization to global or contextual theologies as a possible route to understand the spiritual awakening in many non-Christian cultures. In this journey a recovery of the theology of culture based on God's reflexivity and the "joining" or "intimacy" where all cultures are invited to the space of Israel made possible through incarnation, is indispensable.

CHAPTER TWO

THE EMERGENCE AND GROWTH OF
AKŨRINŨ CHURCH MOVEMENT

In this chapter I track the first epoch of evangelization of the East Coast of Africa through the Portuguese explorers to the second epoch of the modern missionary efforts which brought the gospel to the interior of East Africa, and in particular to central Kenya where the encounter of the missionaries with the local *Agĩkũyũ* culture clashed. Out of this clash of cultures, some *Agĩkũyũ* prophetic individuals, the *Arathi*, felt led by the Holy Spirit to start African Indigenous Churches (AICs) that were closer to their culture. In particular, some of these prophetic figures started the *Akũrinũ* Church.

Early Portuguese Travelers and Explorers to the East Coast of Africa

The early Catholic missions to East Coast of African started when Vasco da Gama anchored on the coast of Mombasa near the present location of Port Jesus on 7th April 1498. He came as part of the grand design of Henry the Navigator, whose aim was expansionism, trade, subduing Islam and spreading the Christian faith as a civilizing agent. Zablon Nthamburi[1] and Sung KyuPark[2] say that Henry was also looking for a legendary African king, Prester John, whom he hoped to make an ally in the fight against the Muslims. Vasco da Gama only found a friendly reception in Malindi along the East Coast of East Africa. He was not welcomed by the Muslim inhabitants who had established themselves along the coastline. Vasco da Gama made no attempt to evangelize. Francisco d'Almeida, who in 1505 followed Vasco da Gama and invaded Kilwa in order to secure the trade at Sofala, like Vasco da Gama, also did not attempt to evangelize. His two Franciscan Friars were just chaplains for the Portuguese soldiers.

However, on Aug 31st 1506, Kilwa reported to have 40 people who wanted to become Christians.[3] Nthamburi reports that it was Dom Petro Mascrarenhas, the Portuguese viceroy of India, who gave orders for the construction of a port at Mombasa and instruction that the gospel be preached to the inhabitants. This was however hindered by the Muslim hostility. In 1585, Mir Ali Bey, a Turk, attempted to oust the Portuguese from the Indian Ocean. He preached jihad and got enthusiastic support. In Pate, a Portuguese named John Robello was dragged around the town and pelted with stones. Two years later the Portuguese avenged Robello's death by razing down Faza Island, killing everyone, and destroying the palm trees. Such brutality did not give witness to the Christian faith that the Portuguese intended to propagate, nor did it improve human relations. Nthamburi concludes that the Portuguese were brutal, of immoral behavior, cruel, and inhuman, all which countered any efforts to evangelization.[4] By 1624 four worship centers had been established; Augustinian Cathedral, The Mesericordia church, the church inside the walled town

---

1. Nthamburi, *Crossroads*, 2
2. Sung Kyu Park, *Christian Spirituality in Africa* (Eugene, Oregon: Pickwick Publications, 2013).
3. Nthamburi, *Crossroads*, 2.
4. Ibid.

referred to as the *Igreja Matrix* (Mother Church) and a Chapel in Fort Jesus. At Faza the Liwali even assisted in building a church.[5]

The struggle for political supremacy and domination between the Portuguese and the Arabs in the East Coast continued for a long time with attacks and counter attacks. On 25th April 1729, the Arabs attacked the Portuguese, killed many of them and the remaining few fled to Mozambique. The Portuguese flag was lowered for the last time. The Portuguese left no mark after the Arabs regained control of the East Coast of Africa. The few Christians were not indigenous but Goans.[6]

To sum up, the Portuguese stint on the East coast of Africa involved baptizing many people but prepared no indigenous leadership to carry on the work, and there was also no attempt to indigenize the church and integrate it within the indigenous culture. These two challenges would continue to hamper the modern missionaries many years later. Likewise, the moral standing of the Portuguese did not support their faith. In the end the church disintegrated soon after the exit of the Portuguese. When the first modern missionaries arrived, there was no trace of Christianity.

The Portuguese's failure to establish a viable Christian movement in the East coast of Africa was a characteristic failure of an approach that generally dogged the missionaries and assured the failure of the gospel. This goes to illustrate further our thesis that for a lasting Christian presence the gospel must be received within the cultural matrix of the recipient culture.

The Coming of Modern Protestant Missions to the East Coast of Africa

John Ludwig Krapf of Church Mission Society (CMS) landed in Mombasa in 1844 after having been in Ethiopia for 5 years. Krapf settled in

---

5. Ibid.
6. Ibid.

Rabai Mpya. Within two months of his arrival he lost his newly wedded bride, Rosina, and their new born baby.[7] With great perseverance Krapf intensified his efforts of evangelization. He studied the local languages and produced a Kiswahili dictionary. In two years, he had translated the entire N.T. Bible into Kiswahili.[8] In 1846, Krapf was joined by John Rebmann and in 1849 by another missionary, Erhardt. Apart from his linguistic work, Nthamburi reports that Krapf who returned to Europe in 1853, baptized only two people, a dying cripple by the name Mringe and a Giriama outcast named Abbe Gunja.

Back in Europe Krapf wrote his famous book, *Travels, Researches and Missionary Labors*. Through this book the Methodists were inspired to start work in Kenya. Krapf offered to help the Methodists in their initial work. He cherished the idea of creating a chain of missions between the East Coast to the West Coast of Africa. He returned to Mombasa in 1862 in order to help Thomas Wakefield, the first missionary of the United Methodist Free Church to establish a mission station in Ribe. Wakefield opened a mission station in Ganjoni (Mazeras), Jomvu, and Chonyi.[9]

In the 1860s, philanthropic attention in Europe focused on East Africa and soon the CMS and the Methodists had to deal with many freed slaves. Sir Bartle Frere a special emissary in Zanzibar encouraged the Christian missions to concentrate on settlement of the freed slaves. CMS established a large freed slave settlement at Freetown in Kisauni. Other centers were Bagamoyo settlement which was founded by the Holy Ghost Fathers. The relationship between the European missionaries and Africans soured due to European racial prejudice and stereotyping, an increasing characteristic of European thought about Africans. The mis-

---

7. Nthamburi, *Crossroads*, 8.
8. Park, *Spirituality*, 86.
9. Nthamburi, *Crossroads*, 9.

sionaries treated Africans as little children who had to be guided and patronized in every way.¹⁰

These observations were not uncommon elsewhere where the colonial administration and missionaries were at work. Among the Zulus in South Africa as mentioned earlier, Jennings reports that the natives were caught in this cultural 'uprootedness';

> The attempt to reestablish themselves and refashion themselves became a permanent characteristic of their existence. On the one hand the people were trying to maintain pre-colonial African institutions with chiefs, *indunas*, headmen on chiefly councilors, and *ibutho*, age-grouped men and women who served the chief by carrying out various duties. Indigenes, who functioned without that kind of institution, wished to remain free of chiefs while maintaining common traditions and practices. On the other hand, the white settler's presence had brought the entire region into a capitalistic system such that no native agricultural practice or tradition involving the land would go untouched or unaltered. All the land and animals, especially the cattle came steadily under settler influence or control.¹¹

Again, like the approach of the Catholic Missions by the Portuguese, the modern missionary approach by the Protestant missions is regrettable. It was dogged by paternalism. Yet this must not crowd out the fact that these missionaries made gallant efforts, often at the cost of their lives.

African Christianity is undoubtedly built upon the graves of innumerable missionaries. Like Mary's expensive perfume, wherever the gospel is preached in Africa, the story of the sacrifices of the missionaries must be told both as a reminder that the gospel is not cheap and as an encouragement to every Christian effort to share the gospel if not

---

10. Ibid., 10.
11. Jennings, *Christian Imagination*, 123.

cross-culturally, at least with the next door neighbor. The lessons on the missionaries' paternalistic approach to evangelization are lessons for all time especially for Africa where tribalism, negative ethnicity, and class differentiation remain an impediment to a genuine Christian "Intimacy" or "Joining."

Nthamburi mentions early outstanding African evangelists such as David Koi who was the first martyr in East Africa (1883), William Jones who was ordained in 1885, Ishmael Samler, George David, John Momba, Thomas Mazera and Stephen Kereri who had responded to the gospel and themselves become propagators of the faith, thanks to the schools that were started in Freetown and other ex-slave communities under the directive of Sir Bartle Frere, to produce the first African teachers and evangelist.[12] Yet even with such initial local leaders, the missionaries remained paternalistic much longer than was necessary.

The Movement of Gospel from the East Coast of Africa to the Interior of East Africa

By 1890's Neunkirchen Mission, a German evangelical mission that had started work among the *Wapokomo* had a thriving work along the Tana River. Dr. James Steward of Scottish mission and David Livingstone's successor in Nyasaland (Malawi) left the coast for the interior on 19th September 1891 with a party of seven missionaries and 273 porters. The original purpose was to go as far as Kikuyu land. He however settled in Kibwezi, but the mission was slowed down by famine and deaths through raids. Because of such dismal results it was later decided that the mission should advance to Kikuyu land forthwith. Rev. Thomas Watson led the Scottish to Kikuyu land in 1898. By 1899 a mission station had already been built at Thogoto.

---

12. Nthamburi, *Crossroads*, 9-10.

The establishment of British East Africa Protectorate and the building of the "Uganda Railway," that begun in 1895 reaching Nairobi in 1899 and Kisumu in 1901, provided an impetus to other missions in the interior. The rail provided a cheap and a safe route across the Savannah and a thorn-scrub country inhabited by the warlike *Wamaasai* and *Wakamba*. By 1890, the CMS had already established themselves in Taveta on an important Arab-Swahili trading center.

The missionary work thrived, and many mission stations were soon opened all over the region. Nthamburi reports that there were even intense competitions among the mission agencies. The major competitors were the CMS, The Scottish Mission, and the Methodists. To ease the conflict, "the spheres of influence" doctrine was enacted thereby easing tension. For example, an imaginary line was drawn between Ngong Hills and Mt. Kenya, with the CMS getting the sphere to the East of the line while the Scottish Mission went to the West of the line. CMS spread to Kihuruko in 1901, Weithaga in 1903, Kahuhia in 1906, and Mahiga in 1908. The Scottish mission went to Nyeri and the southern part of Meru.

The Society of Friends from England begun African Industrial mission at Kaimosi in Western Kenya and thereafter schools, Teachers' Training College, a Bible institute, and a hospital. The African Inland Mission (AIC) began its ministry in Ukambani under the direction of Peter Cameron Scott in 1895. C.E. Hurburnt moved the mission to Kijabe in 1901. A station was opened in Kapropita among the Tugen people in 1907. The African Inland Mission was an interdenominational movement comprising of many Baptists, some Methodists, Presbyterians, and Anglicans.

The Church of God commenced its work in 1905 in Western Kenya with missionaries from U.S.A. The proclamation of the gospel went hand in hand with social services such as education and medical services. At Kima they developed a hospital, a Bible School and a Teachers Training College. The German Seventh Day Adventists (SDA) started their work in

1893 in Mwanza and moved to Western Kenya in 1906 particularly in Kisii and South Nyanza.

The Pentecostal Assemblies of Canada begun their ministry in 1921 and grew rapidly in Western Kenya. They built a Bible School in Nyangori and later a printing press, Evangel Publishing House, in Nairobi. Other late comers included the Southern Baptist who begun their work in Kenya in 1956. The Salvation Army had begun their work in 1921 opening stations in Nairobi, Thika, Malakisi and Embu. After staying at the coast for a long time, The Methodist eventually went to Meru and opened a station at Kaaga and a Hospital in Maua.

For all their faults, the missionaries invaded Kenya with a zeal that can only be described as God directed. Almost all parts of the country had a missionary presence. I have deliberately left out the modern Roman Catholic missions (except the early Portuguese explorers), confining myself to the Protestant missions for the scope of this research. The missionaries brought with them education, hospitals, Bible translation and laid the foundation for the modern development. The large Christian presence in Kenya today owes its existence to these missionary efforts. To date the places that the mission work took root, remain relatively more developed than places where missionaries never reached. The Kenyan church has largely grown on denominational lines because of the different missionary efforts.[13] Thankfully one of the amazing features of Kenyan Christians is their ability to overlook their denominational barriers and foster a more largely ecumenical outlook to the Christian faith.

The Growth of African Indigenous Churches (AICs)

The African Indigenous Churches (AICs) have been defined in many ways by different scholars. The 'I' in the middle has represented different

---

13. Park, *Spirituality*, 98.

things to different scholars such as; Independent, Instituted, Initiated, and even International. For our study I will take Kalu's definition to refer to the AICs as the Church movements that emerged from the dawn of the twentieth century either within or outside the institutional framework of mission or mission-oriented churches.[14]

The birth and growth of the AICs within which the Akũrinũ church, the focus of this research, generally belongs, is situated against this background of aggressive and even conflicting missionary efforts, the brutal invasion and confiscation of the African land by the inverted hospitality of the missionaries and the colonial government, and the subsequent denigration of their religious traditions by these hegemonic cultures that sought to flatten the cultures that they confronted in Africa with little or no feelings, as they sought to establish their own culture. Making a reference to David B. Barrett[15], Nthamburi identifies several factors that are responsible for establishments of the AICs: African Traditional culture, African Religion, Missionary paternalism, colonial legacy, and conditions of modern society. Currently (at the time of Nthamburi's writing, 1991), there are 35 million adherents and 7000 denominations of AICs in Africa from when they first appeared in 1862. Nthamburi's statistics are certainly outdated but the growth of the AICs has continued with the same zeal to date.

Indigenous Christianity in Western Kenya

In Kenya most of the AICs are found in Western Kenya among the Luos and Luhyas in the Kavirondo region. By 1920's almost all mission agencies had a presence in the Kavirondo region and with a large following. Interestingly these are the same areas where the AICs thrived most.

---

14. Ogbu U. Kalu, ed., *Africa Christianity and African Story* (University of Pretoria, Pretoria: Department of History, 2005).

15. David, B. Barrett, eds., *Kenyan Churches Handbook* (Nairobi, Kenya: Evangel Publishing House, 1973).

Another interesting feature is that the majority of the AICs had seceded from the historical Churches. They include Mumboism led by Onyando Dunde; Nomiya Luo mission in 1914 by Johana Owelo; Roho movement by Alfayo Odongo. This later became Dini ya Masanda. Dini ya Roho seceded from Friends Mission. Others include Legio Maria, a splinter from the Roman Catholic started by Gaundecia Aoko, and Israel Nineveh Church a splinter from the Pentecostal movement in Nyangori in 1932 led by a charismatic leader, Paul David Zakayo Kivuli.[16]

Indigenous Christianity in Central Kenya

Nthamburi says that the indigenous Christianity in central Kenya is identified with the cultural nationalism that swept the country in 1920's and 30's. The main bone of contention was clitoridectomy (or female circumcision). The issue of clitoridectomy became a cultural definitive matter and precipitated a crisis in 1928 when the Kikuyu Central Association (KAC) made a strong challenge to the missionary's attitude towards it at a conference in Nyeri. The local community made the issue both a religious and a political matter. In making these cultural judgments, the missionary Church came to be regarded by the Agĩkũyũ as being swayed by imperialist motives.

To the missionaries in Kikuyu land female circumcision was barbaric and abhorrent from a medical point of view and the initiation ceremonies incompatible with the Christian teachings. In 1920, the Church of Scotland Mission tried to make it a rule that baptized Church members undergoing the operation or allowing their daughters to do so should be disciplined by being suspended from Church membership. The missionaries did not see the social implication of their injunctions. To the Agĩkũyũ community, it was necessary to have the initiation ceremonies as a way of graduation from adolescence to adulthood, the equivalent of certification.

---

16. Nthamburi, *From Mission to Church* (Nairobi, Kenya: Uzima Press: Kenya, 1991), 17.

Circumcision was the outward sign that pointed to deeper and religious values of the community. While the physical operation was not the most important aspect, it was nonetheless essential as the culmination of instruction (given to the initiates in seclusion as they healed from the circumcision wound), and a gateway to initiation into womanhood. It was the duty of the community to prepare its members to become trustworthy persons and circumcision and clitoridectomy fulfilled this role mentally, spiritually as well as physically.[17] For the Agĩkũyũ, it was their culture and not Christianity that was at stake. What appeared as stubbornness or "the work of darkness" to the missionaries, to the Agĩkũyũ was a legitimate attempt to prevent the disintegration of their culture which was basic to their identity.

By 1929 and 1930 the matter had reached a crisis point as the people had started establishing their own schools where they could practice their culture without inhibition. The Kikuyu Independent Schools Association (KISA) and the Kikuyu Karing'a Education Association were formed with a sole purpose of providing education in direct opposition to mission education, which up to that time had monopolized education.

When some of the mission schools closed their doors to those who refused to conform, the only alternative was for the people themselves to start their own schools. Many people were opposed to the missionary type of Christianity but at the same time wished to retain their Christian faith. Thus, the emergence of independent schools was accompanied by the founding of independent or Indigenous churches. These included the African Independent Pentecostal Church (AIPC) which came out of KISA, while out of Karing'a schools was formed African Orthodox Church, which was later renamed African Greek Orthodox Church.

Nthamburi mentions that other churches emerged out of the dissatisfaction with the leadership and paternalism of mission-founded Churches. They include the African Christian Church and Schools

---

17. Nthamburi, *Mission to Church*, 18.

(ACCS), which were formed in 1947 by the members of the African Inland Mission in Murang'a District. African Brotherhood Church (ABC) in Ukambani parted ways with the mission in 1945 because of the mission's reluctance to allow Africans to exercise leadership. In the 1940's *Dini ya Kagia* also called *Arata a Roho Mutheru* (The Friends of the Holy Spirit Church) was formed. The Apostolic Faith of Africa and the Holy Church of Evangelistic Apostles Faith are charismatic churches that came out of the Revival Fellowship. Other spiritist churches such as *Akũrinũ* (also written as *Akorino*), *Aroti* (dreamers), and *Anabii* (prophets) sprung up. All these wear turbans for which they are referred to as "*Andu a Iremba*", i.e., Turban people. The colonial government called them *Watu wa Mungu* (people of God) in 1930's.[18]

Nthamburi says that the *Akũrinũ* churches have similar characteristic with the *Roho* churches found in Western Kenya. They trace their origin in 1920's. They rejected western education, western culture, western medicine and other amenities. Such a reaction happens whenever people's culture is threatened. It may not be far-fetched to draw a parallel of this to the current jihadist movement such as Boko Haram and others. The *Akũrinũ* also rejected some of their *Agĩkũyũ* traditions and sought guidance from the Scriptures and the Holy Spirit. They are influenced mainly by the Old Testament. After Kenya gained political independence (in 1963) when many of these groups were registered as *bona fide* churches they took various titles such as; The Holy Ghost Church of Kenya, the Christian Holy Ghost of East Africa, the Kenya Foundation Prophets Church, the Holy Spirit of Zayun, The African Mission of the Holy Ghost Church and God's Word, and Holy Ghost Church.[19]

Nthamburi reports that in 1991 there were 180 Indigenous Churches [i.e., denominations] in Kenya. As a general characteristic, the AICs in

---

18. Jomo Kenyatta, *Facing Mt. Kenya* (New York: Vintage Book edition, 1965), 279.

19. Nthamburi, *Mission to Church*, 20, quotes Jocelyn Murray, "Varieties of Kikuyu Independent Churches," in Barrett et al, *Kenya Churches Handbook* (Kisumu: Evangel Publishing House, 1973), 129.

Kenya are not founded by theologians or clerics; they are founded on the initiative of lay people who are concerned about the authenticity of the Church and as expressions of their cultural identity. They resent the moral decay that they feel that the missionary Christianity tolerates, a situation that they associate with the erosion of their African cultural values. They look for a spiritually buoyant church that is truly a reflection of African spirituality. On the whole the indigenous churches attach great importance to community life and human relations. They give women a prominent place in leadership unlike the historical churches. Their worship is lively and meaningful to their members, a challenge to the more archaic and somewhat dull services from the mission-founded Churches.[20]

The Socio-Cultural Background of the Emergence of the *Akūrinū* Church

Before tracing on the birth, growth, and spread of the *Akūrinū* movement, I will first analyze the *Agĩkũyũ* pre-colonial traditional culture and religion that formed the backdrop of the founding of the *Akūrinū* church. Bediako informs us that religion as a manifestation of social and cultural behavior will remain as an important indicator for understanding African life.[21] In this effort, I will appeal to Kenyatta's seminal anthropological work, *Facing Mt. Kenyatta* and Ngũgĩ wa Thing'o's book, *The River Between*, besides other sources.[22]

---

20. Nthamburi, *Mission to Church*, 20.
21. Bediako, *Christianity in Africa*, 262.
22. Here we acknowledge that religion has been a source of blessing and pain. Many atrocities in Africa and elsewhere have been committed in the name of religion. For example religious reasons were cited in some African cultures for killing new born twins as a sign of bad omen. Our usage of religion here is rather in introspection from our current Christian understanding into the African past in areas where religion most closely reflected something of the true God and goodness. For contrast purpose we also reflect on religion as it negated the true God due to the fallenness of humanity.

Agĩkũyũ traditional cultures have metamorphosized and found new ways of expression in a globalized world all the while borrowing from the heritage of their traditional culture. Yusufu Turaki sums up these thoughts;

> There is a false assumption that African tradition culture and religion are obsolete and have no influence over modern Africans. Some of the old institutions, social structures and values have been replaced by colonialism and Christianity, but some have remained — not necessarily in institutions or social structures –but in the minds and in the worldview of Africans. These traditional values continue to exert very powerful and pervasive influence over Africans, whether modernists or Christians. As a result of colonialism, Christianity and Islam, some traditional values, cultures and social institutions have been transformed into new social formations and values that are neither traditional nor Western.[23]

I underscore that our reason for this study is not a quest for a return to the old traditions so as to escape present realities, but rather to understand the old traditions and their pervasive and profound influence upon Africans, whether modernists or Christians. I also do not intend to elevate a certain cultural aspect to produce "cultural Christianity." Instead, I aim to engage modern Africans in terms of the worldviews and values that shape and mold their attitudes, behavior and social life. A large portion of this is embedded in the heritage of their traditional culture.

---

23. Yusufu Turaki, *Christianity and African Traditional Religion: A Systematic Examination of the Interactions of Religions* (Unpublished).

Chapter two

An Introduction to the *Agĩkũyũ* People

When Kenyatta wrote his book in 1938, the *Agĩkũyũ* numbered about 1 million people rising to about 3.2 million in the 1979 general census.[24] They mainly occupied the western and southern slopes of Mt. Kenya, with Mt. Kenya standing to the North. They occupied four main districts (today referred to as counties): Murang'a (then called Port Hall), Kirinyaga, Kiambu which boarders Nairobi City, and Nyeri. Later on, when their land was taken by the colonial settlers the Kikuyu moved further to the West to Nyandarua in the Aberdare ranges in search of land or as workers in the colonial farms. To the South and East, Kikuyu land border Kianjahi ranges also called Ol Donyo Sabuk and Kiambiruiru, or Ngong Hills.[25]

While Kenyatta included the *Ameru* and *Atharaka* people who live in the Eastern slopes of Mt. Kenya as part of the *Agĩkũyũ* people, my present understanding is that these two claim a different cosmology. Though their customs are very close to those of the *Agĩkũyũ*, for the sake of this study we will not be considering them as part of the *Agĩkũyũ*.

Economically, the *Agĩkũyũ* are great farmers and shrewd business men. Besides farming and business, the *Agĩkũyũ* were involved in small scale industries with professions such as bridge building, string making, wire drawing, and iron chain making. The *Agĩkũyũ* had a great sense of justice (*kihooto*). Because of their enterprising spirit and business acumen, today they are found in every part of the country especially in Rift Valley. They were forced to move to Rift Valley mainly when their land was taken by the colonial settlers and later on as their small farm holdings continued to diminish with growing population. Their population is currently estimated at about 9 million or about 22% of the country's

---

24. Godfrey Muriuki, *People around Mt. Kenya: Kikuyu*, (Kenya: Evans Brother Limited, 1985), 2. More recent demographic records show that the *Agĩkũyũ have grown to more than nine million people as demonstrated above. Again though there are more recent studies, the Kenyatta's is considered as a standard treatment of the Agĩkũyũ culture.*

25. Muriuki, *People around Mt. Kenya: Kikuyu*, 2.

population forming the largest voting block and the wealthiest ethnic grouping.

The Cosmology of the Agĩkũyũ People

The Agĩkũyũ have a legend that explains their origin. They claim that the whole tribe descended from one man who was called Gĩkũyũ and a woman called Mũmbĩ. One day God appeared to Gĩkũyũ who did not have a wife and showed him the beautiful land with forests and pastureland. In the middle of the land was a tall mountain called Kere-nyaga or Mt. Kenya which God said was to be the sign of God's glory. God took Gĩkũyũ to the top of Mt. Kere-nyaga and from there asked him to descend the mountain and build a village close to where there were big figs or Mũgumo trees. When Gĩkũyũ went down to the place he was shown he met a beautiful lady whom he called Mũmbĩ (meaning creator or molder). Both lived happily and had nine daughters but no sons.[26] Today this place, Mukurwe wa Gathanga, houses a museum.

Gĩkũyũ was disturbed by the fact that he had no sons. When he took the matter to Ngai, Ngai instructed him together with his wife and daughters to make a sacrifice near the fig trees and then go home and return to the fig tree at night alone. Gĩkũyũ did this and when he returned, he found nine handsome young men whom he took home and who married his daughters. These had many children and grandchildren until the land could not contain all of them together.

The nine daughters continued to be the heads of their families. With time when the land was too small to contain their numerous numbers, the daughters gathered their families and moved further away occupying the vast land of Kikuyu land. Muriuki records the names of the daughters who formed the nine clans or Moheriga of the Agĩkũyũ as; *Anjiru (Wanjiru), Ambui (Wambui), Aceera (Wacera or Njeri), Agaciku (Wanjiku), Akiuru or Ethaga or Ambura (Nyambura), Angeci or Aitherandu (Wangeci*

---

26. Muriuki, *People Around Mt. Kenya*, 3.

or *Waithira*), *Angui* or *Aithiegeni* (*Wangui* or *Waithiegeni*), *Angari* or *Aithekahuno* (*Wangari*) and *Airimu* or *Agathigia* (*Wairimu* or *Gathigia*)[27]. E.N. Mugo adds one more clan to the list, *Aichakamuyu* (*Wamuyu*). He says ordinarily the *Agĩkũyũ* would not give an exact number of their clan only saying they are nine "plus one."[28] One thing is sure, the name *Wamuyu* is today common like the rest of the nine names among the *Agĩkũyũ*.

Muriuki says that the land that the *Agĩkũyũ* occupy today was first occupied by the *Gumba* who were of small stature and the *Athi* people. Both of these were hunters and gatherers. These people traded with the *Agĩkũyũ* and intermarried with them through adoption and peace treaties. Before the *Agĩkũyũ* moved to their present land, they lived in the northern part of Meru, in Tigania and Igembe region. It is not known why they moved away but perhaps they were running away from the Galla people who were coming southwards from Ethiopia.[29]

The *Agĩkũyũ* are of Bantu origin were among people from the southern regions of Africa who moved northwards up to Equator where the Northern streams of Negroes, Hamites and Nilotes stopped them.[30] The *Agĩkũyũ* settled around Mt. Kenya near the Equator and were subsequently influenced by their neighbors the *Maasais*, a Nilotic tribe with whom they have intermarried over the years. For example, in his research, Father Cagnolo noted similar dress codes with the Masaai, identical vocabulary to refer to God — N*gai*, offering of sacrificial meat, and hair styling using ochre and fat, piercing of ears, and similar circumcision ceremonies, indicating unrestrained contact between their peoples.[31]

---

27. Ibid., 4.

28. E. N. Mugo, *Kikuyu People: A Brief Outline of their Customs and Traditions* (Nairobi, Kenya: Kenya Literature Bureau, 1982).

29. Muriuki, *People around Mt. Kenya*, 5.

30. Cagnolo, *The Akikuyu*,18.

31. Ibid,

One may be puzzled by the fact that the Agĩkũyũ Cosmology has similarities to that of the Jews recorded in the Bible. The neighbuoring Ameru people tell a similar legend. Those similarities need to be explored.

The Traditional Culture of Agĩkũyũ People

I am of the opinion that it is this religious heritage that Akũrinũ vernacular theology builds on. Contrary to the popular belief by missionaries that Africans had no previous knowledge in religion before their coming and that they had an empty religious slate, *tabularasa*, upon which the European missionaries endeavored to scribble the first possible religious consciousness, the fact is that all people learn new knowledge in religion through the lenses of the residue of that which they have tasted and approved in the past.

On this Cyril C. Okorocha, says that a new scheme of faith can find a hearing only by appealing to religious instincts and susceptibilities that already exist.[32] And it cannot reach those [instincts] without taking into account the traditional form in which all religious feelings are embodied, and without speaking a language which men accustomed to these old forms understand.[33] To this I add that religious consciousness is built into the created order. God created a human being who can respond to God. However, it is a distorted the response due to the fall. Yet, belief in God seems to be universal across humanity.

The Religion of the Agĩkũyũ People

The Agĩkũyũ were very religious. They were conscious of good and bad spirits. This religiosity was seen best during the initiation ceremony called *irua* where at very many points in the ceremony that lasted sev-

---

32. Cyril C.Okorocha, *The Meaning of Religious Conversion in Africa* (Vermont, USA: Gowa Publishing Company Limited, 1987), 2.

33. W. Robertson Smith, *The Religion of the Semites* (New York: 1957), 2 quoted in Cyril C. Okorocha, *Religious Conversion*, p.?

eral weeks, rituals were performed to ward off evil spirits [almost akin to exorcism] or attract the benevolence of the good spirits.[34] Religion pervaded every aspect of life. There were religious rituals for virtually every activity and season of life. For example, the beginning of a planting season was attended by special religious rituals, and so were the harvesting season and all other stages in between.

The God of Agĩkũyũ

The Agĩkũyũ believe in one creator God called Ngai (Mugai), the giver or the divider, who dwells in the sky, Matuinĩ, but who occasionally descends on the mountains when he wants to bring blessing or punishment to the people. In prayer and sacrifices the Agĩkũyũ address God as Mwene-Nyaga, the possessor of Kere-nyaga, the mountain of brightness, or Mt. Kenya. They pray facing Mt. Kenya because they believe it to be the official resting place of God.[35] Ngai is also referred to as, "Revered Elder."[36]

Ngai gives man free will and does not interfere with man's daily activities only intervening in crisis points; birth, initiation, marriage, and death, or when calamity and disaster strikes.[37] In these crisis points prayers are made to God. In other times when for example an individual has offended and needs to be cleansed, the appeal is made to the offended ancestral spirit by a medicine man on behalf of the particular individual. God is not

---

34. A more comprehensive reading of ceremony of the irua, circumcision for girls, is given under the topic, 'The Great Ceremonial Dance (Matuumo)', in Jomo Kenyatta's, Facing Mt. Kenya, 133-134,. So much care is taken to protect the initiates from any ill will from evil spirit, witchdoctors or anyone with a bad eye. Caution is taken to ensure the initiates are kept in excellent hygienic conditions. The process is done away from the presence of men ensuring no immoral feelings are entertained. Herbs with medicinal values are used to ensure the wound heals quickly and the pain is numbed using various methods. Throughout the process, the elders and the communicants keeping on uttering words of peace, Thaai-thathayai Ngai thaai.

35. wa Thiong'o, River Between, 15.

36. Kenyatta, Facing Mt. Kenya, 248.

37. Ibid.,225.

approached by individuals but by the community or the family. The place of the father in religion is critical. The family is a religious unit.

Other minor homes of God include *Kea-Njahe* (the mountain of the Big Rain) on the east; *Kĩa-Mbiroiro* or the Ngong Hills (the mountain of the clear sky) on the south, and *Kĩa-Nyandarwa* (the mountain of sleeping places or Hides) on the West. The *Agĩkũyũ* have no temple made with hands of man but instead worships under certain trees. "All sacrifices to *Ngai* were performed under a sycamore tree (*Mũkũyũ*) and if one was not available, a fig tree (*Mũgumo*) would be used. The olive tree (*Mũtamaiyũ*) was a sacred tree for women." These trees were like the Christian church building. This practice has continued in varying degrees to date.

Ngai is not visible to mortal eyes but instead manifests himself in various ways such as the sun, the moon, the stars, rain, rainbow, lightning and thunder, through which he can reveal his love or anger. When a man is struck by lightning, he is said to have attempted to look at *Ngai* when he was preparing to fight his enemies. Thus, it is a taboo to look to the sky when there is thunderstorm. *Ngai* is not to be bothered unnecessarily and people do not pray daily. However, when they meet for public affairs, they offer prayers for guidance and protection.[38] Sacrifices are made only in serious matters such as drought or outbreak of epidemic, great distress, or serious sickness.

The *Agĩkũyũ* believe that God will answer their prayer as a reciprocal of the gift offered in sacrifice.[39] This in essence suggests that the worship tends to be manipulative. This does not in any way suggest that the prayer is not genuine. They only understand God in reciprocity terms. In the recent years 'prosperity gospel' originating both from West Africa and North America has found ready market in Kenya. One can only speculate that this approach to seek benevolence from God after offering him an offering is tied to the concept of reciprocity, meaning if you give to God,

---

38. Kenyatta, *Facing Mt. Kenya*, 226.
39. Ibid., 230.

he will be more inclined or obligated to attend to your prayer. Some pastors have exploited this seeming African religious understanding to the maximum. It is not far-fetched to imagine that this belief is embedded in the African traditional culture and religion, given its widespread acceptance. Cyril Okorocha reminds us that, "Every religion that is worthy the name is a blend of universal principles and local setting...which [when] lifted out and made clear, speak to man as man, whatever his time or space."[40]

Another understanding of God that shows the imperfection of all religions, Christianity included, is the unhealthy fear that the Agĩkũyũ had for God. Ngũgĩ says that the Agĩkũyũ had more fear than love for God. They interpreted his benevolence as sinister, preceding a disaster. For example, when there was a good harvest, the people feared what may follow.[41] This inability to trust God fully and to read sinister motives is not entirely absent even today among African Christians. Yet we know that the fear of God is esteemed in the Bible. Proverbs 9:10 tells us that the fear of the Lord is the beginning of wisdom, and knowledge of the Holy One is understanding. The contrast is that the fear that the Bible sanctions, contrary to Agĩkũyũ fear of God, is the awe and reverence that a person feels before the presence of God because of God's sublime greatness and holiness. Such a fear is healthy and is to be encouraged. But the distrustful Agĩkũyũ fear for Ngai is based on cultural understanding or misunderstanding of God. This may basically be explained by the fact that the Agĩkũyũ did not always differentiate spiritual phenomena – attributing both good and evil to God, a further testimony to the depravity of humanity and degeneration of human cultures.

As I have said the Agĩkũyũ thought God is not to be bothered unnecessarily. If one is sick for example, ordinary knowledge of medicine is applied. If the sickness persists, a diviner is sought to appease the offended

---

40. Okorocha, *Religious Conversion*, 2.
41. wa Thiong'o, *The River Between*, 36.

ancestor. If the situation persists e.g. when death threatens, the father of the family organizes an appeal to Ngai through a sacrifice in which the whole family, the living and the dead, are involved. The understanding here is that the departed ancestors are part of the community. Ngũgĩ says that during such a ritual both the spirit of the dead and the living would be invoked to join in the ritual.[42]

In case of the injury caused by nature, such as lightning, actual treatment of the individual is done and sacrifice to appease God is done in hope that God will not further visit wrath to any other member of the family. This sacrifice is made to God, but the ancestors are also present with the living. Since Ngai speaks through nature such as lightning, the Agĩkũyũ are in constant touch with nature. Unfortunately, this has often been mistaken for "nature worship by some Western scholars."[43]

Sacrifices in Agĩkũyũ Religion

Religion involved everyone, children and women besides the elders who were the priests. The select children in particular were important for the learning and continuity of the religious rituals. The inclusion of the whole family in religious matters echoes Judaism which should serve to interrupt today's tendency to divide the family during worship where the teens, the children, and the parents all worship under different roofs in the same Church. This greatly hinders mentorship and learning of religion through observation and asking questions by the young.

In the Agĩkũyũ culture, there was a religious attachment to every aspect of life from planting, weeding, to harvesting, and virtually every aspect of life, integrating religion seamlessly into everyday life. All these events and seasons were attended with different sacrifices. The dichotomy between the sacred and the secular was not known.

---

42. Ibid., 11.
43. Kenyatta, *Facing Mt. Kenya*, 231.

Sacrifices were the means through which contact with Ngai was established. They were done under sacred trees. The sacred trees were an institution in Agĩkũyũ religion and people have great attachment to the trees. Such trees marked their unity as a people, their family integrity (for their fathers sacrificed around it), their close contact with the soil, the rain and the rest of nature, and to crown it all, their most vital communion with the most High God of the tribe.[44]

The idea of 'clean and unclean things' was well known among the Agĩkũyũ. For example, if a person touched a dead body, he or she was unclean, and a cleansing ceremony was conducted. This in itself taught the idea of boundaries and self-control. Likewise, the practice of 'holy and unholy things' was also well known. For example, the instruments used for sacrifices were declared holy and used exclusively for religious purpose.[45] This was so critical that even a sacrificial ram was not only expected to be of one color, but even its history had to be a clean one, e.g. one that had not been stolen or in any dispute. Even a digging stick that was used for the religious planting ceremony was cut from a holy tree. This stick held the sacrificial animal during the offering of a sacrifice. Again, the stick had to be one that had resisted burning during a sacrifice.[46]

During any sacrifice young children boys and girls not above 8 years formed part of the procession of holy elders who also included the elderly women who had passed the age of child bearing and had become mothers of the community. No person with any known tint of sin, *thahu*, would be allowed to take any part in the religious ceremonies.

As I shall demonstrate in this study, the leadership of the AICs is closer to the African traditional religions. For example, the place of women in AICs church polity showed significant influence of African traditions.

---

44. Ibid., 240.
45. Ibid., 230.
46. Ibid.

Unlike in some historical churches which until recently were ambivalent to the ordination and inclusion of the women in their leadership, the Agĩkũyũ traditional religion had a special place for women. It recognizes women as equal and able leaders with men. The Akũrinũ church in particular has a lot to teach us on this area, as our research will show.

Priesthood in Agĩkũyũ Traditional Culture

Priesthood was so important to the Agĩkũyũ Kikuyu community[47]. Sacrifices were made by elders, who Kenyatta describes, as chiefs or sub-chiefs, high profile political officers, who performed in the sacrificial ceremonies simply in their role as elders of various grading, Athuri a kiama i.e. "council of elders." Kenyatta describes sacrificial elders as individuals of high moral caliber standing tall above the ordinary mortal. Perhaps a long quotation from Kenyatta is appropriate here;

> In this category of sacrificial elders, some of them are, "wise men', or seers (Morathi, sing.; Arathi pl.). These men are believed to be endowed with powers beyond human beings. They are to be in direct communication with Mwene-Nyaga who gives them instructions, generally during sleep. Mwene-Nyaga assists and directs them in executing their sacred duty. The powers so given, it is said, are never to be used for personal purposes, but only for the welfare of the community. For it is feared that if anyone dared to misuse such powers, thus acting contrary to Mwene-Nyaga's instructions, the result would be disastrous, not only to himself but to the whole of his family. A Morathi uses no magic or medicine in interpreting the messages or instructions given to him by Mwene-Nyaga. He is commanded not to seek earthly aid in executing his sacred mission. Thus, a seer was in a very delicate position, for while he was in direct communication with Mwene-Nyaga on the one hand, on the other hand his

---

47. Kenyatta, Facing Mt. Kenya, 232-233.

life was in danger, especially a beginner's. Unless he had heard the message from *Mwene-Nyanga* repeatedly and was quite sure that he had got them accurately, he dared not deliver them to the people, because if his prophesy proved false he would be taken to be a pretender, and the punishment for an act of this nature was death.[48]

This might suggest that the Agĩkũyũ had a concept of the nature of God who is holy and who demands holiness from his creatures especially those who serve as the priests for the people. Ngũgĩ, echoes the same sentiment on the respect accorded to the elders by the Agĩkũyũ. "Elders are respected especially those who are wise and knowledgeable of the ways of the tribe and the community."[49]

Waigwa concurs with Kenyatta also that a *Morathi* or *Mũrathi* was a significant religious figure, usually doubling as a traditional healer, for it was God who told a traditional healer what a client was suffering from, the cause of the ailment, and what herbs to use.[50] Usually, diseases were believed to have a spiritual cause, and this required a *Morathi* to identify and to deal with it. A *Mũrathi's* main "national duty was to foretell the future and to advise the nation how to prepare for what was in store. One such prophet among the Agĩkũyũ was Mũgo wa Kĩbirũ who prophesied the coming of the Europeans into the country. In his dream, a horrified Mũgo wa Kĩbirũ had tried to intercede for his people, persuading *Ngai* to spare them from the imminent predicament of foreign invasion. Like Jacob's struggle with Yahweh at the Brook Jabbok, (Genesis 32:22-32), Mũgo wa Kĩbirũ engaged God in a futile intercession and struggle. Bruised and exhausted, the prophet obeyed *Ngai's* command to go and warn the people. *Ngai* told him that strangers would come from across the large body of water into Gĩkũyũ country. The color of their skin

---

48. Ibid., 225.

49. wa Thiong'o, *The River Between*, 11.

50. Solomon Wachira Waigwa, *Pentecost without Azusa: An Historical and Theological Analysis of the Akorino Church in Kenya* (Unpublished PhD. Dissertation), 1991.

would resemble that of the small light-colored frog which the Gĩkũyũ call *kĩengere*. Their clothes would not be skins. They would wear clothes that look something like the wings of a butterfly.

Mũgo said that the strangers would later bring an iron snake with as many legs as a *mũnyongoro* "centipede" which would traverse the whole country from the large body of water on the east to the other body of water to the west. The sign to show that the intruding strangers were near was to be a great famine that would devour the entire land. That would be the beginning of suffering, not only for the *Agĩkũyũ* but also for their neighbors.

Mũgo wa Kĩbirũ urged his people not to take up arms against the encroaching foreigners or even try to kill their iron snake. To do so would be disastrous because the long magical sticks (guns) that the foreigners would carry, would spit a fire that would kill instantly upon contact with the body. Since those sticks could kill from a distance, the warriors' spears and arrows would be no match to them and a confrontation with the strangers would lead to the annihilation of the tribe. The great seer said that the best thing would be to establish friendly relations with invading strangers.

Waigwa adds that the beginning of sorrows for the Gĩkũyũ people did come just as prophet Mũgo had said. Between 1889 and 1892, a rinderpest epidemic swept through most of Africa. Ninety per cent of the cattle were destroyed. That catastrophe was followed by a severe drought that enshrouded the whole country causing a great famine which the *Agĩkũyũ* call *ng'aragu ya Rũraya*, "the famine of Europe" since it was around that time that the first Europeans begun to visit *Gĩkũyũ* country.[51]

Further on the priesthood, Kenyatta says that in all religious ceremonies, political, and social gatherings, the elders hold supreme authority. The custom of the people demands that the elder should be given his due respect and honor, not only when he is present, but also when he is

---

51. Waigwa, *Pentecost without Azusa*, 130.

absent.⁵² The position of an elder is respected. He offers his service to the community freely and in return he is respected by the community. He attributes his wisdom and success to his ancestors and will often pour libation to the ancestors in appreciation.

The Agĩkũyũ do not worship their ancestors but they commune with them reserving worship only for God. The West has accused Africans of worshipping the ancestors. Kenyatta tells us that this is not worship but communion with ancestors. The communion with the ancestors can be equated to the West's respect for the graves of departed heroes especially soldiers. Year after year there are memorial rituals to remember the departed heroes of war among the European races.⁵³

Among the Agĩkũyũ the father's or mother's position is critical being strengthened by religious sanctions. The father is in particular the priest of his household and is alone entitled to offer family sacrifices. In doing this he is supported by the will of the ancestral spirits. Where there is strife or dissension in the family the spirits can intervene and punish the wrong-doer. These kinds of spirits are known as *ngoma cia rohuho*, i.e. the spirits of the wind.

Among the Agĩkũyũ, religion is not propagated the way Christianity is spread through evangelism and missions. There is no official priesthood and no religious preaching. Religion is interwoven with traditions and social customs of the people. It is assumed that through childhood teaching, every member of the community has acquired the necessarily religious teaching. The parents are entrusted with this responsibility.⁵⁴ Through the parental teaching coupled with stringent adherence to social institutions, sanctions and taboos, every member of the society conformed. Again, this calls to mind the injunctions of the parental obligation to teach children in the Old Testament. Abraham's primary

---

52. Kenyatta, *Facing Mt. Kenya*, 254.
53. Ibid.,255.
54. Ibid., 232.

mandate was to teach his family, Genesis 18: 19: "For I have chosen him, so that he will direct his children and his household after him to keep the way of the Lord by doing what is right and just, so that the Lord will bring about for Abraham what he has promised him."

The role of the parent in teaching and training children in the Agĩkũyũ customs was as indispensable as in the Old Testament. Deuteronomy 6: 6-9 says:These commandments that I give you today are to be on your hearts. Impress them on your children. Talk about them when you sit at home and when you walk along the road, when you lie down and when you get up. Tie them as symbols on your hands and bind them on your foreheads. Write them on the doorframes of your houses and on your gates.

King Solomon knew this value of social conformity, Proverb 22: 6 (NET) — 'Train a child in the way that he should go, and when he is old, he will not turn from it." Like in the Jewish traditions, besides the parental training to the children and the young people, religious ceremonies formed the picturesque on the mind of the young and elicited important questions for their meaning from the children; which always offered the parents an opportunity to teach children.

The Agĩkũyũ religion can be summed up as being based on belief in a supreme being, Ngai, and on constant communication with nature. The most solemn religious service is sacrificing to Mwene-Nyaga. This privilege and duty belong to the elders. These people are believed to be endowed with power beyond those of ordinary human beings[55] and are held to be in direct communication with Mwene-Nyaga who gives them instructions, generally during their sleep as I have noted above.

This may explain why dreams and visions are so vital in the Akũrinũ church. Dreams are part of a familiar custom. It is also interesting to see how religion is tied to language. A linguistic analysis of a word like Arathi or Morathi, which referred to the wise men of the community was

---

55. Kenyatta, *Facing Mt. Kenya*, 232-233

the same word that was used to describe the new religion at its inception in late 1920s before the name *Akũrinũ* was adapted in 1940s. The community recognized the new Christian *Arathi* in the category of their own traditional wise men and thereby accorded them the same respect. The Bible, which is full of reference to dreams and vision as a way of communication by God to people just came to affirm what was always known and practiced in the *Agĩkũyũ* culture. Again, it is interesting how the *Agĩkũyũ* found resonance with the Old Testament on the sacred places. The Israelites had sacred places such as the Mt. Sinai and it is in the same breath that *Kere-Nyaga* can be an official resting place of God and the *Mugomo* tree a place of worship, while the lightning is like a theophany akin to the "burning bush." Again, the family was a religious unit just like in the Old Testament where the religious rituals were led by the fathers with all family members participating. The place of men in Church is critical but today in many churches a gradual feminization of the church is discernable. It would seem that either the men take the lead, their natural orientation, or they will withdraw all together. The *Akũrinũ* church can teach us the value of putting the male figure in the forefront in religious matters and by so doing solicit his participation, again borrowed from a rich traditional culture.

A seer is not in the same category with a witch doctor (*murogi*) or medicine man (*mondo mogo*) whose professional duty is to help the elder in carrying out certain rites, such as purification, ceremonies, and trials by ordeals and healing of various maladies. The medicine man has no power above his professional duty. Thus, the duty of teaching morality or religious ethics is vested in the elders in their capacity as parents.

If Christian pastoral office today invokes its understanding of leadership from the *Agĩkũyũ* cultural understanding, the pastoral office might claim a more respectable place. Today's abuse of the pastoral office had no such equivalence in the African traditional cultural discipline for a spiritual leader. Instructively, when Christianity finds resonance in the cultural practices, it may gain a more effective and permanent value. ATR has a lot to teach us on such values as family life. The kinship ties and family values in African tradition culture should aid the African Christian in fostering a truly Christian communion while the high expectation of the traditional religious leader should be applied to the Christian leader especially those who hold Pastoral and teaching ministry. The beliefs and values in the ATR may be a tool in Christian discipleship — a very elusive dimension of Christian faith especially in Africa.

The Tribal Organization or Political Life of the *Agĩkũyũ*

The *Agĩkũyũ* life was organized from birth to death. Life was organized around religious rituals that climaxed in various transitions — rites of passage. At an early age a young boy underwent the second birth. At about the age of 16-18 a boy was circumcised and became a full man, *Mondo morome*, while a girl underwent clitoridectomy at 10-14 years. This rite was the most important transition and marked the entrance to full participation in the life of the community. After the circumcision the young men entered the junior warriors' council, *nyama ya anake a mumo*. Next was the senior warriors' council, *nyama ya ita* (war council). After this, there was marriage when a man entered the "council of elders" in the first grade of eldership, *kiama kia kamatimo*, or "the carriers of shields." In the next stage when one's first born son reached the age of circumcision, the man entered the "council of peace," *kiama kia mataathi*. The final stage of eldership was the religious sacrificial council, *kiama kia maturanguru*. The elders of this grade assumed the role of the holy men or high priests. In the induction ceremony at this stage the elders dedicated their lives to God and the welfare of the community. Only few elders reached this stage[56]. The fact that life moved progressively to this stage of service to God ordered life's ultimate purpose as religious.

---

56. Kenyatta, *Facing Mt. Kenya*, 80.

Kenyatta says that the Agĩkũyũ tribal organization was based on three factors; *mbari* or *nyumba*, *moherega*, and *riika*. In a recent unpublished study of leadership in Kenya, Kimathi et al argue that the family level referred to as '*mbari*' or '*nyomba*' ('*nyumba*') brings together all those who are related by blood[57]. They include a man, his wife or wives, children and grandparents and even the great grandparents. The man is the head of the home apart from the far past when legends say the Agĩkũyũ were matriarchal. The man or the father is referred to as *Muthuuri* which literally means "the one who chooses or decides."[58] At the second level, several *mbaris* form the clan, referred to as '*moherega*' or '*muhiriga*'. The representatives of the *moherega* would meet during special occasions such as marriage, initiation, or circumcision ceremonies. The representatives, who were elders of the community, would bring with them young members from each of their respective *mbaris*. The purpose for this was to induct them to the future leadership by educating the youngsters on how the leadership was structured. The goal was to promote unity in the whole *moherega*. Each *moherega* was governed by certain rules or behavior to maintain harmonious relationship in the community. Many *moherega* (s) form the whole tribe, *ruriri*.

Kimathi further says that at the *mbari* level, the patrilineal system was in place. Here the father was treated as the supreme ruler of the homestead. His position in the community largely depended on the type of homestead he kept and how he managed it. The ability to manage one's homestead well was taken as a testimonial that one was able to manage public affairs. The father was to be shown respect by his family members. Also, the members of the children's age grade were to address the father

---

57. Jacob Kimathi, Alexia Njambi, and Lillian Mugure, *A Leader for Kenya* (Unpublished Manuscript).

58. Edmond Cavicchi, *Problems of Change in Kikuyu Tribal Society* (Bologna, Italy: EMI-Via Meloncello, 1977).

in the same manner as his children do, that is, in a gentle and polite tone, and calling him 'Baba' (Father).[59]

Traditionally the Agĩkũyũ family consists of all members of the family both living and dead. Anything that disturbs this family fellowship is evil, and nothing disturbs the dead more than an offence against the family unity and loyalty. For example, if by any harshness or indifference to family claims that the youth may bring, divine vengeance may be visited on the whole family of which the youth is a member. Thus, early and late in the life of the youth and the young people, by rules of conduct in individual instances, by regards and punishments and fears of ceremonial uncleanness, the younger generation learnt respect and obedience due to parents. The older generation did likewise. Ngũgĩ says that through deep conviction and strong teaching and ritual, each generation strived to pass on the way of life of the tribe to the next generation. The highest honor that a son, especially, would give to his parents was to remain true to the tribal values.[60]

In the Agĩkũyũ community there is no really individual affair, for everything has a moral and social reference. The habit of corporate effort is but the other side of corporate ownership; and corporate responsibility is illustrated in corporate work no less than in corporate sacrifice and prayer.[61]

The third organizational factor is the age-grouping or *riika*. Jocelyn Murray says that almost every year (circumcision took place after every four years) many young boys and girls go through initiation or circumcision ceremony. All those who go through this ritual in the same year from across the whole tribe, *ruriri*, form one age group, *riika rimwe*, irrespective of their *mbari* or *moherega*. They have a very strong broth-

---

59. Kimathi, Njambi, and Mugure, *A Leader for Kenya*.

60. wa Thiong'o, *The River Between*, 37.

61. Kenyatta, *Facing Mt. Kenya*, 115

erhood and sisterhood among themselves in all matters of the tribe. The activities of these age-sets stabilize the whole tribe.[62]

Though I have demonstrated the life of the Agĩkũyũ as seamlessly religious, the standard of this religiosity was a matter of public rating and approval. Anything that was done in the open and in agreement with the community was acceptable. For example, wife sharing among age mates was acceptable as long as it was done with mutual consent and agreement. Such things needed the discipline that biblical teaching brought to the African Church. Thus, when early Agĩkũyũ believers such as the Akũrinũ read the Bible, they found a much higher righteousness by which they critiqued and rejected some of their previous beliefs and customs.

The Traditional Education of the Agĩkũyũ People

In the Agĩkũyũ *traditional* system of education the instruction is always applied to an individual in concrete terms unlike in the European education system. Commenting on the difference between the education of the Europeans and Africans, Kenyatta observes;

> The rising generation is trained in beliefs and customs necessary to the self-maintenance of the tribe and the interrelation with the neighboring tribes. The fundamental needs of reproduction, extraction of food from the environment, and social solidarity are recognized and met. The tribal society not only maintains its existence but secures the continuity of its distinct features over against other tribes.[63]

The main difference between the European and Agĩkũyũ system of education is the primary place given to relationships. In the Agĩkũyũ

---

62. Jocelyn Murray, *Proclaim the Good News: A Short History of the Church Missionary Society* (London: Hodder and Stoughton, 1985), 87.

63. Kenyatta, *Facing Mt. Kenya*, 115.

education system, each official statement of education must be the building of character and not the mere acquisition of knowledge.

I sum this difference thus: to the Europeans, "individuality is the ideal of life" to the African the ideal is the right relations with, and behavior to other people.[64] The European education alienates the educated from the community while the Agĩkũyũ system of education on the whole socialized people to fit and function best in the community.

The Agĩkũyũ system of education focused on practicality of life. For example, children followed their parents to the farm and participated in the farm work as age allowed. When they were of age, they were given small portions of land for themselves. Whatever they cultivated was theirs. They could sell the produce and keep the income for themselves. The boys followed after the craft of their fathers. They learnt to grow and harvest honey in the field. No one needed to be away from home and the tribe in order to acquire education. Education had an immediate value. There was no competition, but effort was recognized and rewarded, sometime with leadership responsibility.

Ngũgĩ wa Thiong'o adds that the education that the missionaries gave had strings attached. It was primarily to alienate the people from their traditions. Those who insisted on holding onto their traditions were viewed with trepidation. The community reacted to this by forming their own independent schools. The Agĩkũyũ community loved education. They thought that education held the key to the wisdom of the white man. However, they were uncomfortable with the way education was implemented by the missionary schools — not with education itself. The point being encouraged here is that every culture, given time, is capable of deciphering what is useful in another culture and what in its own culture is no longer relevant. This process should not be hurried and made a bone of contention. Time always makes this happen.[65]

---

64. Ibid.,118.

65. wa Thiong'o, *River Between*, 21.

It is from this perspective that Kenyatta advised the early European educators to Africans;

> As a teacher his first concern should be to establish a good understanding with the people amongst whom he works, and to learn how to appreciate what is good in the tribal law and custom of that particular community. The importance of this point is that such an attitude would serve as a connecting-link between the pupils in the schools and the rest of the community.[66]

Kenyatta is lamenting that the European approach of education was that of "civilizing and uplifting poor savages," a policy that was based on the preconceived ideas that the African cultures were "primitive," and as such, belonging to the past and could only be looked upon as antiquarian relics fit only for the museum.[67] The Europeans should have realized that there is something to learn from the African and a great deal about him to understand, and that the burden could have been made easier if a policy of "give and take" could be adopted.[68] This paternalistic attitude has remained largely unchallenged to this day when it comes to the way the West view Africa.

Kenyatta's observation shows that the general attitude of Europeans on anything African was paternalistic. It is unfortunate that even today many of the missionary sponsored theological institutions in Africa have followed the same path where the curriculum is imported from the West and is expected to meet the vast needs of the African Church in the same way it has worked for the West. The African who is being civilized looks upon this "civilization" with great fear mingled with suspicion. Above all, he finds that socially and religiously he is torn away from his family and tribal organization. The new civilization he is supposed to acquire does

---

66. Kenyatta, *Facing Mt. Kenya*, 120.
67. Ibid.
68. Ibid.

not prepare him for the proper functions of a European mode of life or for the African life — instead he is left floundering between two social forces.

This can be said also of the missionary Christianity. It produced a Christian who was neither at home in his culture nor settled in the western culture. Suggesting how this discrepancy in education could have been narrowed, Kenyatta quotes his professor, Malinowski who says,

> All words which express religious beliefs, moral values, or specific technical or ritual proceedings, can only be rendered by reference to the social organization of the tribe, their beliefs, practices, education and economics. The study of the native language must go hand in hand with the study of culture.[69]

The Sexual Life of the *Agĩkũyũ* people

Like many African communities sex before marriage was forbidden among the *Agĩkũyũ* system of education. In my own community, the *Ameru*, children born outside the marriage union were rare. A lady who got pregnant outside wedlock was shunned and this greatly reduced her chances of marriage. She could only be married as a second wife and by an elderly man for that matter. Sexual abstinence before marriage was enforced through sexual taboos. Among the *Agĩkũyũ* traditional culture, sexual play or fondling, called *ngweko*, (sex without penetration), among the initiated, and masturbation among the boys (but never girls) was allowed and encouraged[70]. Wife sharing among age mates was allowed as part of shared of life.

The *Akũrinũ* church has carried on this tradition of sexual chastity. Sex before marriage is not permitted. The *Akũrinũ* will find it difficult

---

69. Ibid., 121.

70. The practice of fondling (*ngweko*) is elaborated by Kenyatta under the topic, "How Ngewko is Organized," *Facing Mt. Kenya*, 152-3.

to conduct the wedding of a couple who have consummated their union before the official wedding date. If the couple has engaged in sex before marriage, the Akũrinũ leaders claim that the Holy Spirit will reveal this and such a marriage may be canceled. In the modern culture, sexual chastity among the young is frowned upon while promiscuity is celebrated.

The argument that I am advancing here is that once the cultural and social sanctions against immoral behavior are broken, like it has happened whenever missionaries' and colonialism's attitude of frowning on the traditional moral injunctions has destroyed the moral fabric of traditional communities, immorality among the young people is bound to exacerbate. Here it must be noted that I am not suggesting in any way that the African communities were morally perfect. I am only saying that they had developed a moral system, a way of enforcing and even sanctions for all deviants. All these were rendered untenable when the moral radar was hinged away from its base in familiar culture to foreign little understood parameters.

European Inverted Hospitality

Kenyatta notes that with the coming of the Europeans, there mushroomed a number of religious sects other than the African traditional religions. He gives a number of reasons that caused this. First Europeans, especially the missionaries, came with pre-conceived ideas of what they would find and what they would do with Africa. Obviously, most of the ideas they had about Africa were as inaccurate as they were stereo-typed. Africa was not yet opened to exploration and discovery. Unfortunately to this day more than a century later, the West gets inaccurate and biased information about Africa. The western media depicts Africa as a lost case when they focus on the isolated crisis points such as the slum life or some few remote parts of Africa as the true representation of the entire continent. Whereas it is true that Africa is still developing, the challenges in Africa are not unique to humanity. In fact, it can be argued with a degree of accuracy that Africa has done so well within a short time, achieving what the West took centuries to achieve.

Secondly, given that Africans were considered mere savages, the European colonial government and missionaries did not deem it necessary to send any personnel of high education qualification to Africa, so that the colonies became like clearing-houses for failures and worse. This approach had a much longer history and philosophy. Jennings in his book, *The Christian Imagination: Theology and the Origins of Race*, tells part of this history. He picks the story from Allesendro Valignano (1529-1606) who had observed that the Europeans had replaced Israel and substituted it by Europe as the elected people of God, supersessionism, also sometimes called "replacement." In this way the idea of elected people became an idea without authentic compass and thereby subject to strange new human discernment.

In this displacement Valignano even discerned those capable of salvation and those capable of ministry, priesthood and ecclesial leadership. The lesser capable are Jews, the Moor converts and the Africans whom he deemed to be of very low intelligence, no culture, and are given to savage ways and vices, who live like brute beasts.[71] Jennings adds that they are born to serve with no aptitude for governing. In his categorization, only European and Japanese and some Chinese are worthy of Christianity and leadership with Africans, Jews, Moors, and Indians incapable of Christian leadership — they are reprobate.

As a result of this scaling of human beings the most qualified missionaries were sent to the Japanese and the Chinese who were deemed more intelligent and capable of understanding Christianity, while the least qualified were sent to Africa. It is plausible to imagine that some of the missionaries who were sent to Africa were like job seekers trying to improve their own lot in life as I will demonstrate a little later. The

---

71. Jennings, *Christian Imagination*, 34.

complexity with this approach to the missionary work in Africa is that these missionaries did not have enough intellectual capacity to understand let alone sympathize with African religiosity. It can be argued, as I have noted earlier, that once these missionaries met Africans whom they could at least outclass, themselves being of low social class in their countries of origin, asserted their superiority by mistreating the African — it made them feel worthy themselves. However, I note here that it would be an overstatement of facts to blanket all missionaries who came to Africa as of low class, yet this attitude is discernable.

Jennings argues that the Europeans succeeded in distorting the identity of the people they colonized the moment they uprooted them from their land. Referring to the invasion of the Latin America by the Portuguese conquistadores, Jennings suggests that space and place give people identity.[72] The European colonial expansion failed to capture the spatial disruption that took place in the colonial process. In the colonial enterprise, space, bodies, land and identity were reconfigured. In this reconfiguration the Portuguese and the Spanish connected the land and the body. The Portuguese and the Spanish stand between the body and land and he adjudicates, identifies and determines. This displacement was most marked in Africa.

Once space and place ceased to be the signifier of the identity of the native and slaves, Jennings says that their skin complexion took the role of the new identifier which graded people into three degrees; the white who are fair to look upon and well-proportioned, the mullatoes who are in between whiteness and blackness, and those who are as black as Ethiopians whose existence is deformed. In this way a scale of existence with the white on one extreme and the blackness at the other end with others in-between is invoked. With this, whiteness became the new organizing conceptual framework and the blackness on the other hand

---

72. Ibid., 27.

appears as the fundamental tool of that organizing conceptuality.[73] The whiteness became the benchmark for racial scale where people were viewed from how white or black, they were.

Our argument here is that if the missionary personnel sent to Africa were of such low caliber as Jennings argues, then they were bound to present a distorted mission. This does not in any way suggest that there were not good and godly men among the colonial administration and missionaries that were sympathetic to the cause of Africans. Africa is forever grateful to the likes of William Wilberforce who fought for abolition of the most diabolical treatment of Africans through slavery that for centuries had decimated her population. Likewise many missionaries both recent and far back lost their lives in Africa. Africa, with her tropical climate and strange diseases devoured the white man mercilessly.

But the white man persisted and insisted. Stories of how husbands would lose their wives within days of arrival in Africa abound. The missionary babies would succumb to the malaria parasite with abandon. Ludwig Krapf lost his newly wedded wife and child on the East coast of Africa two months after arrival at a tender age of 27 years as noted earlier. David Livingstone died on his knees praying for and in Africa right in the deepest interior of Central Africa. These are just few of the examples of the gallant sacrifices of the highest sublime humanity. As Paul says many preach out of strange motives, but the gospel is somehow preached. And the results are vivid. A distorted presentation of the gospel is far better than none at all. The gospel has a power of its own once presented — the motive and attitude of the presenter notwithstanding.

Whereas many Africans may be justified to think that all Europeans were altogether heartless to the African cause, there were still many well intended missionaries and even colonialists of good will. T.F.C. Bewes, the African Secretary, Church Missionary Society (CMS) was one such a missionary with great love for Africa. Having been a missionary in Kenya

---

73. Jennings, *Christian Imagination*, 25.

for twenty years earlier, he was later sent by the Archbishop of Canterbury at the height of the Mau Mau uprising to console the Church that was under intense persecution. As one familiar and sympathetic to the African cause, he had this to observe,

> The Kikuyu cannot easily differentiate between one white man and another. They do not realize that it is often the European of the poorest cultural background and of the lowest and most insecure wage group who would actually be rude to them, but they are certainly constantly aware that we do not always speak to them as courteously as we speak to each other. You will often hear them discussing this point together. Most of us have had, at one time or another, to apologize to an African for the rudeness of a fellow-countryman, or indeed perhaps for our own, only to be met with a shrug or a smile, 'don't bother about that; we are quite used to it'.[74]

Jocelyn Murray furthers singles out other missionaries that were sympathetic to the plight of Africans.[75] For example, in the 1920s Handley Hooper, a missionary in Kahuhia, himself a son of a pioneer missionary from coast, Douglas Hooper, helped the young African Christians at Kuhuhia with their magazine, *Mwiguithania*, at the expense of his reputation. In the same period another missionary Archdeacon W.E. Owen risked his reputation with the settlers and administrators in defending the rights of Africans in Western Kenya. Murray mentions others who during the Mau Mau warfare stood out and even spoke on behalf of the African church. They include Rev. David Steele, Minister of St. Andrews Presbyterian Church in Nairobi, Leonard Beecher, and Peter Bostock among many others. All in all Murray says that; "The CMS (and other societies) can be proud today that their missionaries did not run away;

---

74. T.F.C, Bewels, *Kikuyu Conflict: Mau Mau and the Christian Witness* (London: The High Press, 1953), 43.

75. Murray, *Good News*, 244.

that they did not seek to protect themselves with arms; and that they did speak out against injustice, even in high places."[76]

The Conflict Between the *Agĩkũyũ* and the Missionaries

With the inverted hospitality that I have painted above, conflict between the European colonial administration and the missionaries and the Africans was bound to happen sooner or later. The missionaries in the *Agĩkũyũ* land looked at all the *Agĩkũyũ* traditional cultures with suspicion as already demonstrated. They therefore treated them as evil and even preached against them. They singled out clitoridectomy as the most barbaric practice that they needed to fight at all cost.

The missionaries attacked customs whose real significance in the tribe they did not understand and probably would never understand. The best example was circumcision.[77] Ngũgĩ says that circumcision was an important ritual to the tribe. It kept people together, bound to the tribe. It was the core of the social structure, and something that gave meaning to man's life. End the custom and the spiritual basis of the tribe's cohesion and integration would be no more.[78]

People's culture with its customs and beliefs defines and gives meaning to life. For example, when Muthoni is asked by Waiyaki why she rebelled against her father and went for circumcision, all she could say is that she has really not rebelled against her Christian faith; "I want to be a woman, made beautiful in the manner of the tribe; a husband for my bed; children to play around the hearth." [79] To Muthoni, life should be defined by culture. She could not be different from her age mates.

---

76. Ibid., 247.
77. wa Thiong'o, *The River Between*, 38.
78. Ibid., 66.
79. Ibid.,43.

In 1929 the Church of Scotland barred children who had gone through clitoridectomy from their schools as noted earlier. Because of the protest that followed, the House of Commons and a committee of parliament was appointed to investigate the matter in 1930. Kenyatta was invited to give his view. In the meantime, the community deserted the missionary schools *en mass*. As a result, the *Agĩkũyũ* formed their own independent Kikuyu schools and the *Kareng'a* (which means "pure" referring to a desire to preserve the pure Kikuyu culture) schools which were completely free from missionary influence both in education and religious matters.[80] This period is of great interest to this research. As I will demonstrate, it is the same period of time that the *Akũrinũ* church started.

As I have said above, one of the fiercest culture battles between the missionaries and the *Agĩkũyũ* society was the issue of the circumcision for girls, clitoridectomy. It was one of the customs whose value the missionaries completely missed. Kenyatta has demonstrated to us that the value of clitoridectomy is not the surgical removal of the clitoris. Like the circumcision for boys, clitoridectomy held great value in the tribal psychology in which the institution carried with it tremendous educational, social, moral, and religious implications. The initiation, called *irua*, (clitoridectomy for girls and circumcision for boys) gave the boys and girls the manhood and womanhood status among the *Agĩkũyũ* community. The moral code of the whole tribe was bound up with the custom that symbolized the unification of the whole tribal organization.[81] The blood of sacrifice during the circumcision ritual was the link between men and God. During circumcision, Ngũgĩ writes this of the Waiyaki, the main protagonist in the story, when he was circumcised, "Henceforth a religious bond linked Waiyaki to the earth, as if his blood was an offering."[82]

---

80. Kenyatta, *Facing Mt. Kenya*, 120.

81. Ibid.,129.

82. wa Thiong'o, *The River Between*, 44.

Initiation enabled the initiates to enter into the secrets of the tribe. The days that followed the circumcision ritual were days of deep education on the matters of the tribe as the circumcision wound continued to heal.[83] The custom also allowed one to commence participation in various governing groups in the tribal organization, because the real age-groups began from the day of the physical operation. Moreover, the history and legends of the people are explained and remembered according to the names given to various age-groups at the time of initiation. For example, if there was a famine at the time of circumcision the age-group would be called Ng'aragu, meaning hunger. The age-group that was initiated when the Europeans introduced syphilis to the Agĩkũyũ community is called gatego, i.e. syphilis. Without the culture of writing, and if this custom was abolished, the community could not have been able to keep her history.

Kenyatta demonstrates how the coming of the European disrupted the life of the Agĩkũyũ community in the name of civilizing and ending tribal conflicts. For example, about 1925-28 was the time when the *itwika* (change of leadership) ceremony was to take place corresponding to the last *itwika* which was celebrated around 1890-98. The *irungu* or *maina* generation whose turn it was to take over the government from *Mwangi* generation begun to sing and dance ceremonial songs to mark the termination of the rule of *Mwangi* generation. However, the British government declared these ceremonies illegal thereby stopping them and denying the *Irungu* or *Maina* their birthright.[84] This disruption of life without providing an alternative continues to plague many communities in Africa. In my own community of *Ameru*, whom Kenyatta includes as part of the Agĩkũyũ, has witnessed increased idleness among young people that often degenerates to criminal and vigilant groups. This can be attributed to a sudden change in culture without offering an alternative.

---

83. Ibid., 45-6.
84. Kenyatta, *Facing Mt. Kenya*, 189.

The missionaries did not understand how the African welfare was bound with the rigid observance of taboos and rites through which all members of a tribe were bound up as one organic whole and controlled by an iron-bound codes of duties. Once in Africa the missionaries set to condemn customs and beliefs which they could not understand. Among these customs besides clitoridectomy, was polygamy (a practice that was acceptable in many African cultures and one that we may categorize as adiaphora) that ensured that no one in the society was lonely and a permanent spinster. Kenyatta says that faced with this scenario the African set out to look for evidence in the Bible only to discover that some of the heroes of the Bible had many wives. This must have been a rude shock. They thought the missionaries were not taking the Bible seriously by "ignoring" or suppressing what was clearly written in the Holy book. What was more puzzling was that the missionaries were not willing to discuss this with their African converts, just expecting them to take what was chosen by the missionaries for his simple mind without argument.

Kenyatta says that, "the missionaries associated polygamy with sexual excesses, and insisted that all those who want the salvation of their souls must agree to adapt monogamy. In their attempt to break down the system of polygamy and other African institutions, they imposed monogamy as the condition for baptism, and demanded that even those who had more than one wife must give up all but one. No one could be received into Church membership without complying with this rule."[85] Today polygamy remains a challenge in Africa for the Christian and non-Christian. In the West polygamy is subtler. Whereas an African keeps all his wives and concubines with no shame, the European takes one wife at a time, each time divorcing the one he has finished with. It would be plain hypocrisy to say serial monogamy is more Christian than polygamy. Both are equally a result of human failure except on one point — the children in a polygamous marriage are more likely to have an identity

---

85. Kenyatta, *Facing Mt. Kenya*, 261.

while in serial monogamy; identity crisis remains a significance cause of social disquiet in the West.

It is difficult to imagine the confusion that such a requirement from the missionaries must have caused among the Africans. Kenyatta says that, "no African could understand how he could drive away his wives and children [and one could add, drive them to where in the first place? Noting that a women once married had no inheritance in her father's estate], especially in a community where motherhood is looked upon as a religious duty, the children as not just the property of their father but of the clan (*mbari*) and without whom the *mbari* is lost."[86] It was also terribly hard for a woman to be driven away and to lose her status in the society where she was respected as a wife and mother. Clearly here is a double standard. The missionaries were preaching what they could not themselves practice. Paul recognizes that some things may not be easily undone, advising the Corinthian converts to "remain as you were when Christ called you," 1 Corinthians 7: 24. Evidently the missionary approach to the cultural question was too fast and too radical and which consequently failed to serve the intended purpose.

The importance of clitoridectomy will be appreciated if one tries to unravel the crisis its proscription precipitated. Robert W. Strayer says that this cultural issue readily took the function of expressing resistance to the foreign order and for some time the matter became in the hands of Kikuyu Central Association (KCA) an important means of political mobilization. It touched too on the immense sensitive problem of land, for popular belief had it that Europeans would marry uncircumcised Kikuyu girls and through them gain access to steal more Kikuyu land. The clitoridectomy crisis, potent enough in its own right, was linked with many of the other tensions of colonial Kenya both within mission communities

---

86. Ibid, 262.

and in the larger society.[87] The missionaries especially those of CMS and later AIM sought for allies in opposing the practice of clitoridectomy from both African converts and the colonial government. Strayer adds that some African converts joined in the opposing the practice, but they were not necessarily able to persuade the community against the practice. The colonial government was more reluctant to legislate against the practice fearing for political fallout. In the confrontation that ensued a missionary was killed, and the missionaries lost control of the schools with many pupils quitting for the African founded schools.

This missionary's effort at conversion of souls detached from culture failed to address the African worldview. Instead of teaching how the African could deal with his traditional institutions and religious system, it just advocated for a total denial and denunciation. In as much as it did not address the core of his being, namely customs and religious practices, it failed to address and consequently transform the African's worldview. It thereby produced a superficial Christian. Kenyatta says that the result was that Africans resulted to superficial acceptance of Christianity in order to be accepted into the missionary schools to acquire the white man's "magic" — especially the young people. Others formed their own African Independent churches and schools where they could practice the African customs and beliefs that they considered indispensable.

The Birth of the *Akũrinũ* Church

As an African Indigenous Church (AIC) that started without the mediation of missionaries about 90 years ago and continues to thrive, the Akũrinũ church deserves a more serious consideration by theologians and missionaries. In this regard I will confine ourselves to the early years of the Akũrinũ, a period of about 15 years between late 1920s and early

---

87. W. Robert Strayer, *The Making of the Mission Communities in East Africa* (Albany, New York Heinemann, State University of New York Press, 1978), 136.

1940s, and to the last 20 years or so. The current growth and ramification of the Akũrinũ movement point to the future direction that this movement is likely to take. According to Abraham Macharia Prince;

> The Akũrinũ Church traces its roots in a colonial movement of believers referred to as 'Arathi Movement'. The impact of these Arathi itinerant preachers, later known as 'Aroti' and currently 'Akũrinũ', and their proclamations of redemption triggered a wave of liberation. The impact was felt both in the religious and political spheres. Not only did they bring a faith that was to alter the religious configuration of the Kenyan mainland but also effected a transformation in the country's political life. It was the Arathi who first proclaimed about redemption and a coming liberation.[88]

Macharia explains that at the time of the inception, Akũrinũ attracted wide popularity owing to the universality of the path of 'liberation and redemption' that it offered. Though emerging in a volatile period and faced with severe persecution at the inception, the community emerged and established itself as an indigenous Pentecostal community in Kenya with neither a parental mission nor Pentecostal affiliation.

What really distinguishes Akũrinũ from other Pentecostal churches is her claim of a unique call to pray for the liberation of the nation from the colonial government. Macharia adds that, "Although the Akũrinũ does not wholly agree with the African traditional beliefs, the religion is closer to Africanism than many other religions."[89]

Macharia says that the Akũrinũ community was known by several names. At the time of inception in mid in 1920s, they were referred to as the "Arathi" (pl.) or "Mũrathi" (singular) church, which literally means the church of the prophets. This is because of this Church movement emphasis on prophetic messages. The name Aroti, meaning dreamers

---

88. Prince Abraham Macharia, *In Search of Identity: Akurinu Community Demystified* (Nairobi, Kenya: Print View Publishers, 2012) 3.

89. Macharia, *Identity*, 5.

was adopted in February 1934, because of the community's emphasis on dreams, visions, and auditions. The community members referred to themselves as "Andũ a Mwathani" or the 'Lord's People' which is *Watu wa Mungu* in Kiswahili.[90] In his book, *Facing Mount Kenya*, Jomo Kenyatta referred to Akũrinũ church as *Watu wa Mungu*, "people of God" while the colonial administrative files of 1931 refer to them as ' false prophets', a probable racial prejudice.[91]

Macharia says that in the 1940s the name Akũrinũ emerged from groups of Aroti from Meru. The meaning of Akũrinũ (pl.), Mũkũrinũ: (sing.) is highly disputed. One theory says that it comes from a question, 'Mũkũrinũũ?' meaning who is the savior?" It is said that when they emerged, the Akũrinũ were commissioned to preach the gospel of redemption, Uũkũri, and proclaim the redeemer, Mũkũũri. As they proclaimed the message the local community would ask them, who is the savior? "Mũkũrinũũ?" to which they would answer, 'Ni Jesu' (He is Jesus). Another theory advanced by Bishop Elijah Thuuri Kinyanjui is that the name Akũrinũ comes from the Agĩkũyũ word Akiranũ (pl.), Mũkiranu, (sing.), which is a diminutive term meaning "sexually incapable people." Because of the obscene overtones, it was contorted to Akũrinũ (pl), and Mũkũrinũ, (sing). This reference is because of the Akũrinũ's stern stance against sexual immorality.

However, the most probable theory is that the term Akũrinũ comes from the Ameru word-*Gũkũrina or Gũtharũma* in Kikuyu which refers to roaring like a lion, a character attributed to the way the Akũrinũ pray with deep groaning. The Akũrinũ church has also been referred to as *Wagithomo* from the word *Githomu*, meaning learning, because the Akũrinũ say that they are going to learn when they attend Church.[92] Though formerly the mainline church viewed Akũrinũ with suspicion,

---

90. Ibid., 9.
91. Kenyatta, *Facing Mt. Kenya*, 263.
92. Macharia, *Identity*, 9-10.

there has been more understanding of the ways of this church with passage of time.

Waigwa and Macharia credit the beginning of *Akũrinũ* to Joseph Ng'ang'a.[93] Ng'ang'a who was probably born in 1884 at Ng'enda village, of Mang'u, Gatundu in Kiambu District. Although he had received elementary education at the Gospel Mission Station at Kambui, Ng'ang'a did not appear to have been faithful in the Christian teaching as it was presented by the mission. He was not baptized, and he lived like any ordinary *Mũgĩkũyũ*, participating in traditional social life including attending beer parties. He was dramatically converted following an illness after a bout of drunkenness in 1926. One evening as Ng'ang'a was walking home from a beer party, he became too intoxicated to walk and fell asleep on the roadside.

His acquaintances related that in his sleep, he heard a voice calling him and though it stopped, he knew it was God's.[94] He went back to sleep. The strange thing about it was that the voice had called him Joseph and he was not yet baptized. The voice called him again and this time instructed him to pray for himself that his sins may be forgiven. In the morning he looked for footprints of who would have called but found none. He became conscious that it was God who had spoken to him. He took the beer which he was carrying and gave it to others and also the apparatus [with which it was made].

---

93. Waigwa, *Pentecost without Azusa*, 159.
94. Ibid., 139-140.

This incident is recorded in an *Akũrinũ* hymn on God's redeeming mercy:

Ndĩ mũrĩu mũkĩra wa njĩra nĩ anjarĩirie,

Ndarĩ njaga na ndaconokire nĩ anjarĩirie,

Mwathani wakwa ũnjoe,

Na Roho Mũtheru anjoe,

Nĩanjarĩirie.

(When I lay drunk on the roadside, He spoke to me,

I was naked, but he was not ashamed, He spoke to me.

Oh, my Lord receive me,

And may the Holy Spirit receive me,

He spoke to me.)[95]

Macharia records that because Ng'ang'a came from the *Agĩkũyũ* tradition, which was predominantly religious and prayerful, he was able to identify the voice as the voice of God. Macharia also tells us that from this calling was born the *Akũrinũ* practice of "baptism of the Holy Spirit," where the name to be given to a *Mũkũrinũ*, at baptism is always given by the Holy Spirit. Apparently, most of the *Akũrinũ* practice only this kind of baptism with no emphasis of the water baptism.

Waigwa adds that after his call, Ng'ang'a went into seclusion for three years. During the seclusion, two more people were led to him by the Holy Spirit, having themselves been filled with the Holy Spirit. The two were Samuel Muinami and John Mung'ara.[96] Abstaining from ordinary life, Ng'ang'a and his two friends devoted themselves to a life of prayer and intensive Bible study. That retreat, and others by the *Arathi* leaders

---

95. Ibid., 140.
96. Ibid., 151.

is indicative of their understanding of the biblical scriptures as a guide in all matters of Christian life and worship.

After that period of preparation, the trio *Arathi* prophets embarked on an evangelistic and teaching ministry which drew many followers to their group. Their message was 'liberatory," a call to repentance so that God could visit the Agĩkũyũ again and deliver them from the yoke of colonialism. Once the people returned to God from their wicked ways and were filled with the Holy Spirit, then God would remove the British from power and most of them would return to England. God would sweep the Europeans aside and usher in an African self-rule. Other *Bendegothitho* (a term describing people who practiced Pentecostal like faith) joined Ng'ang'a's growing group and identified him as their leader. As a result of Ng'ang'a's ministry, the *Arathi* movement spread in areas beyond southern Gĩkũyũ to parts of the Rift Valley.

Concurrent with Ng'ang'a's ministry, Waigwa reports that another *Bendegothitho* was emerging in Murang'a district. In the same year that Ng'ang'a's group was budding, a similar group was developing around the ministry of Moses Thuo of Gatanga Location in Murang'a district. Like Ng'ang'a, Thuo was born around 1900. As a young boy, Thuo went to school at Githumu African Inland Mission (AIM). Having received a fourth-grade education, Thuo was certainly one of the fortunate people in the area at that time because he could read and write in both Gĩkũyũ and Swahili, and some English. At Githumu, Thuo became a Christian and was baptized.

Thuo left the AIM along with other Agĩkũyũ who felt that the missionaries were hindering progress towards African leadership both in the affairs of the church and its schools. Thuo joined an independent church group led by Daudi Maina Kĩragũ who had formed a fellowship in his home village. In 1926 however, Thuo begun to experience intense spiritual renewal along with repeated dreams and visions, an experience that was "at variance with the beliefs and practices espoused by the larger independent group led by Kĩragũ. That new experience of the Holy Spirit set Thuo's group apart from other Christians because of its outward manifestation.

In addition, this emerging *Arathi* movement was parting ways with the rest of *Gĩkũyũ* independency because the latter focused upon two issues only: "African control of schools and the circumcision of girls." To the *Arathi*, those objectives were only temporal, and failed to meet the deeper spiritual needs of the *Agĩkũyũ* society. At one of their meetings in 1926, Moses Thuo and several others begun to pray involuntarily, to groan or shout and to confess their sins aloud. Thuo describes his own initial Pentecostal experience thus: "I was excited and for a moment I saw my wretchedness before God and how insincere and half-hearted a believer I was. I do not know exactly what happened to bring this about, but someone told me later that I had also started groaning and worshipping more than anyone else."[97]

After this experience, Thuo, like Ng'ang'a went into seclusion and engaged in intensive Bible study accompanied with meditation, dreams, and incidents of speaking in tongues and sorrowful groaning in intercessory prayer. His ministry yielded several groups in the villages of Gatanga. None of the two main *Arathi* groups in Kĩambu and Mũrang'a knew of the existence of the other. *Akũrinũ* oral history maintains that those and other groups that were formed later were introduced to each other by the Holy Spirit. The elders teach that after a group had formed in one area unknown by others, they would be told by the Holy Spirit to go to a specific village where they would find elders who would teach them more about the Holy Spirit. Sometimes individual prophets would be led to join a group in a distant village, or to go and preach the new message about repentance and the gift of the Spirit. Upon arriving at the designated village, the prophet would be surprised to learn that "the people there had been informed about it [by the Spirit] and were await-

---

97. Waigwa, *Pentecost without Azusa*, 151.

ing his coming." These occurrences are still very common among the *Akũrinũ*. When my research assistant and I went to collect data in one of the *Akũrinũ* churches, the members informed us that they knew of our coming well in advance.

Waigwa says that the leaders of the various Arathi *Bendegothithos* engaged in evangelistic activities in their villages and many people joined the new faith. The initial success of the *Arathi* evangelistic activities was due to their holistic messages which touched on the real-life situations of the people. Both Ng'ang'a and Thuo and their followers preached messages that "dealt with the problems which the *Agĩkũyũ* were facing during that time." Such messages touched on the plight of the *Agĩkũyũ* under the yoke of colonialism, the racist attitudes and policies of the colonial administrators and settler farmers, including forced labor and confiscation of their land by the settlers. *Arathi* preachers also addressed existential questions that concerned the life of the *Agĩkũyũ* community under the colonial rule.

Since God is sovereign, and God had ordained lands for each group of people to call their home, (Acts 17: 26) why would God allow foreigners to invade *Agĩkũyũ* land and possess it? Why did God allow *wazungu* to subjugate them to such inhumane ways? Isaiah 59 has always been a key text in *Akũrinũ* evangelism, for it answers the question of suffering under the yoke of colonialism and how spiritual salvation could also have socio-political ramifications. "Surely the arm of the LORD is not too short to save, nor his ear too dull to hear. But your iniquities have separated you from your God; your sins have hidden his face from you, so that he will not hear," (Isaiah 59:1-2). The *Arathi* preached that it was because of their sins that Kenyans had been left at the mercy of evil imperial powers. Just as God had forsaken Israel and allowed Nebuchadnezzar to take them captive into Babylonian, so God had forsaken Kenyans and allowed a foreign King to make them captives in their own land.

The answer to that predicament was found in the book of Isaiah, "'Come now, let us reason together,' says the LORD. 'Though your sins are like scarlet, they shall be as white as snow; though they are red as crimson, they shall be like wool. If you are willing and obedient, you will eat the best from the land; but if you resist and rebel, you will be devoured by the sword.' For the mouth of the LORD has spoken." (Isaiah 1:18-20)

The *Arathi* called all *Agĩkũyũ* to repentance, for if they repented, God would let them eat the good of the land of Kenya which was then being enjoyed by foreigners. Of course, the spiritual aspect of repentance was emphasized, for in the New Testament, the *Arathi* read that sinners should repent of their sins because the Kingdom of God was at hand, (Mark 1:15), but true salvation that followed genuine repentance was understood in holistic terms. It implied healing and restoration of peace of the body, mind and soul, and the removal of unjust, racist and oppressive political power and the institution of a democratic form of government that Africans could call their own.

It has been alleged that such *Arathi* messages were millennium in nature. Waigwa says that the testimony of Father Chilardi from Ruchu Catholic Parish in Murang'a is significant in spite of being rather negative. He testified hearing Moses Thuo calling people to "repent for the Kingdom of God was coming." In support of his theory, Chilardi said that Thuo also led his followers "in prayers for the deliverance of the *Agĩkũyũ* people from colonialism."[98]

The millennial preaching and approach to life among the *Akũrinũ* and other spiritual churches has significantly changed with time. For example Philomena Mwaura notes that when the spiritual churches emerged at the beginning and middle of the 20th century, their ethic (at least, some of them) centered on the belief that they were living in the time of the end after which God would inaugurate "a new heaven

---

98. Waigwa, *Pentecost without Azusa*, 293.

and a new earth."⁹⁹ Before this everyone will account for this life (Matt. 25:31-46). The present life was regarded as transitory and therefore one should lead a life that will eventually lead him/her to acquire his/her own salvation and not get involved with a world that was ending. This however did not entail total withdrawal from reality for they also heeded Paul's command in 2 Thessalonians 3:10, "if anyone will not work, let him not eat." Hence while they preserved themselves for the second coming of Christ, and the final judgment, they were expected to participate in productive activities for their material welfare.

It is worth mentioning here that *Arathi* preaching had two foci. First, it highlighted the plight of the Africans in the face of colonial subjugation. Colonial rule, the *Arathi* announced, had been measured and found wanting for treating God's people in an inhumane manner. Accordingly, God had decided to bring that rule to an end and hand over the country to its owners. A government of Africans by Africans would be established. Since that transition was not going to be an easy one, the *Arathi* claimed to have been called to the ministry of intercession, a role the *Akũrinũ* have maintained hitherto. They were not to participate in any military confrontation with the colonialists as others may do. They understood their office as of priests in the land, bridging the gap between God and the people, in a sustained intercession for the process towards African self-government. Secondly it addressed the issue of personal repentance and holiness before God.

Although the founders claim that they were directed by the Holy Spirit to start their church as I have demonstrated above, from the foregoing analysis of the socio-political challenges, it is likely that they were also reacting to the social, political, economic and cultural upheavals that were being experienced by the *Agĩkũyũ* community. Other sources

---

99. Philomena Njeri Mwaura, "Africa Instituted Churches in East Africa," *Studies in World Christianity*, Vol. 10, Issue 2 (2005):168, accessed March 1 2016, <https://mail.google.com/mail/u/0/#inbox/1533292cdd1814bd?projector=1>.

testify to this genesis. Nthamburi explains that, "In Kenya, this Gikuyu independent Church arose out of the need to preserve African traditions such as female circumcision in the wake of the missionary's attack on such customs as barbaric."[100] Another author, Mary N. Getui, maintains that, politically, the colonial administration had established a new form of government that did not recognize the powers and the authorities of the *Gikuyu* elders, and instead chose chiefs from young men.[101] The colonial administration's hand-picked chiefs, often young men of dubious back-ground, served the interests of their masters and were times worse in oppressing their own kin and kith. The Gikuyu community resented the imposed leadership. Economically the colonial settlers had reduced the people to squatters by taking the prime land, 'white highlands.

The western missionaries in their endeavor to convert the Agĩkũyũ believed that they had to get rid of their traditional customs and beliefs which they termed unchristian. They attacked various Agĩkũyũ customs such as dances, polygamy, and female circumcision. Female circumcision particularly irked the Agĩkũyũ people and generated a great heat and controversy between the Agĩkũyũ and the Protestant churches.

On this, Kenyatta says that the missionaries condemned customs and beliefs that they did not understand. Among other things they insisted that the followers of the Christian faith must accept monogamy as the fundamental principles of the African social structure.[102] This finally resulted to some Agĩkũyũ forming their Churches. Among these were the Independent Pentecostal Churches of Africa (AIPCA) and the Akũrinũ church.[103] But as I have demonstrated the Akũrinũ Church specifically did not begin as a breakaway from the missionary Churches but resulted

---

100. Nthamburi, *Crossroads*, 55.

101. Mary N. Getui. ed., *Theological Method and Aspects of Worship in African Christianity* (Nairobi, Kenya: Acton Publishers, 1998), 96.

102. Kenyatta, *Facing Mt. Kenya*, 261.

103. Ibid., 197.

from the prophetic figures (*Arathi*) who claimed divine calling to their prophetic ministry.[104]

The *Akũrinũ* church has since split into several groups. But all the groups are still identified by a very emotional repentance of sin accompanied by loud prayers and weeping. Francis Githieya reports that by 1978 there were fourteen different *Arathi* groups registered by the government of Kenya.[105] Githieya says that most of these groups borrowed rules from each other such that an outsider may not notice any difference. Macharia lists the current fourteen groups that were registered between 1930 and 1970 from the original group as;

> Kenya Foundation of the Prophets Church, Christian Holy Ghost Church of East Africa (C.H.G.C.E.A.) , Holy Ghost Church of Kenya (H.G.C.K), God's Word and Holy Ghost Church, African Mission of Holy Ghost Church (A.M.O.H.G.C.), African Holy Ghost Christian Church (A.H.G.C.C.), African Christian Holy Ghost Church, Israel Holy Ghost Church of Kenya, Holy Mission of Israel Church, 'Kanitha wa Arathi', Chosen Church of the Holy Spirit in Kenya, Israel Assemblies of Kenya, East Africa Israel, A.K. Israel (African Kanisa Israel)[106]

On the whole, the *Akũrinũ* churches were concerned with religious matters avoiding activist politics, but in silent opposition to the colonial power. Kenyatta describes them as uniquely concerned with religious aspects of life. They assume the role of holy men, to have direct communication with God, *Mwene-Nyaga*, to have the power to know the past and the present, and to interpret his [God's] message to the community at large, hence their name, *Arathi* (prophets or seers).

---

104. Francis Githieya Kimani, *The Freedom of the Spirit: African Indigenous Churches in Kenya* (Atlanta, Georgia: Scholars Press, 1997), 123.

105. Ibid., 145.

106. Macharia, *Identity*, 71-73.

The *Arathi* travel in groups and as a demonstration of their mission, they have given up their property and homes, maintaining that owning property are a sin, and that having chosen to serve God they have no need for accumulating wealth. The groups of *Watu wa Mungu* are harmonious consisting of men and women. They have headquarters in various districts where they have built temporary religious structures where they live, eat, and drink in common. It is amazing that these eschatological tendencies are the same tendency, which we find in the early church where the believers had everything in common, Acts 2, 4.

Kenyatta says that the Akũrinũ believe in certain parts of the Bible, as well as communion with their ancestors. (Kenyatta's sentiments should be taken at face value since though he himself was interested with the Akũrinũ Church he was never one of them and therefore not an insider). It is safer to say that the Akũrinũ Church is more at home with the Old Testament. On communion with the saints, Akũrinũ argue that since the Church (particularly Catholic and Anglican traditions) recognizes the sacredness of the saints, who were but ancestors of *mzungu*, and if the deity can be addressed by the saints and can listen to their intercessions, it will be more likely that the spirits of the *Gikuyu* ancestors will act effectively.[107]

Kenyatta adds that the Akũrinũ included in their new religion most of the ritualistic points that the missionaries had condemned and that by widening their religious ceremonies they were able to get a large hearing, especially among those who were suffering from spiritual hunger. This observation by Kenyatta is immediately telling. That there was spiritual hunger suggests that the Agĩkũyũ tradition religions had not fully satisfied their spiritual quest. The people though practicing their traditional religions were hungering for something more. They were attracted to the Akũrinũ faith.

---

107. Kenyatta, *Facing Mt. Kenya*, 266.

Kenyatta says that at first the group of Akũrinũ was seen as a bunch of lunatics and little attention was paid to their activities. But with time the government arrested the Arathis, accusing them of agitation and incitement which disagrees with Kenyatta's earlier statement. This persecution was not without a cause. Macharia[108] says that Arathis had predicted an impeding war.

Because of this they carried weapons for self-defense. The Arathis would also dig and cover their excreta using the weapons they carried, what the Israelites did in their desert wandering experience. Because they often traveled through forests and for long distances, the Akũrinũ used the weapons for protection against wild animals. But as persecution against the group intensified, as any people would, they had a tendency to be paranoid and even to mount self-defense.

The Arathis were also accused of moral laxity because they stayed together both women and men. This again can be explained. As they became a target both by the colonial administration and fellow Africans, especially during the Mau Mau uprising, the Akũrinũ tended to find safety in seclusion among their numbers. The Akũrinũ also resented giving their daughters in marriage to people whose faith they could not vouch for and who had persecuted them, thus insisting on marrying among themselves, a tradition that has been carried to date.

In the courts and gallows, the Akũrinũ did not defend themselves, which Kenyatta interprets as a demonstration against the foreign institution. Kenyatta says that the Watu wa Mungu neither indulged in politics nor belonged to any political activities. For this reason, many of them were persecuted by their fellow tribesmen when they refused to join the Mau Mau guerila warfare in the agitation for the political independence.

---

108. Macharia, Identity, 36-37.

Chapter two

Ecclesiology of the *Akũrinũ* Church

An *Akũrinũ* museum, which stands in Thika town 45 km to the North of Nairobi, was established in the year 2000 with the aim of preserving and strengthening peace values among the *Akũrinũ*. It started by documenting the group's history, collecting peace material culture, photos of *Akũrinũ* leaders who have been an inspiration to others on pacifism, and their biographies. The museum identified a number of material cultural items that are still held by the community because they are perceived as sacred and are exclusively worn during ceremonies.

One of the vestments is a turban, which is used to identify *Akũrinũ* as peacemakers, the white robe called *kanju*, from Kiswahili *kanzu* for a robe, which reflects the Aaronic priesthood which required every minister at the altar to wear priestly garments. The museum has photographs of *Gaaru*. *Gaaru* is traditionally *Ameru* in origin, where young warriors lived together and underwent rigorous training in military and social responsibility. The *Akũrinũ* adopted the *Gaaru* barrack as a church facility to be used for various activities such as informal meeting for peer learning. *Gaaru* also accommodated travelling evangelists, pastors, and prophets who frequented the church community.

Today, it is customary for each church campus to have two *Gaarus*, for the separate use of each sex. During *Mau Mau* and the violent struggle for independence, *Gaarus* were a refuge to many *Akũrinũ* who were severely persecuted by the *Mau Mau* activists for joining the pacifist faith group. This adaptability to different cultures such as the Ameru is a learning point in cross-cultural missions.

I have shown that when the *Arathi* movement went to Meru it was called *Akũrinũ*, which the founders in the central province did not have a problem in adapting. Again, I have demonstrated how the Meru chapter of *Akũrinũ* introduced *Gaaru* which was accepted across the board. This is what the missionaries needed to observe, namely that the gospel is adaptable to the different cultures who are able to understand and appreciate the gospel within their cultural milieu and even find new epistemology within their culture to help them to relate to the new faith. This must be respected and even encouraged in cross-cultural missions. The gospel animates culture and thrives in culture using the material resource and the idiom of the culture.

Another notable *Akũrinũ* material culture is a white bag, called *modo*, which hung over the shoulders of *Akũrinũ* elders during services and especially during church ceremonies (*magongona*), Inside the white bag are religious literature such as documents of the doctrine and practice of the *Akũrinũ*. Still another artifact is the *Akũrinũ* music, which uses typical African tunes and melodies which reach deep into the African psyche. The music is sung in deep and loud sounds using African drums, and other percussive instruments for accompaniment. Notice how objects such as the traditional drum that have taken on a symbolic (sacred) meaning play such an important part in their worship (the missionaries would surely have not allowed these instruments that they considered satanic).

In describing the *Akũrinũ* church, Githeiya says that they draw their beliefs from the Bible while functioning structurally like the traditional African family or homestead.[109] Interestingly the flavor of Judaism was also a family set up. The father was the family priest. Every member of the family participated in the worship and this was not left to everybody's whims unlike today and especially in the West and Western legacy in Africa where religion is an individual private business. Again, the early Church had a family flavor. Homes were the main meeting places for worship and teaching, (Acts 2: 46, 20: 20).

To be able therefore to understand the ecclesiology and theology of the *Akũrinũ* church, it is important to understand the *Agĩkũyũ* traditional religion that formed the background of the *Akũrinũ* church, a subject that I have developed in this chapter. According to Kenyatta, one can

---

109. Githieya, *Freedom of Spirit*, 222.

safely conclude that Akūrinū's ecclesiology is informed by their cultural beliefs and their traditional way of life on one hand and on the other hand, the Bible especially the Old Testament which has some similarities with the African culture as the next section will demonstrate. Kenyatta says that the Akūrinū have a special characteristic in their religious ceremonies. He rightly observes Akūrinūs' prayers are a mixture of Agĩkũyũ religion and Christianity. In their prayer to Mwene-Nyaga Akūrinū hold up their arms to the sky facing Mt. Kenya; and in this position they recite their prayers. In so doing they imitate the cries of wild beasts of prey such as lion and leopard, and at the same time they tremble violently. The trembling they say is the sign of the Holy Spirit, Roho Motheru, entering in them. While thus possessed with the Spirit, they are transformed from ordinary beings and are in communion with Mwene-Nyaga.

Kenyatta further informs us that in the early days when traveling, the Akūrinū did not carry provisions believing that Mwene-Nyaga will provide for their sustenance. They slept in the open or under caves which provided places for rest and meditation. They hated money and other foreign things. Consequently, Akūrinū have strong nationalistic feelings. They also believe in the miracles that were performed by Jesus especially the raising of the dead and healing of the sick — believing they have this same power which they do not hesitate to exercise sometimes with success. They do not believe in owning property (this has changed with time); instead they have a strong eschatological living perspective. They believe in the Bible (especially the Old Testament). They believe in communication with ancestors and some sections practice polygamy, a practice that divided the movement further. Both of these practices are a case of the Bible interpreted with the lenses of culture. Akūrinū do not indulge in politics, but instead devote themselves to religious life.

Akūrinū shake and jump when praying. They baptize their followers through fire and the Holy Spirit. They believe in visions, dreams and auditions, and speaking in tongues. They frown on modern medicine arguing that the use of modern medicine betrays a lack of faith in the healing power of God through prayer. They use traditional herbal medicines together with faith healing instead. When a member dies, volunteers preserve the body using traditional methods. The "death volunteers" are not allowed to pray or mix with the other members. Following the burial, an eight-day period ensues before a "cleansing day," during which anything the "death volunteers" came across when handling the dead and their household belongings are thoroughly cleansed.

Akũrinũ women do not attend church when they are menstruating. They believe that menstruation makes a woman unclean. The menstrual calendar of the bride and her maids determines the date of the wedding. Since the marriage ceremony is holy, it has to be held on a day when both the best maid and the bride are not on their monthly period. Akũrinũ wedding is strictly conducted on a Sunday as they consider marriage as holy union as Sunday. Today this has changed especially among the contemporary Akũrinũ church where weddings are conducted on Saturdays.[110]

Formal marriage is compulsory for any Akũrinũ member who hopes to hold a leadership position in the church. A mũkũrinũ man cannot be allowed to marry before 25 years old while women must be above 22 years. This is a revision of the Agĩkũyũ traditional culture where formerly circumcision (done within the late adolescent years) was followed immediately by marriage. Among the Agĩkũyũ community and other Bantu communities one is considered immature before marriage and cannot be trusted with any serious responsibility especially leadership. The Akũrinũ marriages are sanctioned by the leadership and marrying outside the Church community is discouraged as we have seen above — theology informs their daily living. Again, this practice is derived from the Agĩkũyũ

---

110. Macharia, *Identity*, 106.

culture where marriage was so central that a non-married person was regarded as a child and would not be entrusted with any leadership role.[111]

As I have demonstrated, the *Akũrinũ's* ecclesiology is seamlessly blended into their way of life. This poses two main challenges. The first concerns hermeneutics. *Akũrinũ* are literalists in their hermeneutics. For example, the elaborate cleansing ceremonies from ritual uncleanliness and polygamy that was associated with a small section of some of the early *Akũrinũ* are based on literal interpretation of the O.T. that does not take seriously the harmony of the Scriptures. The record of polygamous relationship in the Old Testament did not obliterate the original design for marriage. Likewise, the Old Testament ablution regulations served for hygienic purposes with no spiritual significance.

The second challenge is the syncretism that can ferment from faulty hermeneutics that tend to merge biblical teaching with cultural practices. However, this syncretism must be understood here as an interphase that must have ensured at the first encounter of the Biblical faith and the *Akũrinũ's* primal religion — some practices from either side would of necessity overlap. We must appreciate that the early *Akũrinũ* followers were obviously not theologians. They were just attracted by the Word of God from the Bible. Believing the Bible meant for them obeying every bit of it. They actually thought the missionaries were not taking the Bible seriously for example when they disparaged polygamy, a practice that the *Akũrinũ* could derive from the Bible. Interestingly these theological gaps are closing with the passage of time.

Akũrinũ Church Today

In 1978, the Organization for African Indigenous Churches (OAIC) was formed. One of its main objectives was to promote theological educa-

---

111. Oral interview, Abraham Macharia Prince, January, 16, 2016.

tion among the AICs.¹¹² OAIC headquartered in Nairobi has continued to engage the AICs and in particular the Akũrinũ church in various ways including HIV awareness.

While the Akũrinũ Church continues to thrive in the rural with a conservative preservation of most of its age-old practices, a new phenomenon is emerging in the urban centers especially Nairobi city where a third generation of the Akũrinũ churches are growing steadily. It is not difficult to see why. Many of the third generation Akũrinũ were born and bred in the urban centers. Many rural people also move to towns in search of further education and employment. Many of these have lost touch with their rural church. Wanting the experience of the parent church, some of the Akũrinũ leaders have tried to reform the earlier beliefs and practices by forming Akũrinũ contemporary churches. These have adapted to new ecclesial practices while maintaining the essential features of the older ones. Each of these churches has strong roots and even patronage from the older churches with a near fanatical respect for the older bishops and leaders who remain the sponsors and *bona fide* leaders of the Akũrinũ movement.

In 2014 an umbrella secretariat body called, General Conference of the Akũrinũ Churches Assembly (GCACA), was formed with the objective of bringing all the Akũrinũs together. Macharia reports that today the Akũrinũ believers' number about half a million distributed in Central Kenya, Nairobi, Western and Nyanza regions, Central Rift, and lower Eastern province.¹¹³ The secretariat aims at modernizing and demystifying the negative notions that have often been associated with this church movement.

The ending of the Akũrinũ founders is rather sad. Macharia says that on Feb 1934 there was a conflict between a group of three *Watu wa Mungu* and the police in a place called Ndarugu forest where they were

---

112. Waigwa, *Pentecost without Azusa*, 104.
113. Oral interview, Abraham Macharia Prince, January, 16, 2016.

praying in a cave. The police claimed that they were looking for man who had been charged with murder. A confrontation is said to have occurred between the trio and the police. The police shot the three. It is said that of the three, John Mung'ara died on the spot, while Samuel Muinami was taken to Kiambu district hospital where he died later. Joseph Ng'ang'a is said to have been captured and taken to Britain to be interrogated on the objectives of the *Akũrinũ*'s movement. He died on arrival and his body was flown back for burial.[114] Kenyatta says that in the government report of this accident, it was stated as an excuse for this atrocity, that they were shot by accident, and they were preparing for a rebellion.

Kenyatta laments that, "nothing was done to investigate the religious aspects of this group, to show the connection between it and Christianity on one hand and *Agĩkũyũ* religion on the other. A careful study of a sect (as Kenyatta calls it) of this nature would have revealed its real African setting." Kenyatta leaves this study to future anthropological field-workers, a call that I have attempted in this study. The leadership of the *Akũrinũ* continued under the hands of Musa Thuo, until his death in 1978.

Conclusion

In this chapter I have demonstrated that the *Akũrinũ*'s daily lives are regulated by their belief. Faith plays in every aspect of life, including marriage. This is possible because their religion has been interwoven within culture almost similar to Judaism and Islam. The *Akũrinũ* do not therefore in this regard have the dichotomy of life between the sacred and the secular — a break from the dualistic faith of the missionaries that has been accused of precipitating a nominal Christianity in Africa.

---

114. Macharia, *Identity*, 30, quotes the newspaper *East Africa Standard* of 20th February, 1934, and an Oral interview with an Akurinu Bishop, Ezra Mbugua.

The missionaries overlooked much good that could be found in the African cultures. They believed that the Christian religion must go with a European culture and European leadership. In their view, Western culture was Christianity and Christianity was Western culture. One could not be a Christian without adopting Western culture. The two were mutually exclusive. All other cultures were considered anti-Christian and pagan. In African culture, missionaries had found little to praise and much to condemn. There was no attempt to trace evidences of *preparatio evangelica* in African culture as was the practice of New Testament evangelists and the church fathers among whose strenuous efforts were made to discern at what points in the pagan world there could be found a *preparatio evangelica*, preparing the way for entrance of the gospel. The realities of pagan religion were accepted, and the relevance of Christ demonstrated.[115]

It is to this insult of their culture that the early Akũrinũ founders reacted by forming a church they could lead as they understood the reading of the Bible within their cultural lenses and understanding. In this reading they preserved what they found in the culture as being compatible with the Bible whilst discarding any pagan believes that could not be supported by the new faith.

The coming of Europeans brought a social change to the people for good or ill. The missionaries were overly harsh and ruthless to the African customs mainly because they did not understand them or rather because they were different from their own. With this mistake, they did not accurately define the basic essentials that counted for conversion. Denouncing tribal ways and embracing the Western culture marked conversion. In this arrangement the-would-be converts felt slighted and hoodwinked into a new way of life at the expense of their own ways. While this remained a hindrance to their conversion, some yielded, but guardedly, preferring to live in the two worlds. The education offered by

---

115. Waigwa, *Pentecost without Azusa*, 96, 191.

the white man was particularly attractive because through it, the African would know the secrets of the white man. They were, however, less prepared to abandon the ways of the tribe for the new Christian faith.

Without discounting the value of education, I, however, note that the education that the missionaries brought to Africa had strings attached. It was primarily to alienate the people from their traditions. Those who insisted on holding onto their traditions were viewed with trepidation. The *Agĩkũyũ* community reacted to this by forming their own independent churches and schools.

In the next chapter I will single out the main theological beliefs and practices of the *Akũrinũ* church. We will also seek to delineate the *Akũrinũ*'s sources of theology through the findings and presentation of the data that I have collected from the *Akũrinũ* churches, leaders, and scholars.

CHAPTER THREE

AKŪRINŪ VERNACULAR THEOLOGY: DATA ANALYSIS, FINDINGS, AND DISCUSSIONS

A recent newspaper article in a Kenya Daily, poses a fundamental question on how a traditional ritual would make sense in a modern African culture. Explaining recent events in a community near Nairobi the capital city, the article notes the following.

> A sheep is scheduled to die today in this cool suburb of Nairobi where some men have been ordered to stay chaste and women to lie low. Kikuyu elders have since began a two-week cleansing-ceremony under the tree that hosted various gatherings and ceremonies in the past decades...The sheep, chosen to die to save the people of Dagoretti, will be tied up and hung upside down, its terrified face pointing in the direction of the great Mt Kenya, and only young, morally pure boys will be allowed to eat the roast mutton...None of the men who will have important roles to play in the ritual at this Nairobi suburb today has been having sex since the bad news of the fall of a *mugumo* branch broke...[1]

Does this scenario provide a possible glimpse of how to understand what role religious ritual, can play in providing a way of looking at reality

---
1. *The Standard*, Media Newspaper Friday, June, 19, 2015.

for the people of the culture it represents? To put it more poignantly, what role may African traditional cultures play in informing vernacular theologies?

An exhaustive study that describes all aspects of Akũrinũ church is beyond the scope of this book. For our purpose I will restrict myself to the aspects of the Akũrinũ theology that may make a significant contribution to global theology. Githieya[2] says that one of the central questions for which answers are continuously being sought in African religious circles is how the themes of the community in the African Independent Churches (AICs) can be studied as a contribution to a fuller understanding of the Christian church. He says that in seeking the contribution of Akũrinũ church to the global theology, one may have to examine the type of worship, organization, and community life that these churches have developed. Githieya proposes that these elements are rooted both in biblical Christianity and African cultures and are considered of indigenous African contribution to global Christianity which in my study I will consider as an important contribution to global theology.[3]

This research found these elements critical in pointing to a unique African spirituality. In all this, the research has sought to examine how the Bible, the Agĩkũyũ religious traditions and other Christian traditions together with the socio-economic and socio-political factors that were prevalent at the time of her inception, shaped and continues to shape the Akũrinũ theology.

Factors That Led to the Birth of the *Akũrinũ* Church

The factors that led to the birth of the Akũrinũ church discussed extensively in the previous chapter must be placed in the larger context of the founding of other AICs. This is because the causes overlap. I will

---

2. Githieya, *Freedom of Spirit*, 1.
3. Githieya, *Freedom of Spirit*, 1.

discuss specific causes for the birth and growth of the Akũrinũ church after a general survey of the causative agents of other AICs.

Shorter and Njeru say that the AICs were essentially ethnic in origin. They recruited their membership from a given ethnic group and spoke its vernacular. They were a form of adaptive mechanism in a period of social change, helping to replace or buttress the traditional ethnic communities of family and neighborhood. They also provided a fairly intense experience of community at a time when the scale of social relationships was becoming enlarged. Their leadership followed traditional ethnic patterns, being nearly always a form of hereditary "chiefdom."[4]

This suggests that the causes of independency were largely sociopolitical. Since the colonial administration excluded people from political activity, they founded churches where they could exercise civil rights of assembly and association, because church organizations were tolerated and could become a substitute for political activity. Shorter and Njeru further note that AICs also arose as a result of the ecclesial 'kaleidoscope' presented by the missionaries. Earlier I demonstrated how the missionaries outdid each other in registering their presence.

Wellborn and Grace Ogot for their part stress the psychological reason for the rise of independence. Since ethnic religion was no longer attractive and the mainline Christianity was neither sympathetic nor relevant, the Africans created their own religious "home" or mental dwelling-home.[5] Barrett attributes the quest for independence to a failure of love on the part of the mainline churches so that the AICs were the face of humanity before an alienating colonialism which was unfriendly to traditional and cultural institutions.[6] One may safely conclude that

---

4. Aylward Shorter and Joseph N. Njeru, *New Religious Movements in Africa* (Nairobi, Kenya: Paulines Publications Africa, 2001), 1-5.

5. F. B. Wellbourn and A.B. Ogot., *A Place to Feel at Home: A Study of two Independent Churches in Western Kenya*. (London, Oxford University Press, 1966), quoted in Shorter and Njeru, *New Religious Movements in Africa*, 16.

6. Barrett, *Schism and Renewal*, 155-156.

both socio-political and socio-economic reasons combined to fuel a quest for religious independence.

But as noted in the previous chapter, the *Akũrinũ* started, without discounting the prevailing socio-economic and socio-political conditions, as a result of two prophetic individuals, Joseph Ng'ang'a and Musa Thuo who independently felt led by the Lord in a unique way even before they met each other.[7] Upon their call, each of these leaders went through a long period of preparation in seclusion, in which they devoted themselves to reading the Bible, prayer, and fasting. After this period of preparation, they began a very dynamic ministry of preaching in their home and surrounding areas. Our respondent Archbishop Musa Ng'ang'a informed us that the ministry of these two individuals was so powerful that once you met them you received the baptism of the Holy Spirit with speaking of tongues upon contact.

However, when the nature of the preaching of these individuals is analyzed, one cannot help to see that the socio-economic, socio-political, and the socio-cultural troubled time the *Agikũyũ* community was undergoing played a major part in the founding of the *Akũrinũ* church. Sandgren says that Ng'ang'a's messages, usually revealed to him through dreams, spoke of freeing of the *Agikũyũ* from the colonial rulers, and God sweeping the Europeans and ushering a Kikuyu golden age.[8] Githieya says that Ng'ang'a also taught against Western medicine, way of dressing, food, all which he believed were heathen. This reaction may again be attributable to the rapid social changes that the *Agikũyũ* community was undergoing.

Other factors can be attributed to the rise of the *Akũrinũ* church. Foremost of this must be the translation of the Bible into Kikuyu language in 1926 (the *Akũrinũ* church started in 1926). Once the Bible was in the hands and in the language of the people, they begun to read and

---

7. Githeiya, *Freedom of Spirit*, 125-126.
8. Ibid., 125.

seek answers for themselves. They were amazed that God could speak their language. The bible instantly became their book. They in particular saw discrepancies in the issue of polygamy, the importance of the land ownership, among others teachings, and they could only conclude that the missionaries were not interpreting the Bible properly.[9] The Bible remains significant in the *Akũrinũ* church up to the present.

The Major Teachings of the *Akũrinũ* Church

The *Akũrinũ* church has a unique approach to ecclesiology and the use of the Bible from other AICs and the mainline churches that easily distinguishes them. I will consider the major ones in this section. They include the *Akũrinũ* music and worship, hermeneutics, the nature of preaching, healing, and baptism.

Akũrinũ Pneumatology

The theme of the Holy Spirit is central to the *Akũrinũ* Church. Our respondent Timothy Kamau had this to say about the Holy Spirit:

> We really are dependent on the Holy Spirit, and not in small measures. Without the Holy Spirit, there is no *ùkùrinù* belief. Even one of our songbooks is titled Nyìmbo cia Roho (songs of the Spirit) to indicate that we are very much inspired by the Holy Spirit. The Holy Spirit is our help and our strength, the one who was left for us by Jesus.[10]

Kamau adds that the presence of the Holy Spirit in a believer's life is a sign of spiritual maturity. The *Akũrinũ* also believe and exercise the gifts of the Holy Spirit. Kamau says, "we strongly embrace the gifts of

---

9. Barrett, *Schism and Renewal*, 90.
10. Oral interview, Rev Timothy Kamau, November, 13, 2015.

prophecy [which is given by the Spirit]; we are also commonly known as *Arathi* (which means prophets or foreseers) or *Aroti* (which dreamers)."

The Holy Spirit whose communication is received through visions, dreams auditions and other manifestations is seen as a way through which God guides the *Akũrinũ*. To this Kamau says;

> God gives us visions often, even about our country. Politicians and other national leaders acknowledge this and they often ask us what God has shown us. For instance, in March of this year (2015), retired president Daniel Arap Moi called some of our leaders to Kabarak, his home, and inquired about some matters. Likewise, recently when there was a crisis in the Government, we were called to State House to see President Uhuru's mother who wanted to know what God had shown us about the case that was facing the president and his deputy at the International Criminal Court (ICC). God had already revealed to us very clearly that the cases would be dropped.[11]

I have already shown that the *Akũrinũ* Church started early in 20th Century with a single focus on the Holy Spirit. Incidentally, this was also the time of great ferment of the Holy Spirit that started with Azusa Street experience almost akin to say that the experience was being replicated far away in Africa even with no direct human contact, a phenomena that has been described in some quarters as Pentecost without Azusa.[12]

From her inception, the *Akũrinũ* Church emphasized the role of the Holy Spirit. One of her early members who attempted to codify their doctrine, came up with few guidelines for belief and practice which included; appropriation of the Scripture as the norm for belief and practice, wearing white lobes (signifying holiness), the Lord's prayer has a model prayer, discernment of the spirits, and an emphasis on personal holiness.[13]

---

11. Oral interview, Rev Timothy Kamau, November, 13, 2015.

12. Waigwa, *Pentecost without Azusa*, 149.

13. Githieya, *Freedom of Spirit*, 137.

Prayer, discernment of the spirits, and personal holiness, which are still a major preoccupation of the Akũrinũ Church, are all aspects of the life of the Spirit.

First, the Akũrinũ define their church as Kanitha wa Roho, "the Church of the Holy Spirit" meaning that it is the Holy Spirit who calls people and leads them to the Church.

Secondly, the Akũrinũ emphasizes the conversion experience — it is at conversion that a sinner becomes a "saint," one set apart for God, and a parting of ways, from the life of one who has not believed to that of one who has believed in Christ and has been filled with the Holy Spirit.

Thirdly, following repentance and conversion, the new believer can now relate with others in the household of faith with confidence as a child of God. This confidence emanates from the Akũrinũ's understanding of the church as, [Andù a Roho i.e. The People of the Holy Spirit], or Watu wa Mungu, meaning the people of God since those who are led by the Spirit are the children of God, Romans 8:14. To be Akũrinũ therefore, is to be a child of God who is filled with the Holy Spirit, with the evidence of speaking in tongues and [the manifestation] of other charismatic gifts.

Fourth, Akũrinũ Church emphasizes the authority of Scripture where the Bible and the guidance of the Holy Spirit arising from dreams, visions, and auditions are used harmoniously. Such guidance must be verified by Scripture and if they deviate from the Scriptures, they are to be discarded.

Fifthly, is the worship — Akũrinũ Church is a worshipping community.[14]

The Akũrinũ's obsession with the dreams and vision echoes what Clark Pinnock calls the blessing of the coming of the Spirit on the day of Pentecost, i.e., the Spirit gives the ability to dream and see visions (Acts 2: 17-18). The Spirits makes us open to new horizons and new possibilities. We are empowered with hope to transcend situations and limita-

---

14. The Akurinu Religion "Worshiping Jehovah in Truth and in Spirit" (January 2, 2014) <http://www.akurinucommunity.org>.

tions. Therefore, it is important to experience the Spirit and reflect on our experience.[15]

Pinnock laments that the Spirit has been neglected in the Western theology a thought that is shared by Kim and Moltmann.[16] Like Kim, Pinnock laments that the Holy Spirit has been made the Cinderella of theology with even the movements of Spirit being reduced to religious phenomena of individuals or community with no relevance for wider interest. Pinnock and Moltmann calls for recognition of the Spirit's work outside the boundaries of the Church.[17]

Yet the Akũrinũ lack a cosmic view of the Spirit in contrast to Pinnock who says that the Spirit has cosmic function from the beginning to the end. He further says that the Holy Spirit is the power of redemption having first been the power of creation. The Holy Spirit is therefore not to be relegated to the Church and piety, but as one who perfected God's work in creation.[18]

Instead Akũrinũ church is a pacifist movement that rarely takes any active interest in politics thereby limiting their influence on social –political affairs, only resulting to prayer that the Holy Spirit would guide the national politics. They in this way fail to see that by being actively involved, they could influence the politics and bring God's Kingdom and Lordship on such an important aspect of life. They forget that the very inaugural message of Christ in Luke 4:18ff, had socio-political

---

15. Clark, H. Pinnock, *Flame of Love: A Theology of the Holy Spirit* (Downers Grove, Ill.: Intervarsity Press, 1996), 12.

16. Kim Kirsteen. *The Holy Spirit in the World: A Global Conversation* (Maryknoll, NY: Orbis Books, 2007), 2.

17. Ibid., 2-3: "However, if it is to relate to contemporary society, pneumatology must recognize the Spirit's work beyond the boundaries of the church or the Christian heart. Furthermore, a theology of the Spirit for today must take into account the other spirits encountered in an increasingly plural world. It must raise awareness of, and help us respond to, the many different world-views and belief systems that we encounter today. Finally, it must offer guidance for Christians on which modern-day powers to support and which to resist, and how to do so ethically and effectively....."

18. Pinnock, *Flame of Love*, 57.

ramification, 'the Spirit of the Lord is upon me, to set the captives free...." Macharia concedes to this when he says, "Sometimes it is hard for us to get channels through which we can communicate God's messages to the country, considering that we are not outspoken," which can rightly be put, the Akũrinũ church is withdrawn. Likewise, the Akũrinũ church fails to discern the work of the Spirit in scientific discoveries such as modern medicine and technology that has greatly alleviated human suffering, which is indeed an act of God's mercy.

Because of this, just like in the West, the Akũrinũ church has succumbed to *filioque* controversy that confines the Holy Spirit to Christ within ecclesiastical boundaries. Howbeit, before we can fault the Akũrinũ Church on this we must note that they feel strongly that theirs is a priestly calling to the nation preferring to be a prophetic voice (and for all purpose the Akũrinũ do not advertise their prophesies).

Akũrinũ's strong sense of community of believers can be equated to Pinnock who equates the Spirit to the love that bonds the Father and the Son. The goal of the Spirit, Pinnock says is love and fellowship, unity and peace, 1 Cor 1:10, 3:3, Eph 4:2. The Spirit confirmed the Son ship of Jesus with the Father, testifies of our adoption as God's sons and daughters, Rom 8:16, Gal 4:6-7. He draws us into the fellowship between Father and Son, 1John 1:3-. He gives us joy, Rom 14:17, Act13:52, Gal 5:22, 1The1:6, Acts 2:46. Pinnock says that the Spirit choreographs the dance of God and directs the steps of the creature entering God's dance, seals us both as those belonging to God, fostering both love and community.

The Akũrinũ are literally a Spirit-led people. The Spirit guides their liturgy in entirely. For example, when they preach, they do not even prepare the message beforehand believing that the Spirit will give them the appropriate message.

The Akũrinũ also take the powers seriously. They believe that behind the physical causes of disharmony in human life, are evil spirits which they do not hesitate to exorcize. Unlike the missionary instituted Churches that dismiss the powers, the *Akũrinũ* address them. The *Akũrinũ* Church is able to attract people who are seeking deliverance from witchcraft, curses and a variety of evil forces as a result. This makes the *Akũrinũ* relevant to the African context.

Any weakness of the *Akũrinũ*'s pneumatology has to do with their hermeneutics. The *Akũrinũ* hermeneutics as stated elsewhere in this study is literalistic. Because of this hermeneutical approach to Scriptures, the *Akũrinũ* fail to appreciate the progressive nature of revelation. They fail to see N.T. as a fulfillment of the O.T and instead tend to regard the two testaments independently. Again, the *Akũrinũ* Church has no much room for ecumenical thinking being suspicious of other denominations. They are therefore an isolationist group sometimes tending to be separatists all which betray their narrow view of the Holy Spirit.

Akũrinũ pneumatology can be understood in two main ways. First, we must link their pneumatology with the *Agĩkũyũ* traditional believes which themselves have a very strong spiritual basis. Traditional belief in the ancestral spirits which pervades all aspects of [African] life is a given among the AIC's.[19] The *Akũrinũ* world is the same enchanted world of Jesus day that we see in the gospels.[20] Because of this background in *Agĩkũyũ* traditional believes, the concept of the Holy Spirit is close to the *Akũrinũ*'s Christian experience. The Holy Spirit is seen as necessary in combating the cosmic powers.

Secondly, it would seem that the AIC's and so the *Akũrinũ* must be understoood from a plural pneumatologies and cosmologies' pespective rather than from a unitive perspective.[21] Like the enchanted wold of Jesus day the *Akũrinũ* see spirits, both the aggrieved ancestral spirits and the

---

19. Pinnock, *Flame of Love*, 55.

20. Veli-Matti Kärkkäinen, "Spirit(s) in Contemporary Christian Theology: An Interim Report of the Unbinding of Pneumatology," in *Interdisciplinary and Religio-Cultural Discourses on a Spirit-Filled World: Loosing the Spirits*, eds., Veli-Matti Kärkkäinen, Kirsteen Kim, and Amos Yong (New York: Palgrave Macmillan, 2013), 30.

21. Ibid.,31

spirit of demons, curses, witchcraft everywhere. These cause untold suffering and hinder the welbeing of the believer which must therefore be addressed. Life for the African Christian is holistic with no distinction between the sacred and the secular segements of life. For the *Akũrinũ* the world of the spirits is real. In this scenerio pneumatology is central.

In contrast, the subject of the pneumatology is generally suppressed in the missionary Churches. On the other hand, because the place of the Holy Spirit is a central feature in the AIC's Churches, Karkkainen says that the AICs [which address the spirits] are irresistible to the African.[22]

Akũrinũ Music and Worship (Liturgy)

The *Akũrinũ* Sunday worship service lasts for several hours. The service starts at 9.00 am and it does not end before 3:00 pm in the afternoon for most of the *Akũrinũ* churches. 3:00 pm is an important hour of prayer to the *Akũrinũ*. Even after the end of the formal worship, the *Akũrinũ* now go to another period of community time. This is usually an informal meeting where they share a common meal and discuss matters of their community life. This takes place in the *Gaaru*. In Kaguthi in Murang'a, the headquarters of The Kenya Foundation of the Prophet Church, the Archbishop, Musa Ng'ang'a showed us their separate *Gaarus* (for men and women) and both had mattresses where the *Akũrinũ* sleep on some occasions. In the same church a special house for the Archbishop and another for other elders are reserved where they keep night vigils of prayer.

Musa Thuo is buried behind this church standing on Kaguthi Hill in Murang'a. In entering the Church building, men and women use separate doors and sit on separate rows. The men enter and sit on the right while women occupy the left side. On the right of the church is the location of men's *Gaaru* while the women's *Gaaru* is on the left.

---

22. Veli-Matti Kärkkäinen. *The Holy Spirit: Basic Guides to Christ ian Theology* (Louisville: Westminster John Knox Press, 2012), 100 -101.

Crucial to the Akũrinũ worship is their singing. As I mentioned in chapter three, the Akũrinũ sing spontaneously for hours. They jump and dance vigorously. All members are animated to the worship. Kiarie says that the Akũrinũ hymn book is central to Akũrinũ church. History says that Daudi Ikìigu, one of the Akũrinũ early members received the traditional hymns through a vision and wrote the hymn book, *Nyìmbo cia Roho Mùtheru*. Kiarie says they have recently launched a smart phone application for these songs.[23]

There are other songs which were revealed through the Holy Spirit but were not written into a hymn book which are sung by memory. There are hymns for different times of the day, and others for different occasions (prayer meeting, wedding, baptism, dedication, repentance besides others). As I will demonstrate later in this chapter the Akũrinũ hymns are a great source of theology. Some of the songs were revealed to people who did not know how to read and write. Again, some were revealed before even the Bible was translated to local languages and widely distributed among the Akũrinũ.

Yet the songs are not in contradiction with the Bible.[24] The hymns are critical in hearing and discerning the voice of God. The leaders informed us that for example one particular hymn is sung by the elders alone when they want to determine if a prospecting couple has engaged in sex before marriage. When this song is sung, God speaks. The song is dreaded among prospecting couples.

During the Sunday service, the Akũrinũ will sing many hymns as led by the worship leader. Then they sing special songs that various members bring forward, as having been instructed to be sung that particular day by the Holy Spirit. These are referred to as *Nyimbo cia Kũheanwo*, meaning songs that have been given by the Holy Spirit for that day. Then individual members stand and sing special hymns that have ministered

---

23. Oral interview, Dr. Kiarie Mburu, March, 5, 2016.
24. Oral interview, Rev Timothy Kamau, November, 13, 2015.

to their hearts as individuals to which all members join in. They also sing different songs at different times in the order of service especially at transition points from one aspect of the liturgy to the other.

I have dwelt on the topic of music and worship because it really forms the bulk of the *Akũrinũ* vernacular theology, majority of whom cannot read and write especially in the rural areas. By committing these hymns to memory, *Akũrinũ* avail to themselves a great reservoir of theology, as the psalmist advised the young, Psalm 119:9. Singing appeals to the poetic nature of human beings and speaks to them in a way that a sermon may not. What is even more important is that these songs are reflective of the culture both in lyrics, rhythm, and the percussions that accompany them which really touches the African psyche in a unique way.

Singing remains an important aspect of the African church in general. Many young people have left the historical churches because they feel that the music does not appeal to them. Chief among the bones of contention is that the older members of the church do not appreciate the more modern songs which are shorter and expressive — often called choruses — preferring the older slower hymns. The young also prefer more modern musical instruments. They prefer loud speakers in their singing which the older generation detests. In this contention, young people leave the historical churches for the AICs especially of the neo-Pentecostal type. The *Akũrinũ* church has blended modernity and African traditions in their singing. They are very expressive with vigorous dancing. In this way they have appealed to the young especially in the contemporary *Akũrinũ* churches. Some of their artists are very popular in the music industry.

What is distinct between the *Akũrinũ* songs and those from especially the neo-Pentecostal AICs is the wholesomeness of the *Akũrinũ* songs. The *Akũrinũ* songs are rich in theology, often including direct quotations from the bible, and they are sung specially to hear the voice of God through them. The *Akũrinũ* expect to hear the voice of God as they sing to him. This approach to music is found in the Bible. When Elisha was presented with an occasion to discern the voice of God on behalf of King Jehoshaphat and Joram, he asked for a harpist. In that serene moment created by the singing, the prophet received a prophetic message for the kings, 2 Kings 3: 15-16, "But now bring me a harpist." While the harpist was playing, the hand of the Lord came on Elisha and he said, 'This is what the Lord says ....'" Likewise, King Saul would often result to David's skillful singing and playing of the harp to calm him down from the bouts of attack from an evil spirit that tormented him from time to time. When David became king, he organized a priestly order that led worship through music in the Jerusalem Temple.

As in the biblical history, in almost all rituals in African traditions, music plays a significant part. Coming from this tradition the *Akũrinũ* find their singing and worship a great moment of humbling themselves before God and hearing God's voice who speaks to them in this mode. In contrast, in many churches especially of the historical type music is often archaic and uninspiring. This I must add is a general observation and it is certainly not static.

Akũrinũ Teaching and the Ministry of the Word

The ministry of the Word and teaching is central to the *Akũrinũ* church. The gift of teaching is particularly valued. In all the *Akũrinũ* churches that I visited in conducting this research, the preaching of the Word took a very prominent place in worship. There were so many speakers on a single service that the service looked like it was leaderless. Malcolm J. McVeigh has observed that, in the spiritual churches to which category the *Akũrinũ* church belongs,

> Most of worship services are not monopolized by any single individual. In fact, one gets the impression that the services are leaderless, with a succession of persons rising to speak followed by active participation from all in dancing and

drumming. All these persons are led spontaneously by the Holy Spirit to proclaim the Word of God. A visitor sometimes has great difficult identifying the pastor.[25]

It is not uncommon for the leader of the service to consult other leaders loudly on what to do next in the order of service while the service is going on. It is also not uncommon for a member to interrupt the service and ask a question or raise a point of clarification. This does not suggest that the service is chaotic in anyway. In my observation, it is not even easy to tell who the main speaker is and what the main message is as many speakers arise and speak — and all in harmony.

The Akũrinũ teachers are great expositors of the Word. They give relevant examples in their sermon. Some of the Akũrinũ services take almost the whole day. As I have said above, they claim that they must stay on until 3:00 pm which they consider an important hour of prayer. All these many hours are used in spontaneous singing and teaching. The nature of preaching and teaching in the Akũrinũ church takes two forms; first it is based on a spiritual and literal interpretation of the bible. And secondly, it is millennial in nature.

Spiritual and Literal Interpretation of the Bible

The Akũrinũ believers have great reverence for the Bible. They hold its authority as absolute. They believe both in the New Testament and the Old Testament. Philomena Mwaura says that the Akũrinũ were ardent believers in the Bible which provided them with a "principled basis for rejecting any teachings they could not reconcile with the Gospel of Jesus Christ including theology of the mission churches." [26] Unlike the

---

25. David B. Barrett and David Tell, eds., *Kenya Churches Handbook* (Nairobi: Evangel Publishing House, 1973), 139.

26. Philomena Njeri Mwaura, "Africa Instituted Churches in East Africa," Studies in World Christianity, Vol. 10, Issue 2 (2005): ," 25. Accessed March 1, 2016. http://web.a.ebscohost.com/ehost/pdfviewer/pdfviewer?vid=21&sid=25a68f39-b517-4f39-abe5-4b0dc428abea%40sessionmgr4001&hid=4106.

nationalist churches, in Central Kenya, the Akũrinũ had no interest in schools and expressed their antipathy to colonial rule and missionary Christianity by rejecting European dress, medicine and formal education.

However, the Akũrinũ are much more at home with the Old Testament because of its affinity with African traditional religious rituals and practices. Kiarie, commenting on how easily the Akũrinũ adopted the Bible, says that it was easy to embrace the teaching of the Bible, because they found many similarities with their Agĩkũyũ culture such as in the aspect of sacrificing to Mwene Nyaga, God.[27]

The Akũrinũ practice a kind of a spiritual and literal hermeneutics combined together. One of the early Akũrinũ leaders had this to say on the use of Scriptures:

> He [God] showed them [Arathi or Akũrinũ leaders] new and holy prayers, and also new interpretations of the Word of God, and a spiritual way to read it and grasp it in the heart just as the Holy Spirit reveals it to a man. For, a certain part of the Word of God must be read in the light of the prophecy that has reached us at the end of these times, (Emphasis mine). (Read: Acts 2:16-22, and Hebrews 8:8, Acts 2: 38-42; and Luke 24: 47-50).[28]

The Akũrinũ literally wait on the Holy Spirit to reveal to them the message to preach. They seek the Holy Spirit to help them understand the meaning of the Scripture. On some occasions, allegorical interpretation of Scripture, a method that can be used to a good effect, but which can also be extemporaneous, may be discerned. The Holy Spirit leads them to scriptures that they should preach on. But once the scriptures have been revealed to them, they do their due diligence in understanding

---

27. Oral interview, Kiarie Mburu, March, 5, 2016.

28. Barrett and Tell, Handbook, 124 - 127. Kinyanyui was one of the original prophets or Aroti Prophets. He was the president (leader) of Chosen Church of the Holy Spirit, one of the many Kikuyu Spirit Churches.

them. They expound the revealed Scriptures by drawing examples for immediate application.

The Akũrinũ practice a literal interpretation of the Scripture. This approach may tend to lack the harmony of scriptures. It may therefore tend to be narrow and skewed. This has led to many splinter groups because of an overemphasis on a certain Scripture by one leader. The literal interpretation of Scriptures has also led the Akũrinũ to practice what many other believers may find weird. For example, women are treated as unclean during menstruation and the days following child birth. At such times women do not attend church until ritual cleansing has been done. Again, the pall bearers in case of death remain unclean for seven days until a ritual cleansing is done.

Such hermeneutics results from literal and direct interpretation of the Old Testament injunctions have found resonance with the Agikũyũ traditional rules on taboos, a term that I will deal with on its own later in this chapter. We may deduce that the ablution rules of the Old Testament may have had to do with hygiene at an age when piped water and the general sanitary disposal systems were less developed. These ablution rules and ceremonial uncleanness are still held and practiced by the Akũrinũ.

The Akũrinũ's approach and use of Scripture is a unique African spirituality that should be examined alongside the popular grammatical-historical approach of hermeneutics that is common in the western theology. To their advantage the West has the history of scholarship in the biblical languages that the Akũrinũ church cannot boast of. With much archeological research the West has recovered much of the ancient biblical world which is deemed as critical to the understanding of the biblical message. The underlying idea here is that the Bible was written in a context and had an original recipient in mind. The grammatical-historical hermeneutics suggest that we must come as close as possible to the original intended message. Once this is done, the timeless principle is isolated for application to a current situation. Much as this approach is laudable, it should not be held as the only, or necessarily the best approach to biblical interpretation. If this approach is upheld as the norm it would leave out many people who do not have the privilege of the deep educational background that the West has. Here again we see the West holding the Holy Spirit ransom to their scholarship.

Suffice it to say that it is arguably a tall order to recover the biblical history with complete accuracy. The grammatical-historical approach and the high criticism leaves us at the mercy of the scholars and their findings in many Bible commentaries and the ever increasing list of other Bible tools each claiming more accuracy than the others, not to mention the many Bible versions all claiming to be closest to the original manuscripts. One may be forgiven for thinking that the market forces are at play. It is in the same vein that the Rabbis in trying to make sense of the O.T. came up with such writings as *Midrash* and *Mishna*, all in an attempt to make commentary on the Scripture to make it relevant for the ordinary folk. In the process, they developed many human traditions that eclipsed the Word of God.

The *Akũrinũ* church brings to the fore a different approach to Bible interpretation, namely the leading of the Holy Spirit. The Holy Spirit knows the need at hand, and he is able to bring the meaning of Scripture to the people. They can appeal to Jesus' reference to the Holy Spirit in John 14: 26: "But the Advocate, the Holy Spirit, whom the Father will send in my name, will teach you all things and remind you of everything I have said to you."

The approach of hermeneutics of the *Akũrinũ* is to start with the situation and then seek the answers from the Bible. The particular situation at the inception and the early years of *Akũrinũ* church was both the subjugation of the *Agĩkũyũ* by the colonial government that led to the confiscation of their land and the subsequent socio-economic challenges, and the insult that the Agĩkũyũ culture suffered under the hands of the missionary Christianity.

From this socio-political and socio-economic context, the Akũrinũ turned to the Bible for answers. Since the teaching of missionaries about equality and brotherhood seemed to be contradicted by their practices in daily life, many African converts took great interest in reading the Scriptures for themselves. The authority of the Bible took precedence over the authority of the missionaries and their teachings. For this reason, the Bible became a treasured document amongst African converts, in much the same way that it did in protestant Europe after Martin Luther.[29]

Mugambi says that owing to the convergence between African and biblical ontology, the African interpretation of the Bible often became more preoccupied with the search for harmony, rather than a quest for dissonance. Thus, a difference in emphasis is observable, between missionary and expatriate readings of the relationship between Africans and the Bible, and the African perception of that relationship. Whereas the modern missionary enterprise often brought the Bible as a condemnation of African culture, African converts have found in the Bible the affirmation of their dignity as human being created in the image of God. With this affirmation, they have been able to resist the imposition of biblical hermeneutics which sought to fashion African converts in the image of their missionary mentors. This is the context in which African independence churches have proliferated in tropical Africa.[30]

Mugambi says that African theologians have discovered that it is possible to begin their hermeneutics from the actual experience of African Christians of today and proceed to discern what the word of God would have to say to them in the contemporary context. In this approach, they

---

29. Mugambi, *Social Reconstruction*, 90.
30. Ibid., 118.

deal with such themes as "Violence and Peace"; "Democracy and Reconciliation"; Poverty and Affluence."[31]

The Akũrinũ also discovered that the Bible affirms human dignity and freedom. This led the Akũrinũ to join the liberation movement. However, their approach was through prayer and prophetic guidance, and peaceful and silent protest against anything European rather than joining their contemporaries in taking up arms against the colonizers. On this approach to the prevailing socio-political and socio-economic context, Elijah Kinyanyui had this to say:

> These three groups whom God had raised up, the politicians, the Independents [meaning the African Independent Churches that had risen around the same time with the Akũrinũ], and the Akũrinũ Church, each began to establish themselves independently from 1927 onwards, in this land of Kenya. The members of these three groups were very strong in faith, praying to God in one heart, that he would remove the Europeans and send them back to their own country, leaving this country to its rightful owners. It was clearly revealed to some of these prophets [here he refers to the Arathi or Akũrinũ prophetic figures] by the Holy Spirit that the Europeans must in the end go and leave Kenya. This is a matter about which they prayed to God, that in the end that the Europeans would go away from Kenya. [32]

Millennial or Eschatological Preaching and Living

The Akũrinũ preaching and living has been of a millennial type (a kind of reading of the Bible and living in an over realized eschatology). This seems like a normal characteristic of the Christian faith wherever it is born. The Apostolic church shared their possessions in common. They too had a millennial view of Christianity. Philomena Njeri Mwaura says

---

31. Ibid., 121.
32. Barrett and Tell, *Handbook*, 125.

this of millennial teaching, "They [Akũrinũ] also held an eschatological doctrine believing that God was going to usher in a golden age during which the chosen would be blessed with abundance and the wicked overthrown. The end was perceived as near, and they urged people to repent and believe in the redeemer"[33].

The millennial teaching and living can possibly be explained in two ways. First, there was a belief in the immediate return of Jesus Christ among the Akũrinũ founders as it was for the primitive or the apostolic Church. The second reason is persecution. A millennial or eschatological teaching helps believers to cope with persecution by looking forward to the return of Christ. The early church suffered persecution from the Jewish religious leaders. Later in the first three centuries of Christianity the church suffered intense persecution under the Roman Empire. In all this they found comfort in their *Koinonia* fellowship believing in the eminent return of Christ. The Akũrinũ equally suffered persecution under both the colonial government and their fellow Agĩkũyũ community. They found comfort in millennial teaching and living. They believed that Christ would soon come and end their agony.

However, as throughout history millennial teaching has produced Christians who are indifferent to the earthy realities. This may explain why many of the early *Arathi* were not concerned with education or owning property. They could rightly say that when Christ comes all these things will be unnecessary. As a result, many of the Akũrinũ are poor, attracting scorn from the society.

However, this is changing with a number of them involved in higher education and business. Moses Ng'ang'a, the Archbishop of The Kenya Foundation of the Prophet Church told us that one of the major pastoral challenges that he faces daily is in trying to help his members to value

---

33. Mwaura, "Africa Instituted Churches,"168.

the earthly material well-being. In his estimation this is the weakest point of his followers.[34]

Our submission is that attempting to dissuade the Akũrinũ from millennial living may not receive the desired result because they derive these teachings from their reading of the Bible. It might prove more profitable to help them in their teaching to have a balanced use of the Scripture so that they can hold the biblical message of "the already" and the "not-yet" in the right tension. This observable characteristic of over-realized eschatology remains a challenge to some of the Akũrinũ Churches. While the Bible talks of Christ's eminent return, it in the same breath admonishes believers to occupy until he comes. Conversely, it is however worthy to note that when Christians disparage the millennial perspective of life on the other hand, they may be tempted to make this present world their sole focus and live very worldly lifestyles and fall into the curse of a materialistic living.

The millennial living of Akũrinũ believers can be seen as an evidence of the transformation that the gospel brings to a culture. I arrive on this, if Mbiti's argument that African time moves backwards from a dynamic present to a remote past, *zamani* or *tene*, is anything to go by.[35]

Healing in the Akũrinũ Church

Healing is central to the Akũrinũ teaching. Our informant Rev Timothy Kamau says that, "We believe in divine healing without doubt and we have never seen God shame us by not healing whenever we prayed for anybody."[36] To this, the Reverend adds several testimonies of healings that he has witnessed; "When I was in Form two in 1992, a woman called Mama Ciiku had 'run mad'. She was brought to my father tied in

---

34. Oral interview, Arch-Bishop Moses Nga'ang'a, Mwangi, 28, March, 2016.

35. John, Mbiti, *New Testament Eschatology in an African Background: A Study of the Encounter between New Testament Theology and African Traditional Concepts.* (London: Oxford University Press: 1971), 24.

36. Oral interview, Rev Timothy Kamau, November, 13, 2015.

chains because she always wanted to strip. In our church, we do not have negotiations with demons; we attack and command them without giving them time. She was healed forthwith after prayer."[37]

In still another testimony, he explained about his niece.

> I have a niece called Nyambura whose mother had died and some of her relatives went to consult the witchdoctor. As a result, Nyambura became demon-possessed. I went to pray for her together with my mother-in-law. Even before we entered the homestead, the girl was already shouting, 'It is not here! Don't come here!' Filled with the Holy Spirit, I ran toward her and within two minutes, the demons left her, shouting, 'Now where shall we go to?' I told those who were near to leave especially if they did not have a right standing with God or risk themselves being possessed because the exorcized demons would seek someone else to possess. After the demons had left her, Nyambura got up, as if she was from sleep, and came to hug me asking, 'Uncle, you have come to see me?'" Rev. Timothy informed us that, "After such a deliverance ordeal, we are taught to directly go to God and ask him to protect us from the devil's attacks because the devil can retaliate."[38]

This belief among the Akũrinũ, that behind every sickness is a demonic operation, and the confidence that prayer can remedy the situation is again based on African spirituality. To understand the importance of

---

37. Oral interview, Rev Timothy Kamau, November, 13, 2015. In another testimony, he reports: "We recently went to Mathare Hospital [this is the main mental referral Hospital in Nairobi] to pray for a young man who had lost his mind. Upon entering the place where the patients were, the demons started screaming among various patients and even some patients became violent — to the nurses' astonishment. This is because the demons knew that we had gone there for warfare. We had prepared ourselves accordingly because we knew that we were going to a place where the enemy operates. [Here he meant that they had prayed a lot before]. Other patients got healed beside the young man and eventually the place became calm. We cannot hold any discussion with the demons, we command them to go where they belong, to the pit assigned to them until the Day of Judgment. We do not converse with demons — Trying to converse with them is like giving the devil latitude than he does not deserve."

38. Oral interview, Rev Timothy Kamau, November, 13, 2015.

healing in the Akũrinũ church we first need to understand its significance in Africa in general and among the Agĩkũyũ in particular.

John Mbiti tells us why healing takes such an important place in the life of Africans. He says, "Within the African worldview, life is seen in its totality rather than in segments. People are at peace when their relationship with God, the spirits, other people, and the rest of creation is good."[39] A broken relationship [which is seen as responsible for sickness] therefore spells disaster for the individual, and, by extension, for the rest of the family and society at large. Consequently, a remedy has to be sought to bring back the wholeness of life to the people. This process of making right the wrongs responsible for the sufferings can be seen as a healing process in which an attempt is made to mend broken relationships.[40]

Every African community had in place mechanisms of dealing with anti-life forces such as diseases, drought, floods, barrenness, curses, and witchcraft. These maladies, according to the Africans, did not occur by accident, but were caused by certain forces, including human agents through magic and witchcraft. Furthermore, such misfortunes were seen as religious experiences requiring a religious approach to dealing with them.[41]

It is for this reason that the services of the medicine man, diviner or herbalist were sought. The medicine man in particular has been described by Mbiti as the greatest gift and the most useful source of help. The process of healing is both psychological and physical. Mbiti sees the psychological aspect as the equivalent of spiritual healing in our modern times.[42]

---

39. Mbiti, *Religion and Philosophy*, 111.

40. Nahashon W. Ndung'u, "Persistence of Features of Traditional Healing in the Churches in Africa: The Case of the Akurinu Churches in Kenya," Thought and Practice: A Journal of the Philosophical Association of Kenya (PAK) New Series, Vol.1 No.2, (2009): 87-104. Accessed April 2 2016, http://erepository.uonbi.ac.ke:8080/xmlui/bitstream/handle/11295/40850/Full%20Text.pdf?sequence=on.

41. Mbiti, *Religion and Philosophy*, 169.

42. Ibid., 166.

Among the Agĩkũyũ for example, it is the patient or relatives who approach or invite the medicine man. This in itself is an acknowledgement that life is in danger and a remedy is urgently required. According to Kenyatta, the patient was expected to participate in the healing process. He/she had to lead the way by confessing to the medicine man.[43] Africans believe that there are cosmic forces behind every sickness. This is illustrated by Kenyatta when he cites a conversation between a patient and a medicine man. The medicine man says to the patient;

> Sick man, I have come to chase away your illness.
>
> I will also chase away the evil spirits which have brought it.
>
> Confess the evils you know and those you do not know.
>
> Prepare yourself, for you are about to vomit all these evils.[44]

Kenyatta adds that during the cleansing ritual that followed, the patient was to symbolically vomit all the known and unknown evils into a hole with ceremonial water. This he did by licking the ceremonial gourd, Gĩthitu, and then spitting into the hole as he proclaimed, "I vomit the illness and the evil spirits that are in my body."[45] Among modern AICs that claim a deliverance ministry, there is also encouragement of their adherence to vomit when the ministry of deliverance is in the process as a sign that the demons have left. Again, one gets the impression that the widespread practice is informed as much by this African healing process as biblical interpretation.

One striking difference between African healing methods and modern medicine, one that Africans cleave to, is the explanation of the cause of the sickness and the reassurance that it will recur. To this Nahashon Ndung'u observes,

> Through this ritual, the patient was given an assurance that all was well. Perhaps the assurance that the problem will not

---

43. Kenyatta, *Facing Mt. Kenya*, 292.
44. Ibid., 292.
45. Ibid., 292.

recur is what distinguishes the traditional and the modern medical practices. Whereas our modern doctors deal with the physical aspects of a disease, they do not answer such pertinent questions as "why" the attack and "how" to avoid a recurrence, [and I add who is responsible?]. Their advice is that "if you fall sick again, consult a doctor." In the traditional approach to healing however, the patient not only gets the treatment, but also an explanation as to why he/she fell sick, and an insurance cover in form of protective charms against people with evil eyes, or he/she performs an action which forestalls a recurrence of the problem. It is this assurance that is driving all and sundry to the medicine men in the modern times.[46]

Another important feature in the healing process is its communal aspect. In modern medical practice, the patient can keep secret the nature of the disease between himself and the doctor. Modern professional medical ethics bars the doctors from disclosing the nature of their patients' illnesses. In African traditions, however, the problem of an individual is shared by the community. The search for healing is therefore the responsibility of all. This is demonstrated among the Agĩkũyũ by the fact that often family members either accompanied the sick person or went on behalf of the sick person to the medicine man. They had to participate in the diagnosis of the problem.

Ndung'u summarizes the healing procedure among the Agĩkũyũ with four important aspects: First, there was the recognition of the role of the medicine man as one gifted with special powers by God for the service of his people. Second, the individual was required to confess any evil he/she had committed. Third, there was the communal aspect in both the diagnosis and the rituals, and fourth, there was the significance of rituals in the healing process.

---

46. N. Ndung'u, "Traditional Healing," 87.

The traditional healing processes were interrupted by the missionary activities and colonial administration. Ndung'u says that according to the missionaries, the practice of traditional healing, ũgo was at variance with Christian teachings. To discourage it, they set up health centers in their missions, to which they referred the sick among the African converts. However, the missionaries did not come up with a substitute explanation for the causes of the sickness that was satisfactory to the African converts. A spiritual vacuum was thus created. This vacuum has been filled in the African Instituted Churches. The concept of healing in these churches is holistic after the manner of the traditional African approach. It is therefore no accident that these AICs are drawing followers either as part-time or full-time members from the main line churches, which have not addressed these issues adequately.

In this regard, Ndung'u advises that healing in Akũrinũ Church should be seen in the African understanding of wholeness, i.e. in a holistic sense. This implies the putting in order of those systems, structures and feelings which have been disrupted causing imbalances and suffering in the life of individuals and society at large.

The Basis of Faith Healing in the Akũrinũ Churches

The Akũrinũ churches have practiced faith healing since their inception. Ndung'u identifies four factors that form the basis of faith healing in these churches.[47] Among the members of Akũrinũ, it is claimed that in 1930, eight Akũrinũ elders were told through a revelation to go to Mount Kenya to receive the guiding law.[48] Reportedly, the elders' experience on the mountain convinced them that God had appeared to them: There was thunder and lightning, a rainbow and a trembling of the earth, similar to

---

47. N. Ndung'u, "Traditional Healing," 87.
48. N.W. Ndung'u, "Religion, Ethnicity and Identity in Africa," Hekima – Journal of the Humanities and Social Sciences Vol. III, No. 1 (2005), 5-21.

the experience Moses had on Mount Sinai when he went to receive the Decalogue (Ex.19: 16-19).

Among the 11commandments that the *Akũrinũ* elders were allegedly given, two touch on healing. The second Mount Kenya commandment prohibits its adherents from going for treatment in Western-type hospitals due to the Europeans' hypocrisy, since the colonialists were opposed to the new movement of the *Akũrinũ*. The third Commandment requires the *Akũrinũ* to refrain from using the things brought by Europeans, and to reject their teachings.

The founders of the *Akũrinũ* churches therefore rejected western formal education and medicine. Indeed, they made it an ecclesiastical requirement that none of their followers would go to hospital and that their children would not go to school. The main reason advanced for the rules was the fear that the Europeans would use their medicine to eliminate the *Agĩkũyũ* leaders in the same way that Pharaoh had planned to eliminate the Jewish baby boys in Egypt (Ex.1:15-22). This paranoia has been passed on to the current generation of the *Akũrinũ*. Archbishop Nga'ng'a cited the same fear for the *Akũrinũ's* ambivalence to medical science.[49] Again our novelist Ngũgĩ wa Thiong'o would cite that it was believed that the death of Muthoni was perhaps a conspiracy of the missionary hospital.[50]

The *Akũrinũ* claim to be guided by the Holy Spirit, whom, they assert, is continually present among them. They therefore attribute most of their practices to the Holy Spirit, who they say directs them through prophecy, visions, auditions, and dreams. They further assert that when God commanded them to abandon Western medicine, the Holy Spirit directed them to resort to prayers whenever they fell sick, and they would be healed. Furthermore, while some members were allegedly given the power to prophesy, others were reportedly given the power to

---

49. Oral interview, Arch Bishop Moses Nga'ang'a, Mwangi, 28, March, 2016.
50. wa Thiong'o, *River Between*, 55-56.

pray for others. Kenyatta supports this thought when he observed: *Watu wa Mungu (Akūrinū)* being the chosen people, naturally believe that they possess these powers [to heal] and they go about trying to heal the sick. Sometimes they succeed in doing so and this gives them more prestige among the indigenous population.[51]

The Role of the Bible in Healing

The early Akūrinū leaders spent four years (1927-1930) searching for guidance from the Bible on how to steer their new church.[52] Whenever an issue arose such as sickness, those who were literate among the elders turned to the Bible to search for a solution. There they found that prophets such as Elijah and Elisha performed healing miracles (2 Kings 4:18-32; 5:1-14). The Akūrinū viewed themselves as God's prophets (*Anabii*), and therefore believed they had similar powers to effect healing through prayers. Moreover, both Jesus and the Apostles performed healing miracles (Mathew 11:4-5; Mark 6:13; Acts 3:1-16, 8:7, 9:32-42).[53] Before they converted to Christianity, the Akūrinū were leading the Agīkūyū way of life, in which the medicine man (*Mūndū Mūgo*) played an important role in the lives of the people. Thus, the practice of healing was not new to them. The difference was in the new procedure that the Akūrinū adopted based on their reading of the Bible.

The matter of healing is so important to the Akūrinū that it even appears in many of their constitutions. Ndung'u mentions a few of these constitutions in the various Akūrinū movements;

> (i) Holy Ghost Church of East Africa Rule No 8 states: "We do not take medicine or receive medical care. When any of us falls sick we pray for him/her (James 5:3-6)."

---

51. Kenyatta, *Facing Mt. Kenya*, 265-266.
52. N. Ndung'u, "Traditional Healing," 87.
53. Ibid.

(ii) Christian Holy Ghost Church of East Africa Rule 17 states: "We do not use modern medicine (or injection or any medicine) neither do we consult medicine men. We pray to Jesus Christ and he helps us. Jer. 46:11-12, Rev. 18:23-24; Hos. 5:13-14; if any one of us is ill we pray for him."

(iii) African Christian Holy Ghost Church Rule 13 states: "We do not take any kind of medicine or inoculation, and we are not connected with African witch-craft doctors; see Deuteronomy 18:9-16; Jer.46:11-12; Numbers 6:1-5; Rev.18:23-24; Hosea 5:13-14. If our members are sick or get illness we go to his house and pray our Almighty God, we believe in that. See Jacob (James) 5:14, John 11:25, Acts 19:12-13."[54]

These official statements apply to other Akũrinũ churches as well. As earlier noted, the Bible is used as the basis for their faith healing. The Akũrinũ disassociate themselves from the traditional medicine men as well as from witchcraft.

The Healing Procedure in the Akũrinũ Churches

It is also noteworthy that the Akũrinũ do not advertise their healing activities as do the charismatic movements. In addition, while in charismatic movements those who seek healing have usually exhausted all other avenues, the Akũrinũ as noted earlier are not supposed to seek other forms of healing. The law which was allegedly given to their elders at Mount Kenya forbade them to use Western medicine, and so they rely on prayer alone. Whereas the stance against medical science has greatly waned over the years, the conservative members of the Akũrinũ churches continue to hold on to this teaching.

Ndung'u differentiates two categories of healing. First, there is the healing that is conducted as part of the service. This usually comes at the end of the service, when the preacher calls for all those with diverse

---

54. Ibid.

problems (be they physical, mental or social) to come to the front next to the *Kigongona* (sanctuary or place of sacrifice) for prayer. The bishop and the elders pray lifting their hands and voices in unison. Congregations join in pleading the Lord for healing).[55] From this Ndung'u makes the following observations: the ceremony where healing prayer takes place is formal, no diagnosis is involved, the suffering is attributed to misdeeds, broken relationships or sin, God's intervention through forgiveness is believed to restore health, that for the success of the healing the individual takes the initiative and is involved in the prayer, and that there is communal participation which ensures that the sick are comforted by being made to feel that their suffering is shared by the rest.

The second category of healing involves the patient and the prophet healer. This is more of a private consultation. As in the traditional Agĩkũyũ consultations with a medicine man discussed earlier, the patient may be accompanied by relatives to the prophet-healer who deals with all forms of afflictions such as sickness, domestic quarrels, barrenness and unemployment. Their role is to identify the cause of the problem and to provide remedies, and to give an assurance that the problem will not recur. In this respect they compare favorably to the traditional African healers and hence their popularity not only among the *Akũrinũ* but even among the *non-Akũrinũ* who also consult them.

Ndung'u concludes that healing in African context is the reason behind the rapid spread of AICs in our continent. It is because healing in these churches is at the center of their worship. Christians find themselves to be quite at home as the practice of healing is rooted deeply in their minds, having some roots from the African traditional religion.

In summary, I can say that healing is at the center of African spirituality. This, Africans cleave to. But I also find healing central to the Old Testament. In Ex 15, Moses suggests that sickness is a punishment for the ungodly Egyptians and that the Israelites could be free from such if they

---

55. Ibid., 100.

obeyed God. In the same way in the ministry of Jesus and the apostolic church, healing was also central. In one occasion Jesus admonished one who was healed to sin no more, again adding credence to the fact that sickness is attributable to sin, what the Africans see as a disharmony in vital relationships.

It is for this reason that in the Akũrinũ Church, on the basis of both the biblical texts and the understanding of healing from the African traditions, I find an attempt to not only heal the sick but also an effort to explain the cause of disease, and the remedy. Whereas mainstream Churches are following after the missionary preferred mantra, when sickness strikes see the doctor, the Akũrinũ Church and AICs are relevant in bringing healing to their people in a holistic way.

The church is the place of hope — if God is truly there. With a myriad of problems and many modern sicknesses among some which have defied conventional medicine, many Africans are turning to anyone who can promise a remedy. If the Church can provide this, we could stem the tide to the witchdoctors that we so often see in Africa.

But one more point on healing is necessary. In African traditions, a variety of efforts and methods were involved when life was threatened. This is where the Akũrinũ differ with their former pre-Christian traditions. They are fixated on prayer as the only option. Just like all methods are employed in the Agĩkũyũ traditional healing process, medical science should be seen as one of the many ways that is meant to give people a wholesome life. In the tradition, the herbs, the medicine man, the family sacrifice, and even witchcraft were all sought in an effort to save life.

It is with this understanding that the Akũrinũ should seek the modern greatly advanced scientific approach to healing, more so now that there is no longer fear that the missionaries are out to kill the Agĩkũyũ. Thankfully, many of the Akũrinũ have accommodated the possibility of medical science in their quest for wholeness. The two young Akũrinũ leaders I interviewed, Stephen and Jesse, are nursing students in a Roman Catholic nursing school. Rev. Timothy also concurred, "We believe in medical science; our third born brother is a practicing pharmacist.

However, some Akũrinũ do not take it and when forced, they feel wronged. There is a man in our village whose leg was bored by a maize stalk; the wound was so bad that it smelled. With the influence of his sons, some policemen came to force him to go to the hospital. Whenever the policemen held him, they would feel weak and dizzy and when they let go of him, they would feel normal. The policemen refused to hold him again. He is now healed, and I found him the other day grazing his sheep."[56]

AKŨRINŨ CHILDBIRTH AND BABY DEDICATION

According to Rev. Timothy Kamau of Akũrinũ Reformation and Worship Center, an Akũrinũ contemporary church in Nairobi, if a member is blessed with a baby, the church leaders go to pray at the baby's home. After this other people can visit the home of the new born baby. The baby should not be seen by anybody else other than the parents before the elders' prayer. If any anyone visits before the elders' prayer, he or she must wash their clothes once they get back to their homes. The prayers made are first for thanking God for the gift of a new baby. Secondly, they are to cleanse the home, to remove *thahu* as a result of the blood shed during the birth. This explains why anyone who visits the home before the elders' prayer is considered unclean.

According to Abraham Macharia, baby dedication, *Kũiyũkia mwana*, is one of the important ceremonies in the Akũrinũ faith.[57] Rev. Timothy says that if a baby boy has been born, the elders visit the home after seven days to make the cleansing prayers. The baby boy is then taken to church for dedication on the fortieth day. If the baby is a girl, the elders go to pray on the fortieth day, and the dedication done on the eightieth

---

56. Oral interview, Rev Timothy Kamau, November, 13, 2015.
57. Oral interview, Abraham Macharia Prince, January, 16, 2016.

day. If the fortieth or eightieth day falls on a week day, dedication is done on the immediately following Sunday. Some Akũrinũ churches do baby dedication on Friday evenings.[58]

A Mũkũrinũ gets to know the gender of their baby in the womb through the name given beforehand as a result of prophecy in the church. However, the contemporary Akũrinũ are abandoning the names given through prophecy by choosing those they like. When the children are dedicated, they are at the same time given the name that has been revealed by the Holy Spirit. Among the older Akũrinũ churches, the bishop can refuse to dedicate a child if he or she does not have a confirmation of the name which the parent says is from the Holy Spirit. This dedication symbolizes kũamũrwo, that the child has been set apart and dedicated to the work of the Lord. This is ultimately salvation to the Akũrinũ.

In the African Mission Church, specific elders, Atiiri a kĩgongona, the supporters of the sacrifice, who form the highest rank of eldership, are the ones who on the eighth day after the child is born visit the home and pray for the new born. This tradition is derived from the story of Jesus' dedication in the temple. The Akũrinũ do not circumcise the boy child on the eighth day like Christ was, reserving this to early adolescence. Here I see Akũrinũ selectively oscillating between the biblical culture and their Agĩkũyũ traditional culture. Again, here the Akũrinũ clearly differentiates the "thou shall" of the Bible from what I describe as "thou shall do what is culturally right to you." After another forty days, the Atiiri a kĩgongona go home for the newborn and bring it to church for dedication and baptism. The song that the Akũrinũ sing during the dedication service captures the story of Jesus' dedication at the temple and Simon's prophecy. This hymn also carries the Akũrinũ theology of dedication:

---

58. Oral interview, Rev Timothy Kamau, November, 13, 2015.

Jesũ mũiguithania wa ndũrĩrĩ nĩ okire kũhingia

Wĩra wa manabii na atũmwo

Ngoro ya ũria warĩ mũthingu kũu hekaru-inĩ

nĩ yakenire maitho make mona ũtheri wa ndũrĩrĩ

(Jesus the reconciler of nations came to Earth to fulfill

The work of the prophets and apostles

The heart of the righteous man in the temple

Became joyful when his eyes saw the light of the nations)

AKŨRINŨ BAPTISM AND ITS ORIGIN

To Joseph Ng'ang'a, the founder of the Akũrinũ, who heard a voice calling him by his new name Joseph in his drunkard stupor, baptism meant a new name and a change of life that enables one to become a true follower of Jesus Christ. This baptism of the Spirit supersedes the baptism of water. For Ng'ang'a and for the Akũrinũ, baptism is therefore a divine impartation of a new name and life. It involves an inward change brought about by the Holy Spirit in which a believer becomes a follower of Christ.[59]

Accordingly, the Akũrinũ believes in baptism by the Holy Spirit in which a baptismal name is also given often through a prophetic utterance. The church elders wait on God in prayer until the name is given. Most of the Akũrinũ churches do not practice water baptism but instead practice the baptism of the Holy Spirit. This is the most critical point of the Akũrinũ that marks one as a true believer. This seems in our research to happen at no particular age and can take place as early as three years.

---

59. Githieya, *Freedom of Spirit*, 142.

The seriousness with which this baptism is taken among the Akũrinũ is worth noting. It is also consistent with the teaching of the Bible that conversion can only be affected by the Holy Spirit. This can be contrasted with the baptismal ritual in the mission or historical churches where baptism was primarily through water upon going through catechism classes. Upon successful completion of the class one would be baptized and allowed to participate in Holy Communion. In this way, Christianity came to be regarded as acquisition of a certain degree of information and a Christian or baptismal name. This tradition has remained intact to the present day. This undoubtedly produced nominal Christianity. Here Dyrness will remind us that the West generally understood Christianity as acquiring a set of information as cited before.

To the Akũrinũ, baptism is an inner work that is followed by the official installation of the white turban. The turban marks every mukũrinũ. It is like the outside sign of the inner change. No one who wears a turban is expected to behave contrary to the Akũrinũ faith with deviants receiving dire consequences. Rev. Timothy Kamau narrated to us what happened to one who took the turban casually; "The turban is a very basic symbol of our faith, identifying one as a Mùkùrinù. It also identifies us with the good news. Whoever wears it falsely without believing in the Akũrinũ faith seeks evil for himself, like one thief who wore it and was shot dead by the police on the same day."[60]

The Akũrinũ baptism seals the Akũrinũ children for salvation. The Akũrinũ believe that when their children grow up following this baptism, they will follow in the faith. This does not in any way do away with the individual adult personal initiative to their faith. Later the children once they are grown make a personal choice to believe in Christ and follow the Akũrinũ church voluntarily or join other churches. The Akũrinũ children are however brought up in the strictest Akũrinũ faith. There is a saying among the Akũrinũ that says that, ũkũrinũ ndũthiraga. In this they mean

---

60. Oral interview, Rev Timothy Kamau, November, 13, 2015.

that once they have brought up the child in their faith with all the attending rituals and ceremonies, the child will not abandon the faith, just like Proverb 6: 22 says.

Akūrinū Vernacular Theology as an Encounter of the Gospel with the Culture in the Formation of a New Community

One of the observable features of AICs in general is their attempt to fashion their churches as a community from the concept of African communal life. Philomena Mwaura says this of the AICs quoting Jocelyn Murray: these churches are the "salt of the earth" in their communities. Through creative cultural hermeneutical processes, they preserve what is good in African culture, they mediate healing where people are hurting due to various problems and they draw people to faith in Jesus and the full life that Jesus promises to His followers. The concept of *Ubuntu* and peace so important in African communities are central to AICs' spirituality and the idea of the good life. *Ubuntu* is a concept that depicts personhood and humaneness. It expresses the ontology of people and their identity. It is a cultural and ethical worldview. It is expressed in the saying, "I am because we are and because we are therefore, I am."

The meaning and essence of *Ubuntu* is the inclusiveness and interrelatedness of all reality. It finds resonance with the biblical story of creation in which God created humanity in relationship and in the New Testament vision of restoration of all things to God. This implies that,

> [b]eing human is relational and cooperative...the concrete person is a web of interactions, a network of operative relationships. A person is fashioned by historical, cultural, genetic, biological, social, and economic infrastructure. These relationships are not mechanical: they do not allow for competitive individualization which would damage the

dignity of the human being. The dignity of human beings emanates from the network of relationships, from being in community.⁶¹

The centrality of the idea of community in AICs is evident in worship and relationship with one another. Given the pressures on traditional society in modern Africa, this attempt to create a sense of community in AICs is of great significance. As Jocelyn Murray observed about the Akũrinũ of Central Kenya, who had created a "church tribe," in which unlike in the traditional community where relationships and social bonds were dependent on kinship, members are tied together by a common faith.

These communities are reminiscent of the early Christian communities where there was mutual concern for all and sharing. This ethic is also derived from African communal values. This is the framework for celebrating life through various social and religious events. The principle of mutual aid in the name of Christian charity governs Church members and it takes several forms depending on the nature of needs.

Commenting on the Akũrinũ communal life, Philomena adds this of the Spirit Churches, "They are closely related to African culture with a strong focus on spiritual gifts and powers. The Akũrinũ Church is closer to indigenous Agikuyu tradition in their beliefs in prophecy, observance of ritual taboos, they designated themselves as a community in the power of the Holy Spirit with a call to evangelize and set themselves apart from a corrupt and evil world."⁶²

It is on this account that I observe in the Akũrinũ, a church that has developed within the cultural milieu of its adherents all the time trying its best to be sensitive to its cultural roots on one hand and on the other hand trying to be true to the Scriptural teaching though with limited biblical hermeneutical principles but fully allowing the leading and the

---

61. Mwaura, "Africa Instituted Churches," 168.
62. Ibid.

guidance of the Holy Spirit. In this way the Akūrinū church has created a new community in the line of the Agĩkũyũ's understanding of the community while at the same time rejecting any element in the Agĩkũyũ culture that is opposed to the gospel. To understand how this new community works, I will explore the Akūrinū church leadership, courtship and marriage, and circumcision to see how these very important cultural aspects of life have been redefined and assimilated in Akūrinū ecclesiology instead of being suppressed and ignored as it has been done in the historical churches to varied degrees.

The *Akūrinū* New Church Community

The Akūrinū efforts to organize themselves in the category of an African community in line with their communal way of life can be traced to the movement of the Akūrinū church to Meru. Githieya documents that the Akūrinū moved to Meru in the area of Tungu, in the larger part of southern Meru called Chuka and Mwimbi in 1935 through the work of Johnston M'Kiambati. The move to Meru is significant in that the Akūrinū or the *Arathi* organized themselves as a community based on their understanding of the early apostolic church, Acts 2: 44-45, 4:32. They believed that in living together, they enhanced their bond as Christians and equipped themselves for their mission.

To do this and avoid the accusation of moral laxity, the Ameru *Arathis* adopted *Gaaru* which was in Ameru tradition; a building a little away from the main homestead where senior warriors taught the younger warriors' military tactics, discipline, and the moral code of their ethnic group. The Akūrinū adopted *Gaaru* as a place for training in discipleship and also as a residential place for the community. There were separate *Gaarus* for males and females. The *Gaaru* serves many functions:

> On the eve of the marriage the bride and the groom would customarily lodge in a *Gaaru*. Here they were taught and coached on matters of family and marriage, the conduct of

a husband and a wife by select leaders and mothers. This guaranteed stable marriages and explains the low divorce rate in the Akũrinũ community.[63]

The Gaaru idea was adopted in all areas where the Akũrinũ church was established including Murang'a and Kiambu where the church had originally started. Later on, Gaaru was instrumental in hiding Akũrinũ believers who were running away from persecution from the Mau Mau freedom fighters who accused the Akũrinũ of refusing to join the freedom movement. As I mentioned before, the Akũrinũ were a pacifist movement that resisted any armed conflict preferring to pray for God to remove the colonialist by His power rather than engaging them in armed conflict.

Both the Akũrinũ ecclesiology and way of life outside and within the church shows clear expression of African communality. Today Gaaru is found in every Akũrinũ church. After the service the members retreat into Gaaru where they discuss their social matters. It also acts as the dinning place. The Akũrinũ love to share a common meal and eat together after the service. The meal may not be elaborate. Sometimes it is only porridge. McVeigh explains how this impacts the members of AICs:

> The people joined in a communal meal of cooked corn served from a common pot. The sense of togetherness evident in both the service and the meal was striking. Given the pressures on the traditional society in modern Africa, this attempt to create a new sense of community in the independent churches is of great significance.[64]

Gaaru is also a place of residence. This is where visiting Akũrinũ are hosted to seminars and other meetings. With such a hostel, the Akũrinũ do not require to incur extra cost of hiring hostels for their visitors. Gaaru is above all used for discipleship training. This is where overnight

---

63. Macharia. Identity, 106.
64. Barrett and Tell, Handbook, 139.

prayer vigils are held. It is also where special training especially for the youth in done.

Stephen Ndùng'ù and Jesse Njùgùna, the youth leaders and our respondents from African Mission Church had this to say of this community life among the youth.

> In our church we have biweekly meetings for the youth whereby we learn doctrines such as the importance of the turban, and various church rules and regulations. We also have forums in which we encourage and develop one another on such matters as investing. We also take care of each other by contributing Kes.10 during every meeting. Kes.10 is affordable to all, including those who are in school. Such monies are used to tailor vestments for each one so that none of us wears tattered clothes. The monies are also used during festivities such as Christmas — basically we are not limited to what we can do with the monies."[65]

Here is a community of youth who wants to be the same (social class) and not to outdo one another — severe competition is the curse of the postmodern human.

Akũrinũ Church Organizational Structure

The concept of *Gaaru* as a community center is just one of the ways in which Akũrinũ church expresses itself as a community. Another way can be seen in the leadership structure. Here McVeigh says that the AICs are community-centered rather than leader-centered. The leaders though at times wear lofty titles; they generally work closely with their church committees and are careful to avoid arbitrary personal decisions. The fact that Akũrinũ churches are of small numbers raging between 20 and 50 affords them a close-knit community.[66]

---

65. Oral interview, Stephen Ndùng'ù and Jesse Njùgùna, November, 12, 2015.
66. Ibid., 138-139.

To understand the *Akũrinũ* church leadership structure, I will compare this with the *Agĩkũyũ* traditional tribal political organizational structure. Three features that were common in this tradition are; the gradation of eldership from the time of circumcision, to the highest level of eldership reserved for the very old and respected elders. The second feature was the understanding that certain families have been vested with the leadership virtue in which leadership becomes hereditary to various degrees. Here leadership was handed down from generation to generation in these families not necessarily as a rule but as a norm. Thirdly, women were not included in this structure. This does not mean that the women were marginalized in any way. The whole structure took care of everybody. The women were involved in the affairs of the community but with no leadership roles. All the three features are discernable in the *Akũrinũ* church to various degrees.

As noted in the diagram below the circumcision of the young men was the first step to leadership. After the rite the young initiates entered the junior warriors' council, *nyama ya anake a mumo*. Next was the senior warriors' council, *nyama ya ita* (war council). After this was marriage when a man entered the "council of elders" in the first grade of eldership, *kiama kia kamatimo*, or "the carriers of shields." In the next stage when one's first born son reached the age of circumcision, the man entered the "council of peace," *kiama kia mataathi*. The final stage of eldership was the religious sacrificial council, *kiama kia maturanguru*. This last level of eldership was highly respected and of course very few people lived to reach it.

Figure 1: The Agĩkũyũ Tribal Political Organization Structure

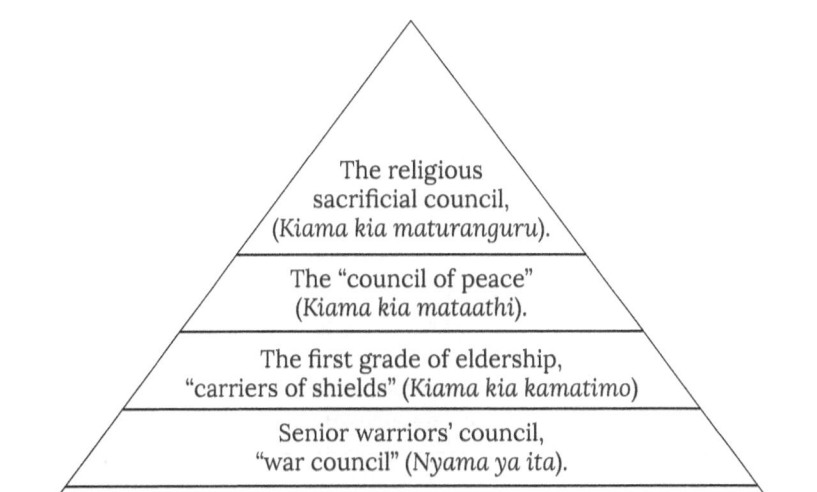

In this community, respect was accorded to the elders for their wisdom, age, and service to the community which they did for no fees, except the sacrificial animal that was eaten by the participants during a sacrifice. Our observation is that respect for the elderly is currently at its lowest ebb in many African communities. The young feel that the elders do not know or appreciate the modern treads. In the political circles, the elder statesmen are viewed as a hindrance to progress. This disrespect is a sign of a fast disintegrating community life in Africa — a recipe for moral degeneration.

Figure Two: Akũrinũ Church Leadership Structure

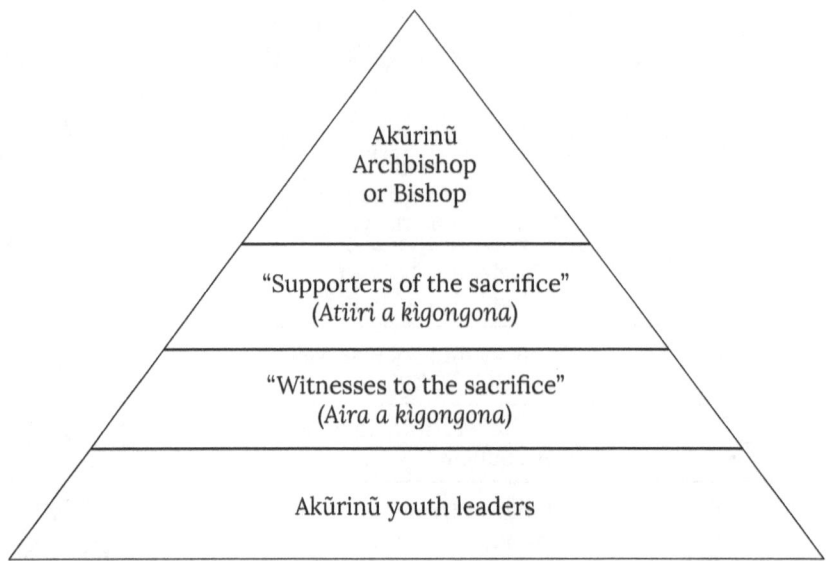

There are similarities in the two leadership structures. In the Agĩkũyũ traditional leadership — whereas women's role in leadership is not disputed — they do not have particular position that they hold. Their interests are subsumed within the interest of the men. The Agĩkũyũ tribal organization structure takes care to protect the children and women. However, during the sacrifices by the highest eldership, a woman who must be very mature who is now seen as a mother of the community and small boys for the purpose of mentorship are involved.

The women in the Akũrinũ church only rise to the level of Aiira a Kigonogona, "the witness of the sacrifice." They witness the ritual worship but do not preside over. However, women play other roles especially as prophetesses, as our informant Kiarie put it,

> Women are recognized in the leadership but only to the level of certain roles. Women cannot carry on ceremonies or pray for someone in the church. In church the women leaders

sit in *itìinì cia ùira* (seats of witnesses) at the front near the pulpit; that is the farthest they go. *Atiiri a kìgongona* (supporters of the sacrifice) are men, but majority of prophets are women. We follow the Old Testament guideline which encourages women to lead up to a certain level. However, nowadays, this is changing, with even some of the women having their own churches.[67]

Leaders in the *Akũrinũ* Church are qualified through various gradations based mainly on age, competence and the sense of the call. Like in the *Agĩkũyũ* tradition, circumcision, which the *Akũrinũ* Church has adopted in its discipleship program, initiates the first step in the journey of leadership. Again, marriage and stability in marital life is a key step in ascending to any leadership position. The admonitions of Paul to Timothy, "He who aspires to be a bishop must be a husband of one wife ..." (1 Tim 3:2) are taken seriously and literally.

In the *Akũrinũ* church as in the *Agĩkũyũ* tradition, leadership is often inherited within the family. The Archbishop of, 'The Kenya Foundation of the Prophet Church', Bishop Moses Ng'ang'a is married from the family of the *Akũrinũ* founder Musa Thuo while Rev. Timothy Kamau, a third-generation leader of the *Akũrinũ* Reformation and Worship Center in Nairobi, an *Akũrinũ* contemporary church is a grandson to the same founder. Such hereditary leadership is not uncommon among the *Akũrinũ* churches.

The *Akũrinũ* Church Courtship and Marriage Procedures

The communal life is also seen when the *Akũrinũ* do their wedding. The *Akũrinũ* courtship and marriage is couched on the *Agĩkũyũ* traditions, where marriage is treated as a community affair. The whole church takes part in raising the monies for the cost of the wedding ceremony.

---

67. Oral interview, Dr. Kiarie Mburu, March, 5, 2016.

Here is how Stephen Ndùng'ù and Jesse Njùgùna describe an *Akũrinũ* wedding ceremony;

> Our weddings are conducted on Sundays. The Saturday before the wedding day, we normally have an all-night prayer vigil, *kesha*, where we dance and celebrate. The following morning, we plan with the bishop and other leaders on how to go to the bride's home to get her and take her to church. The first car in the convoy is for the youth members, and it is the same car that does the video graphing. In church, the pastor speaks to them (the couple) briefly and then the lady is vested with the *gacuka* (this is a kind of apron that is worn across the bust by all married women) — The *Akũrinũ* do not wear wedding rings. Gifts are then exchanged with lots of entertainment and the ceremony ends.[68]

All inappropriate relationships and all kinds of flirting between men and women are proscribed among the *Akũrinũ*. The commencement of courtship must be sanctioned by the leadership. Our two youth leaders had this to say on the courtship;

> During our youth meetings, we teach the youth that it is not wise for an unmarried lady and a gentleman to be seen standing in a lonely place and with no purpose — it is wrong. If a young man is ready to marry, he will first go to one of the elders of the church and inform him that he is ready to settle in a family. This seeking for permission to start a family is important. The elder will then share the information with other leaders. After building a consensus, the young man will be given a letter, *Marua*, to take to the prospective girl or to her church (that is if the two do not fellowship in the same *Akũrinũ* church). If the lady is agreeable, she will sign the letter and the signed letter will be returned to the elders. The letter is valid for a maximum of six months after which the young man must wait until he can request for another

---

68. Oral interview, Stephen Ndùng'ù and Jesse Njùgùna, November, 12, 2015.

letter. This letter gives the prospecting couple permission to be seen together but even then, a third person must be in their company. [69]

With the digital era, it is impossible to restrict interaction but that notwithstanding the Akũrinũ youth are not encouraged to spend time together before marriage least of all the flirting that leads to sex before marriage. If the lady accepts the marriage proposal, the wedding preparations begin. However, any visit to her home by the man must be in the company of another male friend. In this way the relation is kept pure and above reproach. The whole church is involved in the wedding plans. The members raise the money and other items required for the wedding ceremony.

Akũrinũ's Esteem for a Holy Wedding

Chastity among the Akũrinũ is highly valued, and it is for those who have not contaminated their salvation by being immoral. The teachings on purity are learnt in the youth's meetings. All our informants said that sexual sin is viewed as a very serious sin, *Mehia*. If a lady has messed and has possibly conceived before the wedding, she will not be accorded a holy wedding. Unholy wedding is treated differently from a holy one. The holy wedding is highly celebrated. Again, this attitude to moral sin builds on the primal values as well as biblical teaching.

According to our informant, Timothy Kamau, the Akũrinũ elders turn to the Holy Spirit to ascertain if the couple has defiled the marriage bed. In some cases, the Akũrinũ leaders will refuse to officiate over a wedding whose bed has been defiled. Many stories abound among the Akũrinũ churches where a couple that has engaged in sex before marriage and who fail to reveal this to the elders have faced severe consequences in their marriage including death. Sexual sin is treated with utter severity

---

69. Oral interview, Stephen Ndùng'ù and Jesse Njùgùna, November, 12, 2015.

among the Akũrinũ. It is not uncommon for the Akũrinũ to thrash one of their own who persists in sexual sin.[70] Again this moral injunction is both biblical and cultural. Culturally all ladies were expected to be virgins before marriage. Deviants were ostracized and shamed.

Circumcision Ritual Among the Akũrinũ

As we have demonstrated earlier in this book, circumcision (and clitoridectomy) was perhaps the most significant rite of passage to the Agĩkũyũ community. Besides the teaching and training that went with it, it was also the gateway to adulthood. The community secrets were learnt during the rite. No uncircumcised person would be entrusted with any serious responsibility, especially leadership as they were considered as children and unindicted into to the tribal secrets and the way of life. The important function of the circumcision rite was its organizational factor in the age-grouping or riika.

Circumcision and clitoridectomy took place after every four years involving many young boys and girls. As it would be expected almost the whole community life came to a standstill. It involved the most elaborate rituals, collaboration from the eldership across the whole tribe, rurĩrĩ. Those who went through the ritual formed one age group, riika rĩmwe, irrespective of their mbarĩ or mũhĩrĩga. A common name for the age-set was reached by the elders. The age-set formed a very strong brotherhood and sisterhood among themselves in all matters of the tribe. The activities of the age-sets stabilized the whole tribe and unified the tribe as one people.

The Akũrinũ church has taken this great cultural practice and incorporated it into her discipleship experience. Like in the tradition the whole church and the extended family near and far come together in solidarity to help the young people transit through an important milestone of their

---

70. Oral interview, Rev Timothy Kamau, November, 13, 2015.

lives. Our two youth leaders, Ndũng'ũ and Jesse Njũgũna will now take up the story as they narrate the spiritual stages of an Akũrinũ male;

> When you are born, you wear a white hat (called *Gakobia*) because as a child you don't understand the faith; even the hat can fall as you play with fellow children (much care is taken for the turban which is worn by adults). At class 8 (the last class in primary level of education), you undergo circumcision. A *Mũkũrinũ* undergoing circumcision is first prayed for in church but not by his parents. A youth from the church takes me (the circumcision candidate) to be circumcised and stands with me during the healing process; he is like a father to me, and he is called *baba mũndiiri wa kĩroho* i.e. my spiritual father or mentor. (Notice that the idea of a mentor is a cultural practice where each initiate would be sponsored by an older close and trusted relative at circumcision, now re-interpreted in a Christian setting). Even after the circumcision process, we continue to respect him, the mentor. During the healing, we receive advice on how to live as grown-ups. My mentor stands with me and advises me through the process, and also welcomes fellow youth to advise me. After healing, which can take about a week or more, I go back to the church where I am prayed for to be cleansed. I am then vested with the turban.[71]

Ndũng'ũ and Jesse Njũgũna describe this rite of passage further:

> The elders who pray for you in the church before the circumcision ritual also notify the church that for one week that you and your mentor will not be attending church for a period. The elder does not announce this in public but informs only the leaders of the church. These leaders then notify others so that the process does not look like a secret. There is no specific age for circumcision, but after completing primary education. Likewise, for those who drop out of

---

71. Oral interview, Stephen Ndũng'ũ and Jesse Njũgũna, November, 12, 2015.

school, the parents notify the church leadership when they want their sons to be circumcised. Circumcision is done when one is big enough such that they begin to feel uncomfortable interacting with Sunday school children, and they are now ready to join the youth. Ladies should not see me during circumcision. Married women who are church members bring raw food items to my mother to cook for me, but they do not get to see me. (Again, notice that this seclusion period that follows after circumcision was traditionally used for a time of learning the tribal secrets and warfare skills. Women were not allowed to interact with the initiates during the seclusion. Psychological, physical and social means are employed to help the initiate appreciate the transition to adulthood). In our Church, circumcision is done in the hospital, but the healing takes place at home.[72]

Here the Akũrinũ take a traditional ritual and used it in a modern setting in their ecclesiological experience. Traditionally, a traditional circumciser would do the circumcision exercise. This role has been taken over by the medical practitioners. However, the traditional teaching that accompanied the ritual in the past has been maintained and modified and incorporated to the Akũrinũ discipleship process.

The teaching centers both on discipleship and social ethics. The Akũrinũ guide their members in all details of life. Macharia highlights some of the teaching for us. In part some of the rules say: do not spit, relieve yourself on the ground (one had to dig a hole in the ground and cover his or her excrement); you must clean your houses daily every morning and night before retiring to bed.[73] Many of the Akũrinũ churches observe a list of "Rules of modesty" which are taught to the youth and especially during the initiation.

---

72. Oral interview, Stephen Ndùng'ù and Jesse Njùgùna, November, 12, 2015.
73. Macharia, Identity, 114.

Chapter three

Taboo Observance and Practices in the *Akũrinũ* Church

There is a whole range of what can be described as taboos or "uncleanness" among the Akũrinũ. Joshua Gachanga singles out three taboos among the Akũrinũ. These include strict laws on food; impurity that is associated with blood such as monthly periods for women, blood associated with child birth, the possible blood shed at breaking of hymen at the first sexual encounter for the newly wedded woman; and circumcision for both boys and girls. In these occasions, those involved with shedding or emitting blood are considered unclean. They cannot attend Church until a ritual cleansing is done. Again, any sexual intercourse before a significant spiritual ritual or ceremony is considered a taboo and those involved should abstain from sex prior to the event.[74]

Taboos played an import aspect of the Agĩkũyũ community. Many of the ecclesiological practices of the Akũrinũ church can be traced to this culture. To understand how taboos are central to Akũrinũ I will look at how this belief affects the entire Agĩkũyũ culture. Although not all current generation of the Agĩkũyũ holds to the belief in taboos, the idea is still potent in many ways, even holding meaning-making reference. I will quote extensively three articles that appeared in the Kenya daily, *The East African Standard*, in the recent past.

On Wednesday, February 6th 2013, the Standard Newspaper carried an article by the title, "Central Mystic *'mugumo'* tree's fall sparks succession debate." The article reads in part as follows:

> Nyeri residents look at a giant *Mugumo* tree, estimated to be more than 200 years-old, that fell in Ikumbo village in Giakanja area, Nyeri County. To many people, the falling of a tree is a routine and natural occurrence. But to some villagers in Nyeri, when the fallen tree happens to be the sacred *mugumo* (Fig tree), then it symbolizes something important. And with the General Election around the corner, the fall-

---

74. Oral interview, Joshua Gachanga, May, 2016.

ing of a *mugumo* tree has created debate in the county. Market centers are abuzz with news of the sacred tree, with some groups of elders from the village saying it signifies a generational change in the county leadership. According to the talk, the happening at Giakanja village can be described as *ituika*, a word that means change of guard from one age group to the other...it came as a surprise when we saw what had happened to the tree," said Wang'ondu who said the tree could be more than 200 years-old. With many locals believing that Deputy Prime Minister Uhuru Kenyatta has a chance to succeed President Kibaki, the falling of the tree may not just be an ordinary happening... A Kikuyu elder, Harisson Kanyuguto, said *ituika* occurs whenever the elderly are handing over leadership to the younger generation or vice versa. "Whenever it occurs, celebrations are conducted, and sacrifices given. Another *mugumo* tree is planted at the scene of the fallen tree," said Kanyuguto.[75]

The newspaper article continued:

Gikuyu and Mumbi Cultural Museum Executive Director Samuel Kamitha told The Standard that whenever a *mugumo* tree fell in Gikuyu land; it had a meaning to the community. Kamitha notes that in 1963, a huge *mugumo* tree fell in Thika, and this led to the exit of colonialists, who were being fought by a local group, the Mau. The Thika tree, according to Kamitha, a Kikuyu elder, Wanjohi Waweru, was also prophesied by Kikuyu prophet Mugo wa Kibiru. "Mugo prophesied that the fall of a giant *mugumo* tree in Thika would symbolize the end of European rule in Kenya," said Waweru, who is also a hotelier. When the British Colonial Government learnt of the prophecy, they built an iron ring around it to prevent it from falling. "In 1963, the tree split and fell in two parts, hence leading to an independent Kenya

---

75. Accessed April 21 2016, http://www.standardmedia.co.ke/article/2000076717/mystic-mugumo-tree-s-fall-sparks-succession-debate.

> led by Mzee Jomo Kenyatta," said Waweru. Mr. Danson Kamanja, a resident of Thika, said the iron ring still exists at the base of the fallen tree that forced out the white rulers. The traditionalist adds that in 1978, another *mugumo* tree fell in Chania, leading to the death of the founding President Jomo Kenyatta.[76]

Another article in a *The East African Standard* for 5th Oct 2015 reads;

> A fig tree, known among the Kikuyu as *mugumo*, has fallen, causing panic at Gamerock Estate near Nyeri Town. Even though the falling of the tree inside the compound of former Cabinet minister Chris Murungaru would appear normal to many, to the Kikuyu community, it symbolizes something serious… A Kikuyu elder, Mr. Mathege wa Iregi, said if the tree was ever used as a sacred place, then the fall may mean something bad will happen. "And if this never happened, then we shall take it as an ordinary *mugumo* tree in the forest with no serious implications to the community," said Mr. Wa Iregi. "Elders are yet to meet since we received the news. But in a few days, we shall inspect the place before we give a report on whether the tree is sacred or not," Mr. Iregi added…Kikuyu traditions state that *mugumo* trees are not supposed to be cut. The trees were used to perform religious ceremonies such as offering sacrifices and prayers… When the trees fall due to natural causes, they are to be left to rot on their own. If the tree is cut down, another one must be planted at the same spot to avoid a curse…[77]

The third article appeared on Friday, June 19, 2015 with the title, "Today a sheep will die in Dagoretti because a branch fell off this fig tree." It reads (in part);

---

76. Accessed April 21 2016, http://www.standardmedia.co.ke/article/2000076717/mystic-mugumo-tree-s-fall-sparks-succession-debate.
77. *The East African Standard*, Media Newspaper, October, 5, 2015.

A sheep is scheduled to die today in this cool suburb of Nairobi where some men have been ordered to stay chaste and women to lie low. Kikuyu elders have since begun a two-week cleansing-ceremony under the tree that hosted various gatherings and ceremonies in the past decades...The sheep, chosen to die to save the people of Dagoretti, will be tied up and hung upside down, its terrified face pointing in the direction of the great Mt Kenya, and only young, morally pure boys will be allowed to eat the roast mutton...None of the men who will have important roles to play in the ritual today has been having sex since the bad news of the fall of a mugumo branch broke... or so they claim... A sheep, a special sheep, will be slaughtered. Prayers will be said. Chants chanted. Demons chased away. Ancestors appeased. And forgiveness sought.

...Harrison Waithaka, chairman of the Dagoretti council of elders, says a wether (castrated male sheep) "with no blemish" will be slaughtered. The knife for the job will first be purified through an elaborate ritual, and anything that will come into contact with the animal, including the utensils that will collect its blood, must be Okayed by the elders...

Once slaughtered, its innards will be inspected to ensure there is no sign from the ancestors that it is a tainted animal...Should something be found wanting about the animal's internal organs, then it will have to be set aside and another one slaughtered for the ritual. The man slaughtering the sheep, selected carefully from a team of candidates by the elders, will carefully collect the blood, which will then be mixed with the contents of the bowels.

After that, the carcass will be placed on a crackling fire and a container placed underneath it to extract fat, which will then be mixed with herbs to form a sacred concoction.

> This, alongside the Kikuyu alcoholic brew, *muratina*, will be sprinkled on the site as libation.
>
> Although in most cases the meat from such sacrifices is not eaten, today's peace offering will be extended to young boys and young boys only. Their fathers won't eat the meat, and neither will their mothers. The elders, too, can't touch the roast mutton. "Nobody else, not even the one roasting the meat, will eat it," says Waithaka. "He and it has to be a he, cannot even lick his fingers and touch the meat! Only young boys will eat the meat because we consider them morally unsullied." Because the few young boys chosen to feast on the special animal cannot complete the job, the rest of the meat, together with all the utensils used in the ritual, will be thrown into a ball of fire and burnt to chars. As the fire consumes everything, the elders will retreat to watch how the smoke behaves. They expect it to rise directly into the skies as a show of confidence from their ancestors that they have done well. Should it, however, just dance around and scatter all over Dagoretti, the whole affair will be regarded a failure. They will have to slaughter another sheep.[78]

Although I have quoted this particular lengthy article, it is the next part that particularly touches on the issue of taboo that interests us, namely sexual chastity in matters of religion:

> None of the men who will have important roles to play in the ritual at Dagoretti today has been having sex since the bad news of the fall of a *mugumo* branch broke…"Having sex just days to the ceremony is considered dirty for those who will be around the tree," explains chairman Waithaka. Other adherents of the Agikuyu tradition were asked through the media, in keeping with tradition, to also abstain. "Such abstinence will cleanse us in preparation for the ritual, and anybody who has been involved in activities that negate

---
78. *The East African Standard*, June, 19, 2015

inner morality during this period of mourning cannot be present at the scene of the ceremony. "They may wait outside the compound, but they can't come near the tree. If you have sinned, you cannot step on the grounds. You must first go and cleanse yourself, otherwise you will go away with a curse hanging on your back...."[79]

The understanding that before a serious religious ceremony, the participating elders should abstain from sex is rife in the *Akũrinũ* church. It is not difficult to deduce that this understanding is derived both from culture and biblical teaching.

Archbishop Musa Ng'ang'a narrated to us the process of cleansing a woman who has given birth; the elders to perform the cleansing abstains from sex for three days. After this they go to *Gaaru* where they pray over water to concentrate it. They then wash their bodies with this water. They carry part of the dedicated water to the home of the nursing mother where they sprinkle the water at the gate and the house. They also pray for cleansing. The same procedure applies for the pall bearers. After this the cleansed persons are free to attend Church and shake hands with other believers.

As I have discussed elsewhere in this work, sex is seen as a form of defilement before a religious ceremony is derived both from the *Agĩkũyũ* culture and the biblical culture. For example, when ratifying Mosaic covenant at the Mt. Sinai, the Israelites abstained from sex for three days. They also washed their clothes and bodies, Ex 19: 10 – 15. For all its other possible explanations, the solemnity and the commitment that should precede important religious rituals should never be lost. Even today religious matters should not be approached casually and unadvisedly. There is an understanding of the sacredness of the ritual and the holiness of God. Negatively though, there is an understanding that the woman is the one that defiles the man in the sexual act. The abstention from sex

---

79. Ibid.

for Akũrinũ must be understood more in the category of the Agĩkũyũ rules on taboos or the "cleanness" and "uncleanness" which has found resonance with the Bible.

The *East African Standard* article ends with the consequence of the culprits who fell down the tree and the religious importance of the Mugumo tree:

> Gicheru and his worker who are responsible for this damage, and the respective members of their clans, *Mucera* and *Muithaga*, will not be allowed in the ritual. The two have however been given a new leaf; they will go to the elders after the ceremony and plead for forgiveness for assaulting the abode of the Agikuyu god, Ngai. It is expected that they will be forgiven.

The elders know the importance of the fig tree:

> Waithaka, the chairman of the local elders, says that, other than being a part of nature, the *Mugumo* is a canvas on which their culture and early religion is painted. Its presence, physically and symbolically, has a divine meaning. And this is not just any other tree. Word has it that the *mugumo*, and many others in the compound, were planted by the country's founding president, Mzee Jomo Kenyatta, who is said to have lived here briefly. The elders, therefore, cannot understand why anyone would want to hurt this imposing cultural, religious and social monument.
>
> According to Prof Godfrey Muriuki in the book, A *History of the Kikuyu*, the author posits that the *mugumo* is held in so much awe as it is believed to symbolize power. And in Dagoretti today, a group of men and women will gather to protect that power.

After narrating the history and the importance of the Mugumo tree in the article, the elder, Waithaka concludes:

> "...We have the *mugumo* tree to thank for our beginning and progression," Waithaka, the elders' chairman, butts in. "It is the symbol of life. And wherever there is a *mugumo* tree, God is nearby." And so, it is in the tribe's collective psyche that, under the *Mugumo* and facing Mt Kenya, they can commune with God at any time by praying to him.

The idea of tying religious understanding to physical objects that symbolize people's religious understanding and hold 'the tribe's psyche' as the elder puts it, is important to Africans in general. It is this religious culture that suffered immensely at the hands of the Europeans missionaries.

To the missionaries this was sheer idolatry. Here I recall Jennings critique on the missionary's approach to evangelization:

> Rather than the possibility of a new identity rooted in the resurrected Son of God, an identity that draws definition from our cultural realities yet is determined by a new reality of love and belonging, colonialist new identity meant unrelenting assimilation and the enfolding of lives and cultural practices inside processes of commodification.[80]

The story of the *Mugumo* tree is important to us in even a more fundamental way. As Jennings points out, we live in a world whose social imagination is increasing conditioned by economically determined spatial strictures — the result is isolation even for people who live within close proximity, a discernable feature in the West and one that is quickly growing in Africa especially in the urban centers. Such commodification of people remains a barrier to real and meaningful joining of people, entrenching further the woes of the race. How would an identity with nature such as the *mugumo* tree open new ways of joining of people away from commodification?

---

80. Jennings, *Christian Imagination*, 292.

Back to the idea of taboos, the story of the *mugumo* trees confirms how taboos on sexuality and other areas of life continue to condition people's behavior both positively and negatively. As I have demonstrated with the story of the *mugumo* tree, taboos are common in all African traditions. There are taboos associated virtually with all different aspects of life in Africa. For example, John Mbiti enumerates a number of taboos that are associated with child birth. He says that, "in many African societies the pregnant woman must observe certain taboos and regulation, partly because pregnancy in effect makes the mother ritually 'impure' and chiefly in order to protect her and the child."[81] Mbiti mentions a few of such taboos; abstinence from sex for a period of time in the duration of the pregnancy and after the child birth, abstention from certain foods which are feared to interfere with the health and the safety of the mother and child just to mention a few. Among the Agikuyu and Akamba for example, Mbiti says all weapons and iron articles must be removed from the house of the expectant woman before she gives birth. In other communities there are regulations on whom a mother can or can't interact with during the period of pregnancy.

Taboos are not observed by mothers only. During circumcision, the sponsor of the initiates, who is called *Baba Mŭndiri*, or a mentor father stays with the initiates and advises them on matters of life and ensures high hygiene for quick recovery. The sponsor is supposed to live with the initiates and abstain from sex during the period of recovery.[82] The bond of relationship between the candidate and the sponsor lasts for life.

For all other purposes, taboos teach the idea of restraint and boundaries especially to the young people. They help people to know that there are limits to life and that at least they should think twice before acting. This does not in any way suggests a fear to venture and innovate. It simply says man must cooperate with God in exploiting creation and any

---

81. Mbiti, *Religion and Philosophy*, 111-12.
82. Oral interview, Stephen Ndùng'ù and Jesse Njùgùna, November, 12, 2015.

action that is injurious to rules of nature and universal morality is detrimental to the very existence of man. Taboos are similar to the Hebrew dietary laws, and the laws of the "clean and the unclean thing." Restraint is an important discipline today especially where the young indulge in all kinds of orgies with subdued self-control.

Borrowing from the Agĩkũyũ customs, the Akũrinũ have a variety of taboos and regulations that regulate their lives. They adopted wearing of turbans, white robes and observed laws of purity and impurity derived from the Pentateuch but reinforced by Agikuyu traditions.[83] In this argument taboos then become important tools in the life of a Christian aiding in discipleship rather than a tradition that should be done away with. In particular the seriousness with which the taboos were viewed should aid our understanding of the seriousness of sin and in seeking for forgiveness. In most cases breaking a taboo was viewed with ostracism. It called for a sacrifice and even restitution. Likewise, forgiveness for humanity called for the death of the Lamb of God. Following this logic, I argue that in seeking for forgiveness after we have come to Christ should not really replace the idea of taboos, in which case forgiveness would just become "cheap grace" that makes no difference in real life.

The Possible Sources of the *Akũrinũ* Vernacular Theology

As earlier stated, *Akũrinũ* Church was unique in its inception. Certain individual prophetic figures were led by the Holy Spirit to found the movement. These early founders were often people of little education or none at all. Where they derived their theology from is significant. Although authors like Ogbo Kalu suggest that the *Akũrinũ* Church had contact and therefore influence from the Azusa Street Pentecostalism

---

83. Mwaura, "Africa Instituted Churches," 168.

that emerged at the beginning of the 20th Century, this research has demonstrated that this is not so.[84] The earlier founders had no contact with other Pentecostal movements.

Their theology is therefore significant to theologians and church leaders because it lends credence to the fact that the church can be rooted in any culture. The Lord himself has said, I will build my church and the gates of hell will not prevail against it. Through diverse sources of revelation and the guidance of the Holy Spirit, the Akũrinũ church fathers founded an authentic African church that has continued to be perhaps the only church for many people in central Kenya, Rift Valley and parts of Meru, and one that exhibits a truly authentic African spirituality.

Nyamiti says that the sources of African theology are both the Christian sources which he describes as both the Bible and the tradition i.e. biblical teaching as officially proclaimed by the teaching authority of the church, and as found in the faith and life of the entire people of God (the Church). The second source is the African socio-cultural situation seen both in the relation to the past, present and future, which form the non-Christian source of African theology. This implies that any cultural item (traditional or modern), any historical event in Africa, any science, any pastoral activity can and should be made to contribute to the building up of African theology.[85] In delineating the Akũrinũ theology, it is this second source that I will focus on, namely the Agĩkũyũ cultural, the socio-political and socio-cultural situation surrounding the founding of the Akũrinũ Church a period as already mentioned before located around the beginning of the 20th Century.

From our research, it is plausible that the Akũrinũ vernacular theology can be traced from a variety of sources chief of which include Agĩkũyũ traditional culture, the socio-political encounter of the Agĩkũyũ and the

---

84. Kalu, *African Christianity*, 56.

85. Charles Nyamiti, *Jesus Christ, the Ancestor of Humanity: Methodology and Trinitarian Foundations*, Vol. 1 (Nairobi, Kenya: CUEA Publications, 2005), 7.

European colonialist and missionaries, the Bible, the Akũrinũ hymnal, the Mt. Kenya Charter, and the Akũrinũ church tradition from the interaction of the Akũrinũ founders and the historical or missionary churches. In this section I shall attempt to demonstrate how each of these suggested sources has helped in the shaping of the Akũrinũ vernacular theology.

From our findings, it is clear that the Akũrinũ theology draws a lot from the Agĩkũyũ traditional culture. Kiarie had this to say on this: All African faiths are based on African cultural beliefs and practices, and this includes Akũrinũ's. This is why it is difficult to adopt concepts like homosexuality among African cultures. However other churches (by this he meant the historical or missionary denominations) adopted the white man's way of doing things but they still have the cultural link to their God. What the Holy Spirit revealed to the founder of the Akũrinũ to do was just an extension of the Gĩkũyũ belief in Mwene Nyaga who they believed lived in Mt. Kenya. Adopting the Bible was also easy because of its similarities with the Gĩkũyũ faith, such as in the aspect of sacrificing to God.[86]

Kiarie gives an example of this borrowing; The Agĩkũyũ could not eat meat from just anybody. In the Agĩkũyũ culture the father or the eldest son in the family slaughtered an animal for meat. Its different parts were reserved for different genders and age groups. Today the Akũrinũ can only eat meat that they themselves have slaughtered. Here again we see a practice that has been borrowed from the culture and integrated in the Akũrinũ ecclesiology. It is not difficult to see the logic. Given the Akũrinũ's particularity with the issue of blood and other dietary law and the "clean and unclean" teaching that goes with these, the Akũrinũ may not trust any meat whose method of slaughter they cannot verify.

Our concern is the way a cultural practice can be so integrated into an ecclesiological practice without any visible attempt to reflect on its source, almost akin to mixing cultural beliefs and biblical teaching. This

---

86. Oral interview, Dr. Kiarie Mburu, March, 5, 2016.

in itself is not a challenge except when the practice conflicts with the teaching of Scripture. But again, we see a great value, namely; when an ecclesiology practice draws its value in culture, it can expect maximum conformity from the believers. This can be contrasted with practices that are borrowed from other cultures and now integrated in local theologies. A good example is the concept of a wedding gown, the ritual of a wearing a wedding ring and cutting of a wedding cake, all which are concepts from West adopted without biblical warranty. The *Akūrinū* have found it difficult to accept such practices. This has put them at odds with other denominations.

Kiarie maintains that the same God who spoke to the *Agīkūyū* is the same one who spoke to the *Akūrinū*. However, *Akūrinū* abolish some traditions from the *Agīkūyū* culture such as *muuma* (taking of oaths) which involved blood. Kiarie concludes that *Akūrinū* borrowed a lot from the *Agīkūyū* culture, and as a result their faith is within their culture unlike the other missionary churches' religions which disregarded African cultures. Kiarie adds that nothing has been able to bring down *Akūrinū* culture. The informer concludes that it is good to embrace one's cultural way of life for the sake of having an identity. In this research I have endeavored to demonstrate that culture is a signifer of identity.

This attitude is evident among other African writers. Healey Joseph says that whereas African Christian theology is not the same as ATR, it draws from the sources and materials of African Traditional Religion such as religious values, beliefs and practices which derive from the religious systems of people in Africa who are not Christians, for constructing an African Christian Theology, adding that Africa's rich religious and cultural heritage is truly a place of God's revelation today. God is communicating to people in Africa today through African cultures and traditions in the context of contemporary social, economic and political events.[87]

---

87. Joseph Healey and Donald Sybertz, *Towards an African Narrative Theology* (Nairobi, Kenya: Paulines Publication Africa, 1996).

The Socio-Political and Socio-Economic Encounter of the *Agĩkũyũ* and the European Colonialist and Missionaries

I have demonstrated how the interruption of the European colonialists and the missionaries interrupted the socio-political and the socio-economic life of the *Agĩkũyũ*. The colonialist settlers took the prime land, "the white highlands" and reduced the natives to squatters or laborers in their own land. The colonial administration also employed young people of dubious backgrounds as chiefs and home guards as the new administrators, in place of the traditional elders who were the custodian of the *Agĩkũyũ* leadership. The requirement for every male to carry an identity, *kipande*, to police them made the people feel caged like animals in their own country, curtailing their freedom. The introduction of taxation, cash crops such as coffee, all introduced new economic trends that often reduced the people to servitude and resulted to poverty and eroded their dignity.

The missionaries preached against clictoridectomy and other traditional dances as barbaric and incompatible with Christianity. The missionary's education took away the young people from the community setting and estranged them from their customs. As a result, the community was divided. Some saw the value of education while others abhorred the cultural erosion. In the end many started their own schools where they could practice both Christianity and academics without the erosion of their culture.

Positively the western education and the exposure that it brought to the people especially the experience gained by many who were conscripted in the first and Second World Wars as carrier corps and soldiers exposed the weakness of the white man who had been hitherto thought as invincible. When eventually *Agĩkũyũ* took harms against the colonial rule, the exposure and the education became the nemesis for the colonialist.

In all this, either the natives gained or lost, while their socio-economic and socio-political life was changed for better or worse. The Akũrinũ faith is a reflection of this social change. Their current stance against medical science and many other practices whose origin is the western culture can be traced to this encounter. I have demonstrated how the Akũrinũ feared that the missionaries were out to poison them the way the Egyptians attempted to eliminate the Hebrew boys. Long after the western threat has ceased, the stance against medical science has become an ecclesiastical and theological concern.

Politically, the Akũrinũ were sympathetic to the Mau Mau fighters. Though their faith could not allow them to take arms, nevertheless they prayed and even acted as prophetic guides to the fighters. Rev. Kamau puts it this way; "We highly participated (he himself was not even born during the Mau Mau uprising but he regards himself as part of the Akũrinũ elders who were alive them) in the fight against colonization as we informed the Mau Mau what God would reveal to us.[88] In this way one can say they participated in the freedom fight. But their pacific approach has remained to date. They prefer to pray for the government of the day always seeking God's will in matters political and never assuming the place of activism and political involvement. This has meant that they are rarely involved in the affairs of governance something that is very much to their disadvantage.

The Bible plays a central role in Akũrinũ church. Nahashon Ndung'u says that the Akũrinũ Church started in 1927 soon after the translation of the Bible to Gĩkũyũ language (New Testament in 1926 and the whole Bible in 1951). It is reported that the early founders of Akũrinũ church spent long periods of time studying the Bible. For example, Joseph Ng'ang'a is said to have studied the Bible for three years between 1927-1930 in seclusion. Joseph Mung'ara spent a year in a store studying the Bible. The two became the Akũrinũ founders and evangelists. Ndung'u

---

88. Oral interview, Rev. Timothy Kamau, November, 13, 2015.

further says that based on early account of the founding of the Akũrinũ Church, I conclude that it was the availability of the Bible in the Gĩkũyũ language which made it possible for these people some of whom were semi-literate, to read and interpret it to others even though they had no theological training.[89]

Thus, the Akũrinũ founders and elders turned to the Bible whenever they wanted to settle any doctrinal matter. After reading the Bible they were able to distinguish between the demands of the missionaries and what could be supported purely from the Bible. In this way they even found a biblical defense for their customs. Since they did not want to imitate the mission churches, they turned to the Bible from where they identified the teaching and practices which are observed to the present. The following practices offer an illustration;

i. Keeping of uncut hair and beard — Num. 6: 6-7, 1Sam 1:11-13
ii. Restriction from wearing red clothes — Deut 27: 26
iii. Removal of shoes in Church — Ex 3: 4-7
iv. Ritual uncleanliness after child delivery — Lev 12: 1-8
v. Rejection of modern medicine — Jer 46: 11-12. Hos 55:13-14
vi. Wearing white robes and turbans — Lev 8: 9 — 14
vii. Rising of hands in prayer — 1King 8: 22-23, 1Tim 2: 8-8[90].

Here I note as discussed earlier in this research, that the Akũrinũ hermeneutics can be described as simply literal. Without a systematic way of interpreting the scriptures, many splinter groups arose all holding a skewed view of a certain passage of Scriptures and often in total disregard of the harmony of the Bible.

---

89. A more complete article on the use of the Bible by the Akurinu Church can be read in the book by Kinoti W. Hannah and J.M. Waliggo, eds., *The Bible in African Christianity: Essays in Biblical Theology* (Nairobi: Acton, 1997). See also in the same volume, Nahason Ndung'u's "The Bible in an African Independent Church," 61.

90. Ibid., 61.

Another important observation is that the Old Testament is really the book of the Akũrinũ, an observation that is true to most of the African believers to date. Along with other AICs, Akũrinũ can be grouped among Hebraic Churches that Alward Shorter says are strongly influenced by the Old Testament.[91] This does not in any way suggest that they do not read or believe in the New Testament. It only suggests that they easily identify with the Old Testament whose beliefs were closer to the ATR. Alward says that the Bible played an important role in the development of the AICs as this enabled them to discover the discrepancies between the Bible text and the practice of the mainline Church.

The Bible plays even a greater role to the Akũrinũ. It is the plumb-line by which all teachings, practices, and prophesies are measured.[92] The Bible is the ultimate authority in doctrinal formulation. The respect that the Bible holds for the Akũrinũ is captured in one of their hymns, *Mbuku ya Ngai ni itheru*, the Word of God is Holy. To the Akũrinũ Church the whole Bible is the Word of God, *Ibuku ria Ngai*. In particular the Ten Commandments play a significant role in the Akũrinũ faith. Macharia says at the inception of the Akũrinũ movement, the commandments were read before the commencement of any Sunday service. The Akũrinũ believed that the law is the foundation of the gospel and the teaching and the key to the kingdom of God — a deep theological understanding indeed.

Also, key Scriptures such as Isaiah 58 are so important to the Akũrinũ. This certainly speaks to the kind of changing socio-political circumstance that the Akũrinũ found themselves at the inception of their church in the hands of the colonial government and missionary churches. The Bible was a liberating tool. The passages that talk about deliverance, healing, and eschatology such as Isaiah 58, became very popular. Again, this is because the Akũrinũ believe that the Bible is the absolute Word of God and as such it can be trusted completely.

---

91. Shorter and Njiru, *New Religious Movements*, 15.
92. Macharia, *Identity*, 3.

The *Akũrinũ* believers are not only committed to read the Bible and live by it, they also strongly believe that they have been called to interpret it and teach it to others. They in particular believed that the missionaries distorted it and that they were called to correct this distortion. Kenyatta says,

> The members of this religious sect believe strongly that they are the chosen people of God to give and interpret his message [that is the Bible — this is how important the Bible is to them] to the people. They proclaim that they belong to the lost tribe of Israel. [93]

Though some members cannot read the Bible they have memorized some portions (and much more as hymns which I have said are basically Bible quotations). When they share their testimony in the church, they support this by asking someone in the congregation to read the verses that they have committed to memory, further demonstrating the authority the Bible is to their faith.

The *Akũrinũ* hymnal as elaborated in the next section should be seen as an extension of the reading of the Bible as I will explain. Negatively, the *Akũrinũ* seem to use the Bible in a mystical way on some occasions. For example, I observed when they pray for people, they lay the Bible on the head of the individuals being prayed for. This may be derived from the traditional culture where amulets or other objects were used as part of the worship as opposed to traditional Christian views that the Bible must be read, understood and obeyed.

In contrast, hymns form a very significant part of *Akũrinũ* liturgy. One may safely say that actually the *Akũrinũ* hymns carry their theology. The hymns are like their official creed. Macharia says this of the hymns, "they (*Akũrinũ*) believe that it is a sacrifice they are offering to God (i.e. when they sing) and therefore does it from deep down their spirit. Macharia adds that the hymns form a vital element of the *Akũrinũ* community

---

93. Kenyatta, *Facing Mt. Kenya*, 264.

worship and the blueprint in which their theology is entrenched.[94] The collection (hymns), entrenched in Scriptures has for a long time served as a biblical educational tool among the *Akũrinũ*. Other than the Bible, much of the *Akũrinũ* theology is encrypted in the *Akũrinũ* Hymn Book, *Nyimbo Cia Roho Mutheru*. This has for decades been the theological blueprint on which is embedded the values and doctrines of the community.

The *Akũrinũ* tell of the origin of their hymn book, one of our informants Macharia explains that originally the hymns were revealed to Henry Maina of Ihiga-ini in Murang'a, one of the four *Aroti* on 'The 1927 Mt. Kenya Retreat'. It is said that an angel informed Maina that he had been given special gift of writing, collecting and teaching hymns through the Holy Spirit. The revealed hymns remained in oral form until Daudi Ikugu published them in 1977. Ikugu lived a life of purity and chastity until his death.

The *Akũrinũ* have incorporated other hymn books in their liturgy. These included: The Golden Bells (translated to Kikuyu), *Nyimbo Cia Kiroho*, (the songs of the Holy Spirit), by Pentecostal Evangelistic Ministries, and *Nyimbo Cia Kũguma Maroho*, (Songs that Enrich the sprit) by the Full Gospel Churches of Kenya.

The hymns advance the objectives of the community such as unity and Christian fellowship. By committing these hymns to their memory, the *Akũrinũ* Church have availed to themselves a great theology that governs their lives. Although many may not be able to read the Bible, hymns form a unique way of hiding the Word of God in their hearts. An example is here quoted;

---

94. Macharia, *Identity*, 117.

Oya rĩtwa riu ria Jesu we ũnyamarite,

Nĩrĩkũhoreragia, ũthĩĩ narĩo kũndũ guothe,

Nĩ riega ni riega o-mũno, o-mũno ma,

Matu-inĩ na gũkũ thĩ nĩ rĩega

Nĩ rĩega kũndo guothe,

Matu-inĩ na gũkũ thĩ

> (Take the name of Jesus,
>
> You who labor,
>
> It will comfort you wherever you will go
>
> The name is good...it is good,
>
> From heaven above and here on earth.)

Macharia says that there are different hymns for different occasions; hymns for praise, for morning, for worship, for evening, for ceremonies etc.[95] What is clear is that passing vital information through song and music is very much an African characteristic, the equivalent of perhaps of a newspaper to the West. This is in line with the oral culture that Africans are and their poetic nature.

In our visit to the *Akũrinũ* churches, I witnessed first-hand how music forms a very important educational tool. Their hymns are rich in theology. That the *Akũrinũ* claim inspiration of these songs by the Holy Spirit elevates them to a respected position as authoritative sources of theology. The hymns are interchanged with preaching. Whenever the members rise to share their testimonies, they back it up with a hymn with the rest of the members joining in the singing. Whenever members undergo low moments on their spirituality these hymns lift their spirits.

---

95. Macharia, *Identity*, 117.

Chapter three

The idea of hymns as a source of theology brings to the fore the question of how best the grounding of believers in theology should be done. The West is overly pre-occupied with right articulation of theology in precisely written creeds. The believer's depth of Christianity is judged by the grasp of these theological statements. The Akũrinũ on their part learn their theology through the hymns that they have committed to memory and which they sing all the time whether in church or outside. In the end, the church in Africa must rethink the best method of grounding its members in theology.

Any method that is close to the African psyche such as music and dance may prove more profitable than the inculcation of doctrinal issues through right articulation of these truths in the western epistemology couched in the writings of theological *gurus*. Systematic articulation of theology may still be valuable but perhaps for the clergy. The Akũrinũ experience suggests the test of theology should not be based on the mental assent and right articulation of theological statements but rather on the quality of the Christian life lived by the believer being informed by a spiritual formation that is based on the right theology. The strongest defense of faith is not apologetics but obedience of the Word of God by the Church.

The Akũrinũ hymnal is a challenge to other Pentecostal Churches especially the neo-Pentecostal type in another way. In some of these churches, much time is spent in singing western music, but the lyrics of the songs are often poor in content. Often a line from the Bible is taken out of its context and is repeated severally in the name of a song. Besides, songs originating from the West are also popular. Whereas such songs no doubt enrich the church, they cannot be compared to the deep Akũrinũ hymns with a deep African touch that resonates with the African reality. When such songs are sung, one observes a different participation from the congregation. Even the most rigid is moved to action in sync with the song.

Another important source of Akũrinũ theology is what has come to be referred to as the Mt. Kenya charter. Macharia reports that in 1927, a group of seven Akũrinũ leaders from Gathumuri in Limuru and Kandara in Murang'a were instructed to take a pilgrimage to Mt. Kenya to receive God's covenant. Among those in the pilgrimage were Jason Kanini, Henry Maina, Philip M'Mkubwa and a lady called Lilian Njeri. On their way they passed by the home of Joseph Ng'ang'a in Gatundu who prayed for them. It is said that the team stayed in the mountain for approximately two months praying and the angel of God was there to minister to them, including giving them food to eat.[96]

Macharia also reports that on the way up the mountain, the Holy Spirit impressed upon Lilian, the only lady in the team to discard all her jewelry and any other traditional adornment that she had on. These included earrings (Nyori), necklaces (mĩgathe), bracelets (bangiri), and discarded them into river Nyamindi on the foot of Mt. Kenya. The group of Arathi was also instructed to consecrate themselves by washing their feet and hands with the waters of the river before going into the presence of God. Out of this encounter developed the practice of washing of feet before entering the place of worship among the early Akũrinũ churches. A basin of water would be placed at the entrance of Akũrinũ house of prayer. This traditional practice has been abandoned with time with leaders emphasizing more the washing of the heart by the blood of Jesus. However, the Akũrinũ women do not wear any jewelry. They do not even wear a wedding ring. This is one of the practices that keep worshippers from other denominations from joining them. However, the Akũrinũ deep piety attracts many people, as seekers of spiritual encounter and breakthrough. This has led some of the churches to abandon the rules of vestments and dress code. It is not uncommon these days to see members who do wear the Akũrinũ vestments attending the Akũrinũ Church.

---

96. Macharia. *Identity*, 117.

Up the mountain an angel of the Lord guided and fed the pilgrims. God entered into a covenant with the group of the *Arathi* on behalf of the nations and revealed to them great mysteries, one such being the "True Sanctuary" (*Kigongona*) which God had established for all the nations. They were given statutes that spelt out the discipline; conduct required of them and rules to govern the sanctuary[97]. It is reported that Henry Maina committed to write these revelations and statutes into a charter under the guidance of the Holy Spirit. History has it that Maina[98] handed down the original charter to Musa Thuo. It is said that the group of the *Arathi* disagreed on the instructions given, to which God declared that the revelations would not be revealed to anyone until the group came to consensus. The original charter is said to be hidden in a house in Kaguthi in the church that Musa Thuo built. Outside this house is a swarm of bees that guard the place. Moses Ng'ang'a informed us that whenever anyone attempts to enter this house, he has met with a misfortune.[99]

The *Arathi* pilgrims were given instructions that touched on *Akũrinũ* vestments: the turban, (*kiremba*) which signifies the priesthood of the cross (*ũthĩnjĩri wa Mũtharaba*), instructions on how to conduct prayers, the white robe (*kanju*) which signifies the Aaronic priesthood, songs, among many other instructions.[100] The Mt. Kenya charter included many instructions. These and many others that were revealed to various *Akũrinũ* founders were compiled together by Joshua Ng'ang'a Kimani. They remain as authoritative sources of the *Akũrinũ* theology.[101] The songs especially those which came even before the Kikuyu Bible was

---

97. Macharia, *Identity*, 117.
98. Ibid.
99. Oral interview, Arch Bishop Moses Nga'ang'a, Mwangi, 28, March, 2016.
100. Macharia, *Identity*, 117.
101. A list of these rules is documented by David Peter Sandgren in his unpublished 1976University of Wisconsin in Madison Ph. D. dissertation. Sandgren had the opportunity of interviewing Kimani.

translated and widely circulated are held in high regard and they are in sync with the Bible.

The Church Tradition from the Interaction of the *Akũrinũ* Founders and the Historical or Missionary Church

I have credited the founding of the *Akũrinũ* church to Joseph Ng'ang'a and Moses Thuo. Joseph Ng'ang'a had received an elementary education at the Gospel Mission Station at Kambui. Though Ng'ang'a did not appear to have been faithful in the Christian teaching as it was presented by the mission until the encounter that brought him to faith and consequently to found the *Akũrinũ* movement, it would be plausible to imagine that he carried along with him some missionary influence which was at the center of missionary education.

Moses Thuo, the other founder of *Akũrinũ* Church went to school at Githumu African Inland Mission (AIM) where he attained a fourth-grade education and could certainly read and write in both *Gĩkũyũ*, Swahili and some English. At Githumu, Thuo became a Christian and was baptized before leaving the AIM along with other *Agĩkũyũ* who felt that the missionaries were hindering progress towards African leadership both in the affairs of the church and its schools. Thuo joined other independent church groups for example the one led by Daudi Maina Kĩragũ who had formed a Pentecostal fellowship in his home village.

Many who joined the *Akũrinũ* had experience in missionary churches and AICs. They brought along with them such church traditions they had acquired in their Christian experience. This integration of different church traditions is discernable in many independent churches. For example, the African Independent Pentecostal Church of Africa (AIPCA) which I occasionally personally attended as a child observed many Roman Catholic practices such as the use of candles, burning incense, among others in her ecclesiology. The Legio Maria, a Church started by Gaudecia Aoko, as a splinter from the Roman Catholic Church is a mixture of Luo, and Roman Catholic traditions such as observance of the saints in prayer.

The point that is being encouraged is that no church tradition is completely independent of other Church communions. This is true of the Akũrinũ. The practices of the Akũrinũ are particularly reflected in their western Kenya counterparts in the Roho Churches and many Pentecostal movements in Central Kenya.

Conclusion

In this chapter, I have distilled some of the Akũrinũ vernacular theology. The dominant themes include the pursuit of moral purity, joyful worship music and dance, careful attention and respect of the teachings of Scripture, their Spirit led lives, and their millennial focus — all based on their roots in Agĩkũyũ traditional culture and their reading of the Bible. In the next chapter I will propose what these themes contribute to global theology.

CHAPTER FOUR

AKŪRINŪ VERNACULAR THEOLOGY AND IT'S CONTRIBUTION TO GLOBAL THEOLOGY

As I stated earlier, if we seek the possible contributing of Akũrinũ Church to the global theology, one may have to examine the type of worship, organization, and community life that these churches have developed. Githieya says that these elements are rooted both in biblical Christianity and African cultures and are considered of indigenous African contribution to Christianity which in our study I would consider as a contribution to global theology. To this I add that these elements may point to a unique Africa spirituality, a subject that I will consider briefly.

Africans' Unique Spirituality

Akũrinũ vernacular theology points to a unique African spirituality. Orobator E. Agbonkhianmeghe says this of the African spirituality: This spirituality is based on the deep religiosity that is discernable among the African people. Orobator observes rightly that anyone coming to Africa for the first time cannot fail to notice the strong and profound sense of the divine that pervades the ordinary lives of many Africans. The awareness of the divine is so strong that you can see, hear, feel, and touch it in the way people talk, behave, even worship, sing and dance.

Orobator says that the African universe is charged with a palpable spiritual energy, an energy that comes from faith in the existence of many spiritual realities: gods, goddesses, deities, ancestral spirits and so on. African spirituality draws on the energy that comes from this awareness that the human being is not alone in the universe; the universe delineates a shared space between creatures and their creator.[1]

Orobator states further "that African spirituality is characterized by the awareness of the divine presence, an awareness that is consciously fostered and developed through African religion and culture. In African spirituality, the existence of God is more important than the theology or discourse about God."[2] What Orobator is saying here is that the existence of God is assumed and nobody in African tradition tries to prove His existence. Another shared unique African spirituality is the experience of God as the Supreme Being. This experience also offers another character of the African spirituality namely, a unique way of worshipping God. There is no uniform way of worship but diversity. People worship God as they encounter His presence resounding in the hills and the caves.[3]

In Africa, Orobator reminds us, spirituality is practical — experience is more important that theory. Religion takes place in daily and public affair as a very powerful sense of the divine permeates the lives of Africans. In this regard, even eating is a religious experience. God is encountered everywhere and in every activity. God is part of every activity on earth. Living is a discovery of the reality of God's existence that is already present in the realities of our lives.[4]

---

1. Agbonkhianmeghe E. Orobator, *Theology Brewed in an African Pot: An Introduction to Christian Doctrine from an African Perspective* (Nairobi, Kenya: Paulines Publications, 2008).
2. Ibid., 22.
3. Ibid., 141.
4. Ibid., 142

African spirituality derives from the African understanding of life i.e. African spirituality is a spirituality of life, a celebration of life in all its dimensions. The goal and aim of human life are life in its fullness. Thus, all religious celebrations center on life; to protect it from harm, celebrate it as a gift, strengthen, or prolong it in the community.

Another spirituality in Africa is that environment is often protected as a matter of life — this explains the existence of many sacred trees, forests, rocks, mountains, springs, and animals whose existence is linked to the survival of the community. These are considered as the abode or messengers of God. Africans also believe that nature is sacred and holds the cure for many illnesses. This explains why herbal medicine is thriving as an alternative to conventional medicine. Silently, this means in African conservation of the environment was inbuilt with the wellbeing of the community being more important than an individual self-gain.

Another aspect of African spirituality is that of justice, peace and reconciliation. I have already mentioned that the *Agĩkũyũ* had a great sense of justice, *kihooto*. Although there were no written records of transaction, fraud was less prevalence. Once a matter was witnessed, it was sealed. The elders witnessed such transactions as land, dowry. All this was possible because of an inbuilt high sense of justice. Many taboos also restrained people from mischief because of the fear of consequences. This can be said of many other African communities. African spirituality can also be seen in the emphasis of community living and relationships. Relationships in particular are important to Africans. An African would rather be late for a meeting than bypass fellow friends and not exchange pleasantries. Africans also love to celebrate and express their faith in dance and song.

Lastly and most importantly African spirituality is a quest for power. This has found a most cherished expression amongst the African Christians. Okorocha says that African Christians' quest for power is not for the sake of power. It is an over-riding concern for spiritual power from a mighty God to overcome all enemies and evils that threaten human life and vitality.[5]

All these characteristics predate Christianity. Thus, what is new in Africa is Christianity not spirituality. Long before the coming of the missionaries, Africans had developed their ways of expressing and celebrating their experience of God. Such ways included priests and priestesses, prayers and forms of worship, shrines and sacred places, taboos and respect for the ancestors. African spirituality stems from the African primal religions. As Andrew Walls informs us, Christianity is subsequent and represents a second thought of this primal way of things.[6]

The *Akũrinũ* theology is based on many aspects of this African spirituality, a spirituality whose many practices find semblance in the O.T. practices which affirms its place in theological articulation. This theology that sees the whole of life in a spiritual sense is a good challenge to the dualistic western theologies that dichotomizes the world into sacred and secular spheres that displaces God in many aspects of human experience with humanism.

From the foregoing argument, I suggest that *Akũrinũ* vernacular theology brings to the world the idea of a shared approach to theological discourse, ethics and morality that is hinged on culture.

A Shared Approach to Theological Reflection

As I have amply demonstrated, *Akũrinũ* theology is not based on individual findings or efforts. There is no reference to single individual theological figures like in western theology. The whole community of

---

5. For further reading see Okorocha, *Religious Conversion*, and Harold W. Turner, 'Contribution of Studies on Religion in Africa to Western Religious Studies,' in Glasswell and Fasholé-Luke (eds.), *New Testament for African Christianity and the World* (London: SPCK, 1974), 174.

6. Andrew F. Walls, *The Missionary Movement in Christian History* (New York: Orbis, 1996), 121.

faith is involved in defining their beliefs and practices. This does not in any way devalue the place of the founders — Much effort has been made to respect the leading of the Holy Spirit and the revelation that the founders expounded.

The Akũrinũ theology can enlighten the global theology on the dangers of focusing theology on individuals. In the western world one person is often credited with how a particular theological movement flow. This has many advantages. One finds that throughout the history of the redemption story, God's move has greatly been impacted by the great discipline and devotion of individuals. This can be said of Abraham, Moses, Joseph, Daniel and others. It is the same with God's dealing with is His people outside the Biblical history. From St. Augustine, to Martin Luther and John Calvin, to Karl Barth and all other great voices of theology, an individual has always championed the movement of God. Such individuals and their writings become a point of reference and beacons in theological development.

This individual focus for the move of God may not be observable in the same intensity in the Akũrinũ church as in the West. Whereas one cannot underrate the contribution of Akũrinũ founders like Joseph Ng'ang'a and Musa Thuo and even the hymn writer, David Ikigu, the Akũrinũ theology is not simply an expression of such individuals. Other than Ikigu who wrote the Akũrinũ hymnals, the rest left behind no written record of their theological stand. Yet the Church movement they founded lives on. In other words, Akũrinũ church is not founded on written treatises. There are few documents like the legal statutory statements in the office of the Registrar of Societies which act as the constitution of the movement and also what has been referred to as the Mt. Kenya Charter. But these are too few and too scanty to base a viable movement on. The question that then comes to mind is how then is the Akũrinũ theology passed from one generation to another and yet retaining many of its fundamental features?

A few pointers from the *Agĩkũyũ* culture may explain this. These include a strong narrative culture that commits issues to memory, the fear of taboos, and especially, the gradation of eldership. We will single out the gradation of eldership as a clear pointer to the continuity of the *Akũrinũ* church. As I have demonstrated in the earlier chapters; the elders are the custodians of all matters of culture and practice. Their services are sought especially during the crisis points of life. Once while conducting a funeral, the *Agĩkũyũ* elders informed me that the body of the dead man must face the sunset. The women and youth were least concerned but obliging. It was the same when I recently buried my father (My Ameru culture is related to the *Agĩkũyũ* culture). The elders said that an elder like my father must be buried in a prominent place near the gate and not far from the homestead and never behind the homestead. In the case of my father, he retains his respect in death and life and so are all elders among many African communities. These might be issues that one may consider lightly, but they hold meaning-making in organizing communities, and perhaps even a pecking order in the traditional communities.

Whenever a decision was needed in the *Agĩkũyũ* culture, the elders were consulted. The elders also understood themselves as the custodians of the beliefs and hence the wellbeing of the community. In this regard, and being greatly selfless, they worked for the welfare of the community. The elders were therefore highly trusted; a saying in Kiswahili says, "*palipo na wazee, hapaharibiki neno*," meaning "wherever there are elders, nothing goes wrong." Again, the elders do not work as individuals but as a kind of council, *kiama*, allowing consultation in all matters. In this way they are able to carry forward the wisdom of the community from generation to generation.

The cultural way of recognizing and appointing leadership through various gradations is discernable in the *Akũrinũ* church just like in the *Agĩkũyũ* leadership. The *Akũrinũ* elders carry forward the deposit of faith entrusted to their care with great reverence. These elders, chief of who are the bishops and the Archbishops devote themselves exclusively to pray for the wellbeing of their Church movement. Induction to eldership is taken seriously. Voting is never encouraged. Archbishop Ng'ang'a informed us that before leaders are conferred leadership responsibilities, the elders spend days and nights in much prayer and reflection.

In such sessions the discernment of the Holy Spirit is sought. Any misconduct of the leaders is severely dealt with.[7] The leaders, just as in their traditional culture, are not paid for their services. And since there is no direct benefit, only the very devoted sign up. These leaders are never novices but those who have been graded through various levels of eldership and mentorship and for a long time. In modern language we can describe the elders as the opinion leaders of their Church and community and indeed this is what they are.

The Akũrinũ leadership procedure is comparable to the Bible. Paul instructed Timothy not to lay hands on any one quickly, least of all a novice, only limiting leadership responsibility to the tested and proven. Many of the challenges of the African church and elsewhere would be avoided if the selection to the leadership was more guarded. Key to leadership is mentorship. I find Joshua serving under Moses for 40 long years before taking over from him. Samuel was mentored by Eli for many years before becoming a judge, a prophet and a priest for the nation of Israel. He in turn mentored King Saul and David for a long time.

Jesus lived with his disciples for three years before conferring apostolic ministry to them. Judas was replaced by Mathias who had been with the apostolic band from its inception. Peter mentored John Mark. Barnabas mentored Paul who in turn led Timothy to Christ, became his mentor-father and circumcised him (talk of a case of a *Baba Mũndiri wa Kiroho* as in the *Akũrinũ* Church), went with him to many missionary journeys before charging him directly with the responsibility of the ministry in Ephesus. The same can be said of Titus and Onesmus. In all these cases

---

7. Oral interview, Arch Bishop Moses Nga'ang'a, Mwangi, 28, March, 2016.

a passing on and a transfer of a leader's heart and what Paul calls "his manner of life," and not just a transfer of an office and change of guard, is in the focus. One of today's pitfalls of leadership whether in its democratization or spiritualization is the disconnect that happens between the incoming and the incumbent especially when the vote determines who holds the leadership office. In such arrangement, continuity is greatly undermined. The Akũrinũ elders are the custodians of faith and practice. This responsibility is not vested on an individual.

The Akũrinũ theology is based on the community of faith rather than the efforts of individual theologians like in the West. In a sense this empowers every child of God to be a complete entity respected and valued before God not for their achievement but for their faith in God. Everyone's faith contribution is valued, and everyone's burden is the burden of the community. In the Akũrinũ theology, the goal of faith is not to champion a new or even esoteric knowledge but to conform to what has been tested by the community of faith being handed down through the generations.

As I have mentioned, this has a great implication for leadership succession. The Akũrinũ elders take time to discern the next leader. They build a consensus through the guidance of the Holy Spirit. In the West and especially in some of the charismatic movement as well as in Africa with some of their Neo-Pentecostal movement, the church is the property of the founder. Small wonder some of these founders are so rich that they own private jets, a missiological mismatch indeed. Imagine such a near-sighted missiological vision in a world where only 30% of the population has been reached with the gospel, and where many more people sleep hungry and die of the simplest ailment? This is most painful in my country because the coffers to these church founders' kingly lifestyles are the poor, the "mama mboga," a term that refers to the women who sell or hawk vegetables on the road side unable even to afford a store, who hope to improve their lot after the admonition of their leaders who never tire to remind them that they too were once as poor.

Like in the West this personal ministry is eventually bequeathed to the wife or the son of the founder often with a disastrous ending. And in all this approach the founders are never questioned — having elevated themselves to a defied position — a recipe for divisions where the upcoming leaders in these churches feeling sidelined, in rebellion form their own churches so as to control the resources that they have been denied and as it may be expected, unfortunately continue to perpetuate the same legacy, having never learnt a different approach.

The Akũrinũ shared theology and leadership has no space for individual leader's excesses. This ensures cohesive and continuity and much confidence on the leadership who take great care to attend to the welfare of each individual member. The most common slogan on the neo-Pentecostal movement in their preaching is, "it doesn't matter what you are going through, just give to the Lord," whereas in the Akũrinũ church, you can easily read on the faces of the leaders, "it matters to us what you are going through." This ability of the leaders to consider themselves at the same level as their members at the foot of the cross is based on the understanding that all of us are forgiven sinners who need God's grace on a daily basis, never outliving it just because of the trappings of the asymmetrical power or wealth that goes with a leadership position, an heritage that we neither see in Jesus who at death only owned a tunic, nor on his apostles all who died as martyrs for their faith, except John whose eyes were gorged at the Island Patmos.

Developing Culturally-Based Morality

Another contribution that the Akũrinũ theology can make to the global theology is in the area of developing morality for the modern Church. The degeneration of morality among the youth in Africa today is a major concern for governments, the schools and parents. Cases abound of students who have set their school on fire while frequent strikes in universities target innocent motorist often with fatalities and much loss of property. The police in Kenya can hardly cope with the rate of crime among the young people. Much of this is attributed to the high rate of unemployment, drug and substance abuse, broken family values, and the scapegoats are many.

Whereas none of these realities can be taken lightly, they still cannot adequately explain the proliferation of such criminality that is being witnessed in Nairobi and other major African cities. This book suggests that the moral breakdown being witnessed in African societies today is a reflection of a broken cultural injunction on moral values. The *Akũrinũ* vernacular theology based on the *Agĩkũyũ* cultures teaches us the value of learning and even borrowing from culture in doing theology and building a strong moral base for the society. Our argument is that once morality has been detached from cultural injunctions as it has happened in many African cultures with missionary Christianity and modernity undermining culture, the moral compass becomes *radar-less*.

The dialogue between biblical tradition and different human cultures is from antiquity. Flavius Josephus tells us that few non-Jewish civilizations can claim the biblical inheritance with as much justice as the civilization of Africa. It is in the land of Cush, and hence in Africa, that the Jewish literature places Moses' retreat in preparation for his vocation. Josephus says that Moses was initiated there in the native religion and married a woman of that country.[8] The Israelites lived in Africa for over four hundred years before going to Canaan carrying with them a great wealth of cultural assimilation from Egypt, such as architecture, embalming of the dead and above all the culture of writing. One can add that Jesus Christ found succor in Africa away from the brutality of

---

8. Father Engelbert Mveng S.J, *Christian and the Religious Culture*, quoted in Kenneth Y. Best, ed., *African Challenge* (Nairobi, Kenya: TransAfrica Publishers, 1975), 1.

Herod, and even a helping shoulder in his hour of need on his journey to Golgotha from the hands of an African from Cyrene.

I also add that God was pleased to use circumcision, a cultural practice that was not originally practiced by the Jews but the communities of Ancient Near East (ANE) as a seal of ownership and a sign of the covenant that God had made with the Jews. This is the learning from culture that the missionaries abused in their evangelization of Africa then, and presently by some of the western trained theologians — which must be disabused — when they found no dialogue partner in the African cultures in their evangelization enterprise.

Here I note that not all missionary efforts were completely opposed to any learning from the African cultures. The Roman Catholics, particularly coming from the idea of "points of insertion" in recipient culture, sought areas where they could hang the gospel. Mveng says this on such efforts; the instruction of the Congregation for the Preparation of the Faith in 1659 affirms that when bringing the gospel to pagans, the missionary must respect the work of the Holy Spirit who had for thousands of years already preceded the arrival of the envoys of the gospel.[9]

Cameroonian theologian Engelbert Mveng adds that:

> The missionaries who landed in Africa in the seventeenth, eighteenth and nineteenth centuries were sent by the Congregation for the Preparation of the Faith itself. They were therefore directly inspired by the doctrine of the Preparation of the Gospel, the doctrine of 'the points of insertion'. This doctrine was to give to extremely thorough investigations, which were to climax in the twentieth century with the establishment of a new theological discipline, that of missiology. This effort was particularly focused on the study of the local languages of Africa and the translation of the Bible.[10]

---

9. Ibid.
10. Ibid., 2.

Our argument is that morality should reflect people's religious experience and when it is removed from peoples' cultural experience it loses its compass.

Kinoti decries the morality of few affluence Africans that is breeding consumerism, materialism, greed for power, misuse and ostentation. She notes that on the other hand the result of poverty is hardness against moral injunction. Kinoti gives the example of the *Ik* people who occupy the *Kipendo* valley of north Eastern border of Uganda bordering Kenya and Sudan. When the government turned their land into a game park, and banned hunting, and settled the *Ik* people in villages to cultivate semi-arid deserts, the *Ik* people lost everything. They become highly individualistic with jungle survival tactics. The *Ik* cosmology told of how their God *Didigwari* lowered their first ancestor from his abode through a long vine and advised them to live by hunting and gathering. But when the men refused to give women meat, *Didigwari* become angry and cut the vine so that man could no longer climb back and reach him. *Didigwari* retreated far back into the skies.

The *Ik* knew that their moral laws were given by God. This is the culture that they passed to their children. But under the new arrangements, they were hardened against this morality. They told their children about it less and less until they told them no more. Poverty dehumanized them, as their moral base lost its anchor from this rich culture that placed God as the giver of morality.[11]

Morality is a question of right standing before society and God, placing it at the highest level of accountability, the Supreme Being. Like the *Ik* people many African communities knew that their morality was from God. And when morality was removed from this level of accountability and became a question of how best one behaved or failed to behave in

---

11. George Kinoti and Peter Kimuyu, eds., *Vision for a Bright Africa: Facing the Challenges of Development* (Kampala, Uganda: African Institute for Scientific Research and Development, 1997).

imitating the European, it became of secondary importance. Perhaps this may explain the current drift of morality to its lowest ebb that is being witnessed in many parts of Africa today.

One possible way of containing the run-away morality among African youth is to tie moral injunctions to culture. I peg this on the great conformity to culture that I find in Africa. A good example of this cultural conformity is circumcision. Among the communities where this is practiced there is a high rate of conformity. It is unimaginable how one can bypass this practice. There is not even a single parent – Christian or not, modern or postmodern, that would dare to advocate a deviation (except on the process on how this is done). As I have mentioned before among the Agĩkũyũ, circumcision was the way that men and women were qualified as full members of the society. Through this process the young people were taught the values of the community and boundaries were drawn. Deviants were ostracized by their entire age-set.

This rite remains one of the most important rites of passage for many African communities even among the urban elite. What is needed in the church today is for the church to take over this rite and redefine it in Christian terms while retaining its main important cultural value and incorporate it into the discipleship programs. It is more urgent because of the single mothers' crisis being experienced today especially in the urban population. Here single women feel most helpless to venture into a rite that is essentially masculine as their son's approach adolescence. They often look to the Church which has on the other hand been socialized to demonize it and place it in the category of the secular domain, one that the church does not need to be involved in, leaving it to individual families. Thankfully the Roman Catholic Church and our Akũrinũ Church have found a gem in the practice and are using it to ground morality for the youth in the postmodern-culture -confused world.

But the circumcision rite must be seen within the wider range of the values that other rites of passage portend. The rites of passage are basic to the African culture. Whereas much of other cultural practices have lost their value, the rites of passage are still highly respected. They are the most important milestones in the life of an African. Traditionally they were the points at which culture was taught and experienced in its fullest. The Church would do well to incorporate the rites of passage in her discipleship program.

The *Akũrinũ* is leading the way. At birth the *Akũrinũ* church takes great exception in the ritual cleansing of the mother, in dedicating the new born baby, in baptizing the baby and demanding a name that is given by the Holy Spirit, to which parents must seek God diligently to receive. All these constitute the earliest inception to discipleship. Compare this with the majority of the mainstream churches where the birth of the new born baby is the matter of the parents and at most the grand parents who demand to be named and more. I need to explain this more with two recent practical examples.

In the first example, I was called by my neighbor's workman to take their two-month, and six-year old children to the hospital with severe malaria. I really feared for their young lives. In my interaction with the couple, I found out that the family had been upcountry the previous week where the children contracted the disease. The reason — the grand parents had demanded to see the younger baby and do the traditional *Abaluya* head shaving. Clearly this family was so financially needy that the journey was an ordeal. Yet they had to comply or risk a curse. So, they obliged, and the baby was shaved, and ancestors were appeased. I asked whether they couldn't have waited for the baby to grow a little. I received no good answer except the fact that culture demands it and it has to be done. I wondered whether the pastor of the church that this couple attends is aware of the new born or even interested in the first place. The ritual performed is supposed to link the child to the ancestors. It is basically done to please them. As such it is not necessarily in the light of the Christian faith. Dedication to God through Christ the Supreme

Ancestor is all that is important. But with a church that is ambivalent to the all-important rites of passage, she has created a wide vacuum that the traditionalists are exploiting to the detriment of lives of the likes of my neighbor.

The second example is a case of false teeth that on rare cases children are born with. The false teeth are called *nguani* in my language. As far as my research has shown, no medical doctor ventures into the surgical removal of such. When I asked the medics why they do not operate on such children, they said that the condition does not fall under the category of conventional medicine. But they also admitted that there are certain cultural procedures that they recommend to the interested parents. If not removed, the babies become anemic and die sooner or later. The only viable option is a surgical removal by traditional experts. The traditional surgeons do this in what may be medically described as crude, but it works perfectly. The challenge is that many local pastors condemn the traditional cure just as they have been taught to condemn anything associated with traditional culture. In the confusion, the parents of such unfortunate babies face the option of going to the culture and risk being ostracized and possibly excommunicated from their church besides being the topic of preaching for next several months by their pastor, or watch their little ones face the inevitable death. In my ancestral village my neighbors were recently caught in this cross fire of culture and faith. They opted for faith as taught in their church and lost their child in the process. As far as my research goes, the process is purely a traditional medical process just like the traditional childbirth, one with no spiritual consequence and one that a Christian should not feel guilty participating in.

Here I recall Apostle Paul's instruction on food offered to idols and later sold in the market place. Paul disapproved the eating of the meat before the idol which would have meant participating in the worship of the spirit behind the idol but saw no reason why the same meat cannot be bought from the market and eaten since, 1 Corinthian 8:6 ...for us *there is* one God, the Father, of whom *are* all things, and we for Him; and one Lord Jesus Christ, through whom *are* all things, and through whom we *live*.

Why should the Christian faith condemn everything in culture even one that has such great medical value? What difference would the Church make if she began the discipleship of the new born at birth by taking over and redefining all the traditions that attend to a child birth? What incredible support and love does the *Akũrinũ* mother receive when the elders visit to cleanse her, and the church collectively prays to receive a name for the new born from the Holy Spirit?

The same can be said of the *Akũrinũ* church marriage process where again every young person knows that there is an accountability before the church; that the leaders will be concerned that the right marriage suitor is ensured, the marriage bed kept undefiled, the wedding ceremony is the church's affair and that even the young couple will come for ritual cleansing after the one month absence of honey moon, and every other time they get a new baby. The *Akũrinũ* church also having taken the circumcision rite from culture has incorporated it in her discipleship process as discussed earlier with the whole church involved. The same support is accorded at death when the bereaved family is so distraught. The *Akũrinũ* even appoints poll bearers and offers ready help whenever it is needed by the grieving family.

These are things that one may take for granted but which are making life much lighter for the *Akũrinũ* followers all because the Church has provided a way of support for all her members from womb to tomb without leaving the members to themselves at the crisis points of life, because they have taken their traditional culture seriously. All these helps give the community a moral focus and an ethic to live by. When people on the hand are left to their cultural practice alone without Christian faith reflection, much harm is done. Here I cite the case of wife inheritance among some communities in Kenya, where HIV Aid is having heyday, among other cultural practices.

All African communities like the case of the Ik people of Kipendo valley knew that their morality came from God. Such teaching was handed down from generation to generation through culture. When this meaning-making culture was replaced by colonial/missionary culture, peoples' moral compass was unhinged from the God who gives morality, to such references as the ability to read and write, speak the colonial language and general conformity to the new dominant culture. The new culture was particularly enforced through the missionary school system. The elders and the age — sets that governed morals were replaced by the police and the prisons, things that were foreign to Africans and which are incapable of containing the basal morality that is being witnessed all over Africa today.

Development of Authentic Ecclesiologies

Another important contribution of the Akũrinũ church contextual theology to the global Church is that it is possible to develop an ecclesiology that is based on traditional cultural systems. The particular Akũrinũ ecclesiology ensures that all the members have a sense of belonging by having their needs being shared by the church. This fosters a sense of unity in a world where not even the church is spared disunity. This suggests that a surer way of developing a cohesive and caring Christian community would do well to borrow from the existing culture to develop such ecclesial communities whether as disciple groups, support groups, peer groups, or mission groups that cut across the denomination barriers. Small churches can enhance their mission by uniting around their common cultural mooring in the light of Scripture. Mega churches can enhance their cohesiveness by organizing themselves into small fellowship groups or "cells" based on contextual theological understanding.

Contextual theologies are able to organize their communities to respond to their psycho-social, socio-economic, and socio-political needs where the organizing factor is the values that are derived from culture. Contextual theologies can help ease tensions in conflicting communities.

Contextual theologies can also contribute to regional ecumenical efforts; given that cultural values are common to the people they belong to. Although the Akũrinũ Church has divided into many independent entities, they are all united by certain characteristics in their common ecclesiologies based on their contextual theology.

The Akũrinũ's appreciation of the role of the Holy Spirit in their lives and their ecclesiology is fresh news in the current theological development that has not given pneumatology a similar emphasis with other theologies. Peace seeking, a strong desire for holy living, and life of worship all go to show that the Akũrinũ have truly encountered the third person of trinity. Their understanding may be limited and even sometimes exaggerated or skewed but there is no doubt that this Church movement can teach the global Church a few lessons on pneumatology.

The Akũrinũ's dalliance with the Holy Spirit speaks deeper into their quest to seek and receive guidance from God in their day to day lives. But again, the quest to seek guidance from the Holy Spirit is based on the Akũrinũ's determination to please God and do His will.

Akũrinũ's quest to seek guidance from the Holy Spirt in all matters of faith connotes a marked effort to live holy lives which cannot be seen in the same intensity in the historical Church. Consequently, social sciences seem to be competing with the Holy Spirit as the source of guide for the Church. Sensitivity to hear the voice of God is important in establishing Christians in discipleship.

Conclusion

The significance of AICs and in particular the *Akũrinũ* in this study is in their ability to fashion an ecclesiology and a theology that is authentic from their traditional cultures and their reflection of such practices from their understanding of their Christian faith. Although in this process they may not always arrive on the best way of life, they nevertheless call attention to the possibility of taking culture seriously in their way of life. In this way they have been able to engage and address issues of culture in a way that the historical churches are not doing.

I conclude that doing indigenous theology calls for a closer investigation of varieties of cultures. This in itself leads to a different way of understanding, away from the hegemony of dominant cultures of the West. Whereas 'contextual theologies' is fairly a recent phenomenon, having been lost after the early church to universalizing of western theology, it nevertheless portends a new possible way of understanding the Christian faith and thereby enrich the mission of the universal church.

The *Akũrinũ*'s contextual theology is significant to the global theology. In this chapter I have highlighted four lessons that the global church can learn from the *Akũrinũ*' namely; Sensitivity to the Holy Spirit, developing authentic ecclesiologies, a shared approach to theological reflection, and developing culturally based morality.

CHAPTER FIVE

Conclusion and Recommendations

In this research work we have endeavored to demonstrate how culture, as a way of life familiar to people and having been passed on from generation to generation, is critical in giving people a predictable life and in socializing them to be worthy members of their community. We have shown that people generally resent any forceful imposition of another culture, at the expense of their own. Where this has happened, it has displaced people who have lost their identity. Having lost confidence in themselves, their institutions, and even their personhood, they can easily fall for anything. When people lose their identity, they succumb to external value-setting that determines and directs their outlook to life. Such people seek validation and direction from anywhere or anybody who may claim to know the way; always playing catch up. This has certainly happened to many African communities.

In this scenario morality is particularly difficult to enforce once the parameters that judge moral values have been unhinged from peoples' familiar culture, and made to adapt to a new one that they do not fully understand or appreciate. Such people are neither comfortable within their culture nor at home in the new culture.

But this research has also demonstrated the value of religious culture to any people. We have shown that culture can be a source of dynamic Christian theology which is indispensable in developing contextual theologies. Such kind of theology responds to people's most important needs as it addresses the core of their being and thereby ensures that the people's worldview is transformed by the gospel.

Unfortunately, missionaries glossed over African religious culture and sought to introduce their own culture as they propagated the gospel. Africans accepted this initially, but with ambivalence. They accepted a thin veneer of Christianity in order to acquire the white man's magic - education. This kind of Christianity has found it hard to give answers to life's most important questions. This is because the African worldview was never fully addressed by the gospel when their culture was instead condemned and demonized by the missionary enterprise. Such Christians often resort to the African traditional culture to find answers especially during the crisis points of life. Many Africans therefore practice a kind of "schizophrenic Christianity" that oscillates between African traditional culture and Christian or rather biblical culture, leaving their faith rather shallow and at times syncretistic.

In contrast this research has presented the Akũrinũ church vernacular theology as one that has built upon the Agĩkũyũ culture, all the time seeking to place God within the new revelation sought from the Bible and revealed to their founding leaders. One that continued to be revealed through their prophetic figures through prophesies, auditions, visions, dreams, and even music and dance, all in the light of their communal reading of the Bible. As a result, the Akũrinũ Church has sought to fashion an Agĩkũyũ community in their Church ecclesiology; a tight knit and a caring community able to respond to each other's need because of being close to their culture.

Our musing over the matter of culture is informed by the havoc that the inverted hospitality that Jennings describes continues to play in Africa to this day. In particular, the West continues to advocate a reasonable cultural (read western) theology or a rational ordered universal theology. This theology does not allow the possibility of learning of theology from the cultures it seeks to reach but instead poses as host and teacher to the recipient culture. The Akũrinũ vernacular theology on the other hand is a positive step in the search for a global theology and an acknowledgement of the possibility of learning theology from multiple locations of the world. As we have mentioned before, the Akũrinũ church is devoid of much syncretism in their theology, as well as religious activism in their practice preferring to keep the Bible central to their faith. This in itself suggests that it is possible to do contextual theology that conforms to biblical "orthodoxy".

In conclusion, we will present the importance of culture in organizing a community and giving it direction, and thereby being a potential basis of theologizing. We believe culture (which is often overlooked in development agenda) is the place to look in order to transform a community or stimulate a desired end without which any community's transformation will most likely be superficial in the long run.

Theology of Culture

As we look at the importance of culture, we note that the assault of African culture that began with colonialism has continued unabated to date. We will cite two examples; food production and distribution, and sexuality, to show how this Western cultural hegemony continues to impact Africa. One area that poses a major threat to Africa's social determination is the area of food production and distribution. In his book, *The Politics of food: The Global Conflict between Food Security and Food Sovereignty*, Schanbacher D. William shows how the neoliberal policies that underwrite World Bank, International Monetary Fund (IMF), and the World Trade Organization (WTO), have complicated the food situation in the Majority-World countries. For example, the food aid from US surplus has proved disastrous to recipient countries. When such cheap food is dumped in the countries of global South, the domestic food market prices for the recipient countries plummet and these countries enter a dependency syndrome.

Likewise the management of food aid by the Breton Wood institutions and foreign investment especially in agribusiness is another problem. The transnational corporations enter countries; introduce green revolution styles, chemical intensive crops, genetically modified seeds that cannot be replanted and expensive capital input with devastating effect on the environment. As a result, the biodiversity is severely affected. Many indigenous seeds that can stand adverse weather because they are in their natural habitat are at risk of extinction, and being replaced with hybrids and genetically modified types. The result is the African peasant and subsistence farmers who for generations had always selected their seeds for planting from the previous harvest have to contend with a new cost of buying seeds every planting season.[1]

Another area of the Western cultural hegemony in Africa is in the area of sexuality. Increasing cases of divorce and remarriage, same sexual relationships, earlier onset of sexual activity among children and teenagers, pornography, abortion, and other sexual expressions that undermine the biblical understanding of sexuality, and were less prevalent in many traditional African cultures, have now found inroads in Africa. As I write this dissertation, Sierra Leone has legalized abortion after South Africa, Central Republic of Africa, and the list is growing. Writing on this, Obianugu Okoecha has said:

> The West African country of Sierra Leone has taken a most unfortunate step off a cultural cliff as they legalized abortion this week. She continues to wonder; who would

---

1. William Schanbacher, *The Politics of Food: The Global Conflict between Food Security and Food Sovereignty* (Oxford: Praeger Security International, 2010.

have thought that a nation still reeling and recovering from an Ebola epidemic would choose death for their unborn children. Obianugu regrettably notes that it was under the intense lobbying efforts of IPAS, a pro-abortion organization headquartered in North Carolina, that the Parliament of Sierra Leone passed the "Safe Abortion Bill 2015" into law on the 8th of December. She concludes her online article on a rather sad note; "Today Africa laments and groans as Sierra Leone joins South Africa, Tunisia, Cape Verde, and Mozambique [and I add Central Republic of Africa], on a path of violence and death. Today the culture of death has made in-roads in Africa[2].

An important question to ask at this juncture is: why is culture so important in development of theology? Unless this importance is recognized, African cultures and other traditional cultures will continue to be depicted as relics of antiquity with no value for the postmodern man. Consequently, Africa will continue to be estranged from herself, unable to value and respect herself as one who is capable of making a positive contribution to world progress and especially in providing new ways of understanding the Christian faith in the face of dwindling fortunes of the Church in the West and the ever growing encroachment of secularism to the Church – arguably the most virulent threat to the Christian faith. In this conclusion we will examine both the integrative and function of culture in organizing the society, as culture is animated by the reflexivity of God in them, that makes "joining" or "intimacy", a possibility, away from supersessionism, and without which the missionaries remained aloof at the door-step of the indigenes that they sought to evangelize.

---

2. Obianugu Okoecha, The parliament of Sierra Leone legalizes abortion & chooses death for their unborn, Accessed December 10 2015, http://cultureoflifeafrica.com/2015/12/the-parliament-of-sierre-leone-legalizes-abortion-chooses-death-for-their-unborn.html?

The Integrative Value of Culture

One of the most critical values of culture is its integrative function. Tite Tieno says that culture has such an integrative value that it is difficult to separate it from philosophy, religion, and spiritual values. Our attitude towards culture, to a large extent, conditions our theological methodology.[3]

Unfortunately as Tienou observes, we have learnt to think of our customs as pagan even though there have been rarely, if ever, substitutes for those cultural elements. The consequence of this is horrifying; much of practical evangelical Christianity in Africa is terribly syncretistic, while missionaries and the pastors they have trained keep on preaching the "pure biblical message"! This is an important pastoral problem in Africa today. Several evangelical authors have warned of the dangers of syncretism, and with good reason. But syncretism has many facets. There is first the unwitting syncretism produced by inadequate teaching of Christian truth. Second, is practical syncretism where the person will go to the fetish priest, often in secret, or possess a talisman, while at the same time professing to be an "orthodox" Christian. Thirdly, there is theological syncretism where there is mixing of contradictory ideas. It is the second form of syncretism which is practiced by many Christians because they have not been given clear scriptural teaching which has grappled with the realities of African *Weltanschauung*, a problem we have attributed to underestimating the importance of people's culture. Missionaries and pastors need to have a right attitude towards culture by seeing it in the light of God's relationship with Israel, as the special people of God, if they are to help Christians out of this devastating syncretistic way of living.

Tienou informs us that we actually do not preach a de-culturalized gospel because the gospel has won the cultural garb of the western world for many centuries. And for this he advises that African theologians must

---

3. Tite, Tienou. *The Theological Task of the Church in Africa.* African Christian Press: Achimota, Ghana, 1982), 19.

thus be well versed with the three cultures; our African, the biblical, and the Western cultures.[4] Because the Christian faith is lived daily in culture, we need to develop a theology of culture, and examine very closely to see what elements are compatible or incompatible with the gospel message. Tienou says that if we evangelicals develop a theology of culture, we could win back precious theological ground that we have lost, and we could also help churches come out of their cultural ghettos and confront culture with the gospel, at all levels,[5] recalling the thinking of Paul Tillich:

Religion is the substance of culture and culture is the form of religion. Our attitude therefore to culture will determine our attitude to religion. There will be those who will take Tertullian's side, advocating a radical discontinuity between Christianity and other religions (Africa religions included). There will be those who will agree with Clement of Alexandria, recognizing some continuity of Christianity and other religions[6].

Yet we must note that culture must obey the gospel. John Mbiti informs us that African religion generated a spirituality that finds its fulfillment in the gospel. The Christian faith comes, therefore, to enrich, to fulfill, to crown and to say 'yes' to African religion and not to destroy it. The gospel of Jesus Christ both judges and saves or sanctifies many elements in African Religion. But, however rich African religiosity has been, it could not and did not produce what the gospel now offers African peoples. Yet, it tutored the African in religious life, so that they could find in the gospel to which this religiosity pointed within the framework of its own revelation of God.[7] . Mbiti goes on to give what elements can be used by the church in a process of accommodation; He says that some beliefs, practices, traditional prayers, sacred places, morals and values

---

4. Ibid., 29.

5. Ibid., 19.

6. Tite Tienou quotes the words of Paul Tillich by F. Chapey in the, *Introduction to Courage d'être* (2 ed. Castermna), 10.

7. John Mbiti, Christianity and African Religion, paper presented at PACLA, 4.

and the services of (former) traditional religious leaders can be used for the enrichment of Christian life.[8]

Religious plurality is not new and need not be feared for its latent syncretism. African theologians should not be drawn into the baseless battles of ridding the earth of this plurality of religion by condemning all aspects of African Traditional Religions. Tienou advises that the bible addresses itself to the question of multiplicity of religions in the world, both in the Old and in the New Testament. He notes that the exegesis of such scriptures as Acts 14:15ff, Acts 17, Rom 1 and 4 leads to the following observation: That non-Christian religions show that all men seek after God and have a certain knowledge of him, (Acts 17: 26, 27; Rom 1: 21); The seeking of non-Christian religions is at the same time a deformation of the knowledge of God, for man loves to domesticate God, (Rom 1: 18, 23), that this undermines the ambiguity of non-Christian religiosity; and that the non-Christian religion seeks God but it suppresses knowledge of Him. This leads us to conclude that no non-Christian religion gives a true knowledge of God, for without the light of Christ, all men are without God, *atheoi* (Eph 2:12). Man's religiosity can only make him be without excuse, Rom 2:1.

The fact that non-Christian religions show that all men seek after God and have a certain knowledge of him as Tienou notes, reminds us that the African religions were not altogether bankrupt of any knowledge of God however basic. This adds credence to the thinking that the missionaries should have enlisted such cultures as dialogue partners in their mission efforts like the efforts of Bishop Colenso in Natal.

To do this calls for critical contextualization. Such contextualization must take seriously both the biblical text and the cultural context where the message is given.[9] Tienou observes that the AICs are filling a gap (sometimes not very adequately, but it is true) in the cultural, social,

---

8. Ibid., Mbiti, PACLA, 4.
9. Tienou, *The Theological Task of the Church in Africa*, 28.

emotional, and religious lives of people which the orthodox churches, often are not meeting.[10] Our research on Akũrinũ concurs with Tienou. But Tienou's observation here raises an important issue also. Whereas we concur with Tieno's observations, one cannot fail to ask a fundamental question, what is an orthodox church? If Tienou meant to exclude the AICs from this orthodoxy, one would want to question whether orthodoxy is defined by westernization in the historical or missionary Churches. It is far more defensible to imagine the AICs as authentic Christian expressions that are in sync with the traditional spiritualties of their culture and instead of trying to upgrade them to what Tienou is calling orthodox communions. This allow the possibilities of learning a different but authentic spirituality and theology from them, if we believe in the first place that, 'the wind blows where it wills' - and does so without seeking our permission in the first place. It is our belief that our energy would be better utilized if we followed where the wind is brewing rather than questioning the wisdom of the Spirit.

The Functions of Culture

Among other functions, culture provides lenses of perception, a way of looking at reality, a worldview. In this view, Ali Mazrui says that culture provides standards of evaluation. What is good and what is evil, what is beautiful and what is ugly, what is legitimate and what is illegitimate are all rooted in a criteria provided by culture. Culture also conditions motivation. What motivates individuals to act or refrain from acting, what inspires individuals to perform well and to exert themselves, is partly inspired by cultural factors. Culture too is a medium of communication. The communicative aspects of culture range from language in the literal sense to physical gestures and modes of dress. Culture provides a basis of stratification- a pecking order in the society. There is also a link between culture and means of production i.e. between culture and economics.

---

10. Ibid.,48.

Culture defines identity, determining who the "we" in a given situation are and who are the "they".[11] In a sense, culture is therefore so central to the proper functioning of a community, that it cannot be bi-passed.

Mazrui further says that in a cultural revolution the fundamental change may indeed occur when existing cultural visions are inadequate for the new realities. For example, African cultures were not prepared for the sudden Cultural Revolution that came with colonialism and the missionaries. This is because as Mazrui informs us; "the power of the western paradigms in Africa was increased because of a basic alliance between Western science and Western Christianity as transmitted in missionary schools. The carriers of Christianity into Africa were also the carriers of the western education. Missionaries built schools not simply to teach catechism and the Bible, but also mathematics, biology and one or more European languages". [12]

Regrettably the Europeans belittled African cultures which they did not sufficiently take time to understand, ignoring any function they served in the society. On this Mazrui says that black Africans were not regarded as having a "high religious culture" but as having at best "folk" or "tribal" religions. The missionaries could challenge these with impunity, and the imperial power let them do it, confident that there would be no significant backlash from "tribal" zealots.[13] Again it would suffice if this had happened only in colonial history. Unfortunately, to this day African cultures continue to be non-existent as a reference for any development agenda as far as the West is concerned. The Western expatriates, the Bretton woods institutions, the western-sponsored theological colleges, and NGOs often set the agenda for African development and in most cases do not consider it important to consult the Africans who are being helped. Mazrui says that the combined western onslaught on the

---

11. Ali Mazrui, *The Africa Condition* (London: Heinemann Educational Books Ltd, 1980), 65.
12. Ibid., 50.
13. Ibid., 51.

African mind, linking the sacred with the secular, allaying science with religion, created a particularly strong cultural revolution in Africa, not least because traditional African cultures themselves did not differentiate between secular knowledge and sacred wisdom.

For example, in the cultural function of defining reality, Mazrui notes the difference between the gods of Africa and the Christian God; the gods of ATR are gods of justice ready to inflict pain, they are brave and reward warriors for their bravery. These gods also make certain places or trees sacred. This understanding of God through filters of African culture must be evaluated alongside the biblical record. The Christian God on the other hand is a God of love who nevertheless approves of suffering as a way of God, who urges you to turn the other cheek when struck on one cheek, canonize martyrs, and considers only man as sacred. In the end the feminine virtues of Christianity – the softer ideas of love, gentleness, tenderness, forgiveness and patience – were invoked in Africa in a manner which made the "pacification' of Africa easier and their submission to the imperial order speedier. The harder warrior values of the God of Africa – courage, manhood, and even purposeful ruthlessness –were discouraged.[14]

Here Mazrui's observation must be understood purely from a cultural lenses that draws some support from the patriarchal culture of the Bible but which must not be seen as normative; Mazrui being himself an outsider to the Christian faith. If the gospel as presented by the missionaries was intended as Mazrui suggests, or if the missionaries presented the gospel to Africans as they understood it, it remains unclear. But, whether one agrees completely with Mazrui or not, the feminization of the church in Africa remains a hindrance to the full participation of the African man in the church leaving the matter of religion mainly to women and children, especially where traditional cultures are still largely intact. In the areas where African cultures have been integrated with Western cultures, a

---

14. Ibid., 52.

larger number of men are passive observers in the Church while women run the show. This is a strange twist because in African cultures, religion was the preserve of men with women and children following. Might the erosion of the African cultures explain this?

Mazrui mentions a number of ways that the European interaction with Africa has changed the African "identity" for better for worse. This is seen in the identity of the tribe where different groups competed for scarce resources in new territories created by the West, identity of the national state, and the identity of the race which has in part been a reaction of European chauvinism and arrogance towards non-western people in the last few centuries. The African who always defined himself in group mindset has been influenced towards individualism and personal accountability partly by the protestant version of the Christian faith, capitalism, and the western rules of science and education that emphasize personal efforts in the place of collective corroboration. Much of this can be seen as injurious to the African mind. Nonetheless it must be appreciated that the group thinking and acting of Africans has its own limitations also. For example it has the potential of holding every ambition captive to the group thinking, and thereby slowing innovation and creativity. But when you consider the African mindset where the wellbeing of the individual is only useful if everyone is doing as well, the African way of looking at reality makes for human flourishing a possible reality far from the ills of the West individualistic mindset.

Reflexivity in Human Cultures, the Roadmap from Contextualization to Contextual Theologies

As we have demonstrated, contextualization is inadequate to explain the proliferation of new indigenous ecclesial communities that are being witnessed in Africa and other places in the majority world. Dyrness says that formal discussions of contextualizing of the Gospel in the many cultures of the world really only began formally in the 1960s with the emphasis on inculturation, growing out of the Second Vatican Council (1961- 65) in the Roman Catholic Church, observations that he bases on the earlier events of the 16th century cultural developments that led to Protestant Reformation. The cultural changes of reformation changed the way religion was imagined in a number of ways: first the focus of worship based on mass - longstanding set of practices—praying with images of the saints or rosaries, processions and pilgrimages, novenas and so forth, was replaced by an emphasis on specific beliefs set forth in a new set of practices—in preaching, in learning catechisms and reading Scripture and prayer books. Simply put; the focus of worship was no longer the dramatic celebration of the Mass, but the clear preaching of the Word of God. The resulting focus of religious devotion was thus transferred from external objects and practices, to internal reflection and faith. Whereas in the medieval period the whole person was involved in the performance of devotion, after the Reformation the head and heart became the primary focus.[15]

The result of this religious focus is that in this process much of the religious culture of medieval practice, and of monastic spirituality in particular, was swept away. The resources of the mystical tradition were forgotten and rich traditions of material culture, of architecture, painting and drama to name only the most prominent, were mostly set aside. A dramatic change occurred in the way "religion" was construed. Instead of providing a holistic frame that determined an entire way of life, including the political and social structure, the way was open for religion to become an inward and personal matter.[16] Western Protestantism has since grown on this line - a private religion of a private life for a private individual. This is the premise on which the Protestant missionary work

---

15. William Dyrness, refers to Edward Muir, Ritual in Early Modern Europe (Cambridge: Cambridge Interversity Press, 1997) and his earlier work, W. Dyrness, *Reformed Theology and Visual Culture: The Protestant Imagination from Calvin to Edwards* (Cambridge: Cambridge University Press, 2004).

16. Dyrness, *Insider Jesus*, 10-11.

from Europe and America to Africa was predicated, a narrow religion that reigns in the category of individual's private life. This approach to religion was rather strange to the African way of thinking where religion was fully integrated to life.

Dyrness says that though there were many positive outcomes of the Protestant Reformation in the way the gospel was spread to Africa, there were other less positive outcomes from this emphasis on teaching and learning that Willie Jennings and others have recently highlighted. Since the understanding of the Gospel was tied to a particular set of beliefs that resulted from Reformation Christianity, missionaries were insistent on making these beliefs clear in the places (and languages) where they worked. Jennings argues that this resulted in an "inverted hospitality" where missionaries, most exemplified in the translation project, rather than accepting the hospitality of host people and learning from their ways, were more intent on teaching than willing to listen and learn.[17] The "inverted hospitality" came a full cycle in the protestant Project of translation. Unlike in the early Church where the apostolic missionaries went out with nothing for missionary journeys, the 19th century missionaries to date come loaded[18], thanks to an affluent West. The resulting asymmetrical power is heavily skewed to visitor -turned –host, and the victims, the legitimate hosts, are now like the visitors in the new arrangement.

A similar weakness is discernable on the focus on verbal proclamation where the missionaries tended to ignore, and in many cases actively discourage, many of the carriers of indigenous values. Yet the imagination of the cultural people was often expressed in stories, in the myths and legends, and more specifically in the dances, cult objects and music that embodied their values; the kind that is still experienced in the Akũrinũ church to various degrees. All these were often suppressed on the

---

17. Jennings, *The Christian Imagination*, 145.
18. Ibid, 145.

grounds that they expressed idolatrous beliefs - they were also felt to be inferior to the more cognitive forms of meaning making.

This net negative effect of the Christianity as preached by the missionaries to Africa has been ably captured by Ngugi wa Thing'o. In his novel, *The River Between*, one of the protagonists, Nyambura, the daughter of one of the early and staunch converts to Christianity, Joshua, has a grasp of what the real religion is, which she can scarcely see practiced by her father's Christianity. She remarks this of her father's faith: "No! It could never be a religion of love. Never, never! The religion of love was in the heart. The other was Joshua's (Nyambura's father) own religion, which ran counter to her [Nyambura's] spirit and violated love. If the faith of Joshua and that of Livingstone (the missionary) came to separate, then, it was not good. If it came to stand between a father and his daughter (i.e. Muthoni) so that her death did not move him, then it was inhuman. She (Nyambura) wanted the other - the other that held together, the other that united".[19] The African religions held together. They fostered unity in the community where the different missionary groups caused division and competition.

Waiyaki, another protagonist in Ngugi's novel, knew that not all the ways of the white man were bad. Even his religion was not essentially bad, some good, some truth shone through it. But the religion, the faith, needed washing; cleaning away all the dirt, leaving only the eternal. And that eternal was that the truth had to be reconciled to the traditions of the people. A people's traditions could not be swept away overnight, as the missionaries attempted. That way laid disintegration. Such a tribe would have no roots, for a people's roots were in their traditions going back to the past, the very beginning, *Gikũyũ* and *Mũmbi*.

A religion that took no account of people's way of life, a religion that did not recognize spots of beauty and truth in their way of life, was useless. It would not satisfy. It would not be a living experience, a source of life

---

19. Thiong'o, *The River Between*, 134.

and vitality. It would only maim a man's soul, making him fanatically cling to whatever promised security, otherwise he would be lost. Perhaps that was what was wrong with Joshua. He had clothed himself with a religion that was decorated and smeared with everything white. Renouncing his past, he cut himself away from those life-giving traditions of the tribe. And because he had nothing to rest upon, something rich and firm on which to stand and grow, he had to cling with his hands to whatever the missionaries taught him promised the future. If the white man's religion made you abandon a custom and then did not give you something else of equal value, you became lost. An attempt at resolution of the conflict would only kill you, as it did Muthoni.[20]

Sadly, many African Christians in Africa remain suspended in a cultural vacuum so created by the way the gospel was introduced. This cultural suspense may be the single most familiar cause of identity crisis to many Africans and consequently the underdevelopment that one witnesses there. Africans have lost their roots. They are now blind hostages to every foreign ideology that volunteers to show them the way out of the crisis.

The shallowness of the Christian faith in Africa is well documented. That the African Christian often falls for anything makes growth in discipleship a serious challenge. Church leaders faced with this scenario resort to more exhortation to Christians to read the Bible more, memorize it, and read it in a variety of current electronic gadgets in the ever expanding technological space. This is besides a host of commentaries,

---

20. In this novel, Ngugi wa Thiong'o. 1981. *The River Between.* (Heinemann: Nairobi, Kenya) Page 136-138, the author paints vividly the clash of culture that occurred when the missionaries brought Christianity to the Agĩkũyũ nation of Central Kenya. Muthoni the daughter of Joshua refuses to embrace Christianity and secretly gets circumcised at the hands of her aunt. Her father has nothing completely to do with her own daughter who she accuses of joining the pagan ritual. Her other daughter, Nyambura remains royal to the father's faith but never forgave him for what she sees as inconsiderate religion that alienates its people and does not even mourn a dead daughter. Waiyaki too caught between the education that the missionary has brought and the traditions of the people clearly sees that Christianity is not altogether wrong. It is only clothed with a cultural garb that is not necessarily. In this cultural garb it rejects any other cultural as it tries to endeavor itself to these cultures.

and all other Bible aids that have come to be refered to as, "tools of biblical decanonization", but the results remain dismal. One wonders whether the 'uprootedness' from the cultural rich spiritual receptors may not account for the lack of rootedness and grounding in the Christian faith. Might this explain why the African believer is ever running after every new idea and suggestion from the West that promises to better his faith, often with no intention to implement it – or rather with no capacity to because the suggestions are too foreign to his spiritual receptacles, thus finding no spiritual "hooks" to anchor on?

Dyrness faults the project of contextualization in one more fundamental way. He says that the assumption, mostly hidden, in many evangelical discussions of contextualization is that since God works primarily or indeed solely through the "message" that is being communicated, God has actually arrived in the luggage of the missionary. The truth, of course, is that God was present and working in the culture from the beginning, and the indigenous values and even the religions of these people pay important tribute to this presence.[21] In this reflexivity in which God from the beginning gave to man – to subdue the earth, to multiply and fill the earth, to name all creatures, to cultivate the earth, and to participate in all these relationships, all which men of all cultures have always participated in - herein lays the argument for an alternative way of doing theology grounded in creation and most embodied in culture, away from contextualization.

God is not certainly dependent on the "message", as proclaimed by the missionary, to reach the lost. He goes ahead of the missionary to open the hearts of the would-be recipients of the gospel before the missionary's arrival. How God makes this possible subverts our best missiological efforts and calls us to observe and discern what God may be doing in a culture; rather than being teachers to a new culture, be ready to learn.[22]

---

21. Dyrness, *Insider Jesus.*, 30
22. Ibid., 30.

It is in this observation that contextual theologies open a new vista of learning theology. Peter was to learn this hard lesson in the house of Cornelius. Long before Peter's noon vision, Cornelius was praying and giving alms, the kind that received notice in heaven. While Peter labored to explain the message of salvation, Cornelius and his guests – again notice that having received a message from an angel of God to call for Peter, Cornelius acting from his culture used his influence to call many of his relatives and friends to his house, a kind of group thinking that one so often finds in African cultures – the Holy Spirit ignored protocol, "tarry ye in Jerusalem" and saturated the house, while Peter was still busy putting his theology to test. And with this the gentile harvest had started. While the Jewish harvest had started in the upper room, the Gentile harvest started in a home, in the family set up. No wonder house Churches, not synagogues and temples, became a permanent feature in the early Gentile church; one that did not call for much fund raising to establish, committing all surplus funds to the missionary work. The gospel was taking shape in a different culture – the Jewish apostles could only learn the new phenomena rather than argue with the method.

Critical to the Akũrinũ church movement is the primal religious worldview that undergirds their reception and understanding of the Gospel – that long before the missionaries' arrival God was at work preparing the way. The Akũrinũ church refused to let go of their traditional culture in entirety. They resisted the Western cultural garb in which the Christian faith was clothed. But critical too was perhaps what God was doing in critiquing their culture. It is in this respect that the Akũrinũ believers could selectively reject what they saw as aspects of paganized Agĩkũyũ culture such as witchcraft, sexual excesses, and taking of oath, while at the same time retaining a lot from the same culture in their new religious understanding. Even without any hermeneutical principles, they were already critiquing their previous beliefs.

Recommendations

In this research, we have endeavored to show why contextualization is no longer tenable to understand the growth of emerging ecclesial communities like *Akũrinũ* least of all because contextualization's power is tilted to the contextualizer and the message to be contextualized is understood within the culture, and hence within the epistemology of the missionary culture. Global or contextual theologies are sympathetic to different indigenes where these theologies are mushrooming. It is in this breath that we recommend more phenomenological study of AICs such as the *Akũrinũ* with a particular focus on the traditional cultural milieu within which such ecclesial movements have emerged to understand contextual theologies. This calls for cultural humility from all propagators of the gospel, and especially the theologians.

We also call for hermeneutical humility. The Western hermeneutical approach of grammatical-historical method holds the word of God captive to western scholarship; a luxury that many emerging ecclesial movements do not have. Yet such communities must hear God speak to them through his written word. The Spirit of God who knows the context of the bible world knows the context of these ecclesial communities. He is able to make the word of God alive and applicable to all believers. This is the hermeneutical approach that we recommend for Africa and a lot can be learnt from *Akũrinũ* church - from the situation (we have showed that the situation of the *Akũrinũ* church at its inception was the troubled socio-economic context that was precipitated by the colonial administration and the missionary assault on the *Agikũgũ* culture) - to the biblical message as interpreted to the *Akũrinũ* founders under the guidance of the Holy Spirit. This calls for a thorough interrogation of Western hermeneutics as presently taught in Bible Schools in Africa. Again this does not in any way negate the need for theological education by the *Akũrinũ* church and other ecclesial communities. We are only calling for recognition that God is not to be held captive to Western idea of reality.

Lastly this research recommends a restoration of the African religious order. Our findings lead us to conclude that the way the missionaries brought Christianity to Africa disrupted the existing African religious order in which the role of men was prominent. Men led in religious matters. This unique feature is still discernable in *Akũrinũ* church with men taking full charge of the church leadership. This has a tendency to draw both the women and children to follow suit. The same cannot be said of the mainline churches. Among the historical churches there is a visible feminization of the church with a few men leading at the clergy level while the next tier of lay leadership is mostly women, young people, and children with men assuming a religious apathy. This is most noticeable among African communities whose cultures are still largely intact; here the church seems to be left squarely in the hands of women and children. The argument that we are trying to advance here is that the way the missionaries introduced Christianity to Africa disrupted the religious power balance. Before the advent of the missionaries, religion was squarely the domain of the men. When this cultural religious order was disrupted and the place of men was displaced, they were cut off from religious participation and perhaps this can explain the current feminization of the church in Africa.

Our argument must not be seen as advocating for male chauvinism but rather a concern for the feminization of the church and the unfortunate apathy that men often show towards the church and even as heads of the family. We agree with apostle Peter's teaching on the priesthood of all believers and equal participation of men and women in the church. Yet this does not in any way eclipse our point of contention: that men seem to have left the show to women and children especially among the more traditional cultures in matters religion. A restoration of the African religious order might perhaps bring back more men participants in the church. This observation is both African and biblical. In the Old Testament, fathers were the priests of their families. In Gen 18:19 Abraham was charged with the responsibility of directing his family and household to follow God. Job was the priest of his family. This is the order that the New Testament reinforced whilst recognizing the role of women in the Church.

Conclusion

In this research, we have demonstrated that the gospel that the missionaries brought to Africa was encased in a cultural garb. The gospel was so dissolved in the Western culture that it was at its most crucial points undifferentiated from it. Whereas this is regrettable to the extent that it blinded the missionaries from their own ethnocentrism and in so doing hindered any possible appraisal of the native cultures as potential dialogue partners in propagating the Christian faith, it also teaches us a profound lesson; culture is an indispensable vehicle for the gospel.

This is to say that the gospel is received and understood within a culture. The marriage of the two is so intimate that it is not always possible or even desirable to separate the two. Indeed it was never meant for the gospel to happen in a cultural vacuum. Yet this is what the missionary efforts attempted; to crush the African culture so as to plant the gospel. It would have been expected that they would have let the gospel be incarnated in the native cultures as they had received it in their own culture. The very incarnation of its savior relativizes any attempt to universalize the Western Christianity.

To the extent that the gospel is allowed to interact and transform the recipient culture is the extent to which it will deepen its roots in that culture. It is in this regard that the recipient culture should be seen as an aid in mission work and not an impediment. This point to something more fundamental – theology develops within a cultural milieu with the attending religious culture. Such a theology transforms the culture of the people where it develops. In this regard local cultures should be enlisted in the program of developing contextual theologies – the Akŭrinŭ church as shown us how. It is certainly irresponsibility on the part of the African theologians to accept the insinuation of the westerner's reading of bankruptcy in African cultures and to passively consume western culture. The African culture should instead form the backdrop for innovation and creativity in understanding the Christian faith.

As said earlier the very incarnation of Jesus Christ into humanity once and for all recovered for us the importance of creation in God's economy of redemption. Jesus' incarnation was actually a pattern from the Old Testament where God in many times in the redemption of the Israelites used the existing surrounding culture to carry forward his redemptive plan. There are many examples that one could cite and we have done so. I will cite one more example.

In the citadel of Suza, the culture that kept many women in the harem for the king's use was rife. This is a culture that possibly devalued women because once the king had a one night stand with a woman who did not please him enough, and who was perhaps taken to the harem without her consent, she become a lifetime concubine with no more access to the king nor a possibility of marrying another man. One can say this was a gross violation of women rights. Thankfully the Babylonian culture had other positive cultures. For example King Xerxes exercised democracy in consulting a team of political advisers in discharging his duties. He was clearly not a dictator in this particular instance. Perhaps this culture also recognized a godly family order of authority in the family with the man's headship role respected and guarded. What is interesting however for us in this study is how God used the same culture without necessarily changing it in a fundamental way to save the Israelites scattered throughout the Kingdom of Babylon from a near total annihilation, thanks to Herman's bloated ego. Esther went through the Babylonian 'harem culture' and thankfully qualified for a queen and saved her people. God used this degenerate culture for His purpose. It is for this that we have argued in this research that God seeks to transform other degenerate cultures and even use them as vehicles for His redemptive work without seeking to obliterate them altogether, to accommodate his redemptive plan.

It is our opinion from this research that African cultures are not about to die. They might be modified in a globalized world but they will remain a source of meaning-making in the foreseeable future. We can here recall Bediako's observations:

> The way the African seek spiritual help today (from praying for or dedicating a new house, for fertility, to success in examination etc.) all shows that far from obliterating the African primal view of things, in its essentially unified and 'spiritual' nature and replacing it with a two-tier modern Western view comprising of sacred and secular dimensions, the Christian faith has reinforced the African view.[23]

As we have mentioned before, the African culture has been an asset in the Christianizing of Africa. Bediako as quoted above has reminded us that:

> The primal religions of the continent have thus been a significant factor in the immense Christian presence in Africa. While this cannot be taken to mean that there has not been any 'paradigm-shift' in African religious consciousness, it does confirm that the African apprehension of the Christian faith has substantial roots in the continent's primal traditions at the specific level of religious consciousness. At least we can say that if it did not have the primal religions has its sub-stratum, the story of Christianity in African at the

---

23. Kwame Bediako, *Christianity in Africa*, 176.

closure of the present century [referring to 20th C], would be very different.[24]

Perhaps we should find it necessarily to think that since this African primal spirituality has had great value in entrenching Christianity in Africa, it may hold the same value in developing African theology and making its contribution to the growing search for global theology especially in the face of a disturbing decline of the Church in the West.

This conclusion leads us to something of importance to us. If people's traditional culture is a viable means of developing contextual theology, then it is plausible to suggest that the principle behind these cultures and the institutions that exist in them might set the agenda for a possible new African social imagination that preoccupy Katongole's argument as presented in this study. As we have demonstrated in this study, the nation-state social imagination with its imperialistic tendency has not helped the majority of Africa. The development agenda set by the West overlooks the African *Weltanschauung* and instead of helping Africa, sets her up on a catch up path after the West, as a ready market for the West's manufactured goods or a testing ground for the West's industrial experiments. By denying Africa her contribution to the world progress, the world has denied herself a unique African contribution in human progress.

---

24. Ibid., 192.

Bibliography

Achebe, Chinua. *Things Fall Apart*. New York: Madowell Obolensky, 1958.

The Akurinu Religion. "Worshiping Jehovah in Truth and in Spirit." Accessed on January 2, 2017. http://www.akurinucommunity.org.

Anderson B. William. (). *The Churches in East Africa (1840-1974)*. Nairobi, Kenya: Uzima Press, 1977.

Barrett, B. and David Tell., eds. *Kenyan Churches Handbook*. Nairobi, Kenya: Evangel Publishing House, 1973.

Barrett, David. *Schism and Renewal in Africa*. Oxford: OAIC office, 1968.

Bediako, Kwame. *Jesus in Africa: The Christian Gospel in African History and Experience*. Maryknoll, NY: Orbit Books, 2004.

_____. "Understanding African Theology in the 20th Century." Pages 56-72 in *Issues in African Christian Theology*. Edited by Samuel Ngewa, Mark Shaw, and Tite Tienou. Nairobi: East African Educational Publishers, 1998.

_____. *Christianity in Africa: The Renewal of a Non-Western Religion*: Edinburgh, Scotland: Edinburgh University Press, 1995.

Bewels, T.F.C. *Kikuyu Conflict: Mau Mau and the Christian Witness*. London: The High Press: 1953.

Blackwood, William. *Kikuyu: 1898-1923: Semi-jubilee Book of the Church of Scotland Mission Kenya Colony*. Edinburgh: Foreign Mission Committee of the Church of Scotland, 1923.

Blixen, Karen. *Out of Africa*. London: Putnam, 1937.

Boesak, Allan Aubrey. *Black Theology: Black Power*. Oxford, London: Mow Brays, 1976.

Bottignole, Silvan. *Kikuyu Tradition Culture and Christianity*. Nairobi, Kenya: Heinemann Educational Books, 1984.

Brinkman, Inge. *Kikuyu Gender Norms and Narratives*. Leiden, The Netherlands: Research School CNWS, 1996.

Brown, G. Gerald. *Christian Response to Change in East African Traditional Societies*: Wood Brooke College, 1973.

Bujo, Benezet. *African Theology in its Social Context*. Nairobi, Kenya: Paulines Publications, 1986.

Buxton, M. Aline. *Kenya Days*. London: Edward Arnold & Company, 1928.

Cagnolo. *The Agĩkũyu: Their Customs, Traditions, and Folklore*. Nairobi: Wisdom Graphics, 2006.

_____. *The Akikuyu: Their Customs, Traditions and Folklore*. Nyeri, Kenya: The Mission Printing School, 1933.

Cavicchi, Edmond. *Problems of Change in Kikuyu Tribal Society*. Bologna, Italy: EMI-Via Meloncello, 1977.

Cone, James. *For My People: Black Theology and Black Church*. Maryknoll, New York: Orbis Books, 1984.

Creswell, W. John. *Research Design: Qualitative, Quantitative, and Mixed Methods Approaches*. 2nd Edition. Thousand Oaks: Sage Publications, 2003.

The Standard Newspaper. "Home Breaking News." Accessed on June 3, 2017. http://www.standardmedia.co.ke/article/2000076717/mystic-mugumo-tree-s-fall-sparks-succession-debate.

Deji Ayegboyin and S. Ademola Ishola. *African Independent Churches*. Lagos, Nigeria: Greater Heights Publications, 1997.

Dyrness A. William. *Invitation to Cross-Cultural Theology: Case Studies in Vernacular Theologies*. Grand Rapids, Michigan: Zondervan Publishing House, 1992.

Edgerton B. Robert. *Mau: An African Crucible*: The Free Press, 1989.

Ela Jean-Marc. *Africa Cry*. Maryknoll, New York: Orbis Books, 1980.

Gachanga, Timothy. "Heritage, Museums and Memorialization in Kenya: Exploring the Past in the Present." Accessed on June 3, 2017. www.open.ac.uk/Arts/ferguson-centre/.../tim-gachanga-paper.shtml.

Gathingira, Henry. *Jomo Kenyatta: A Man and His People*. East Africa Newspaper Ltd, 1969.

Gehman J. Richard. *African Traditional Religion in Biblical Perspective.* Nairobi, Kenya: East Africa Educational Publishers Ltd, 2005.

Getui N. Mary, editor. *Theological Method and Aspects of Worship in African Christianity.* Acton Publishers: Nairobi, Kenya, 1998.

Gifford, Paul. *Christianity, Politics and Public Life in Kenya.* London: Hurst and Company, 2009.

Githieya, Francis Kimani. *The Freedom of the Spirit: African Indigenous Churches in Kenya.* Atlanta, Georgia: Scholars Press, 1997.

Groody, Daniel. *Globalization, Spirituality, and Justice.* Maryknoll, New York: Orbis Books, 2007.

Gutiérrez, Gustavo. *A Theology of Liberation.* London: SCM Press, 1974.

Hastings, Adrian. *African Christianity.* Southampton, Great Britain: The Camelot Press, 1976.

_____. *African Christianity: An Easy Interpretation.* London: Geoffrey Chapman, 1976.

Healey, Joseph and Donald Sybertz. *Towards an African Narrative Theology.* Nairobi, Kenya: Paulines Publication Africa, 1996.

Hochchild, Adam. *King Leopold's Ghost: A Story of Greed, Terror, and Heroism in Colonial Africa.* New York, NY: Mariner Books, 1998.

Houston, Dewey. "Ber Rabbit is Dying: The Demise of the Traditional Morality Among the Kikuyu People of Kenya and an Effort to Reclaim It." Doctoral Dissertation. Asbury Theoloical Seminary, 1996.

Howarth, Anthony. *Kenyatta: A Photographic Biography.* Nairobi, Kenya: East Africa Publishing House, 1967.

Jennings, Willie James. *The Christian Imagination: Theology and the Origins of Race.* New Haven, MA: Yale University Press, 2009.

Kalu, U. Ogbu, editor. *Africa Christianity and African Story.* Pretoria, South Africa: University of Pretoria Press, 2005.

Karanja, William K. *Hallowed be Mt. Kenya: The History of Agĩkuyu Culture in Kenya.* Ruiru, Kenya: Gacuiro Publishers, 2003.

Katongole, Emmanuel. *The Sacrifices of Africa: A Political Theology for Africa.* Grand Rapids, Michigan: William B. Eerdmans Publishing Company, 2011.Veli-Matti Kärkkäinen, Kirsteen Kim, and Amos Yong, eds. *Interdisciplinary and Religio-Cultural Discourses on a Spirit-Filled World: Loosing the Spirits.* New York: Palgrave Macmillan, 2013.

Kärkkäinen, Veli-Matti. *The Holy Spirit: Basic Guides to Christ ian Theology.* Louisville, KY: Westminster John Knox Press, 2012.

Kenyatta, Jomo. *Facing Mt. Kenya.* New York: Vintage Books, 1965.

Kimathi, J. Samuel, Alexia Njambi, and Lillian Mugure. A *Leader for Kenya*. (Unpublished Manuscript)

Kinoti. George, and Peter Kimuyu, editors. *Vision for a Bright Africa: Facing the Challenges of Development*. Kampala, Uganda: African Institute for Scientific Research and Development, 1997.

Kinoti. W. Hannah and J.M. Waliggo, editors. *The Bible in African Christianity: Essays in Biblical Theology*. Nairobi, Kenya: Acton Publishers, 1997.

Kirika, Gerishon. *The role of Sacrifice in Religion: Models of sacrifices in Gikuyu Religion*. Nairobi, Kenya: Faith Institute of Counseling, 2002.

Kirsteen, Kim. *The Holy Spirit in the World: A Global Conversation*. Maryknoll, New York: Orbis Books, 2007.

Kiruri, Harrison. *Christianity as a Means of Change in Kikuyu Land. 1958 -* Berlin: Viademica.Verlag, 2008.

Kuhn, Marko. *Prophetic Christianity in Western Kenya: Political, Cultural and Theological Aspects of African Independent Churches*. Frankfurt am Main, Berlin: Peter Lang, 2008.

Leakey, Richard. *The Making of Humankind*. London: M. Joseph, 1981.

Ndung'u, Nahashon W. "Persistence of Features of Traditional Healing in the Churches in Africa: The Case of the Akūrinū Churches in Kenya." *A Journal of the Philosophical Association of* Kenya. 1:2 (2009): 87-104.

Macharia, Prince Abraham. *In Search of Identity: Akurinu Community Demystified*. Nairobi, Kenya: Print View Publishers, 2012.

Magessa, Laurenti. *Anatomy of Inculturation: Transforming the Church in Africa*. Maryknoll, N.Y: Orbis Books, 2004.

Maggay, Melba Padilia. *Transforming Society*. Eugene, OR: Wipf and Stock Publishers, 1996.

Mbiti. S. John. *African Religion and Philosophy*. Nairobi, Kenya: East Africa Educational Publishers, 1969.

_____. *New Testament Eschatology in an African Background: A study of the Encounter between New Testament Theology and African Tradition Concepts*. London: Oxford University Press, 1971.

_____. *Introduction to African Religion*. Nairobi, Kenya: East Africa Education Publishers, 1975.

Moll, Peter. *Mzee Jomo Kenyatta*. Nairobi, Kenya: Trans Africa Publishers Ltd, 1973.

Mugambi, Jesse N. *Christian Theology and Social Reconstruction*. Nairobi, Kenya: Acton Publishers, 2003.

Mugo, E. N. *Kikuyu People: A brief outline of their Customs and Traditions*. Nairobi, Kenya: Kenya Literature Bureau, 1982.

Muriuki, Godfrey. *A History of the Kikuyu, 1500-1900*. Nairobi: Oxford University Press, 1974.

_____. *People Around Mt. Kenya: Kikuyu*. Kenya: Evans Brothers Limited, 1985.

Murray, Jocelyn. *Proclaim the Good News: A Short History of the Church Missionary Society*. London: Hodder and Stoughton, 1985.

Muzorewa, H. Gwinyai. *The Origins and Development of African Theology*. Maryknoll, NY: Orbis Books, 1985.

Mwaura, Philomena Njeri. "African. Instituted Churches in East Africa." *Studies in World Christianity*. 10:2 (2005): Accessed 2016: http://web.a.ebscohost.com/ehost/pdfviewer/pdfviewer?vid=21&sid=25a68f39-b517-4f39-abe5-4b0dc428abea%40sessionmgr4001&hid=4106.

Ndung'u, N.W. "Religion, Ethnicity and Identity in Africa." *Hekima-Journal of the Humanities and Social Sciences*. 3:1 (2005): 5-21.

_____. "Persistence of Features of Traditional Healing in the Churches in Africa: The Case of the Akurinu Churches in Kenya," *Thought and Practice: A Journal of the Philosophical Association of Kenya (PAK) New Series*, Vol.1 No.2, (2009): 87-104. Accessed April 2 2016, <http://erepository.uonbi.ac.ke:8080/xmlui/bitstream/handle/11295/40850/Full%20Text.pdf?sequence=on.

Ngũgĩ, Michael Wainana. *Impact of Christianity Among the Kikuyu people: A study of Kikuyu People Religion and Belief*. Berlin: Viademica, 2007.

Ngũgĩ wa Thiong'o. *Decolonizing the Mind: The Politics of Language in African Literature*. Nairobi, Kenya: Heinemann, 1986.

_____. *Dreams in a Time of War: A Childhood Memoir*. New York, NY: Random House, 2010.

_____. *I Will Marry When I Want*. Nairobi, Kenya: Heinemann, 1982.

_____. *The River Between*. Nairobi, Kenya: Heinemann, 1981.

Njururi, Ngumbu. *Agikuyu Folk Tales*. London: Oxford University Press, 1966.

_____. *Tales from Mount Kenya*. Nairobi: Transafrica Publishers, 1975.

Nthamburi, Zablon. *The African Church at the Crossroads: Strategy for Indigenization*. Kenya: Uzima Press, 1991.

_____. *From Mission to Church*. Uzima Press: Kenya, 1991.

Nyamiti, Charles. *Jesus Christ, the Ancestor of Humanity: Methodology and Trinitarian Foundations*. Nairobi, Kenya: CUEA Publications, 2005.

Obianugu, Okoech. "The Parliament of Sierra Leone Legalizes Abortion and Chooses Death for their Unborn." Accessed on 10th Dec. 2015: http://cultureoflifeafrica.com/2015/12/the-parliament-of-sierre-leone-legalizes-abortion-chooses-death-for-their-unborn.html.

Okorocha, C. Cyril. *The Meaning of Religious Conversion in Africa.* Vermont, USA: Gowa Publishing Company Limited, 1987.

Okot p'Bitek. *Song of Lawino.* Nairobi, Kenya: East Africa Publishing House, 1972.

Orobator, Agbonkhianmeghe E. *Theology Brewed in an African Pot: An Introduction to Christian Doctrine from an African Perspective.* Nairobi, Kenya: Paulines Publications, 2008.

Park, Sung Kyu. *Christian Spirituality in Africa.* Eugene, OR: Pickwick Publications, 2013.

Parratte, John, editor, *A Reader in African Christian Theology.* London: SPCK International Study Guide, 1997.

Paul Jenkins. "The Roots of African Church History: Some Polemical Thoughts." *International Bulletin of Missionary Research.* 10:2 (1986): 20-52.

Pinnock, H. Clark. *Flame of Love: A Theology of the Holy Spirit.* Downers Grove, Ill.: Intervarsity Press, 1996.

Rũkenya, Wanjĩra wa. *Reclaiming my dreams: Oral narratives.* Nairobi: University of Nairobi Press, 2010.

Sam, Babs Mala, editor. *African Independent Churches.* Nairobi, Kenya: OAIC, 1983.

Sanneh, Lamini. *Translating the Message: The Missionary Impact on Culture.* Maryknoll, New York, Orbis Books, 1989.

Schaeffer Franky, editor. *Is Capitalism Christian?* Westchester, IL: Crossway Books, 1985.

Schanbacher, D. William. *The Politics of Food: The Global ConflictBbetween Food Security and Food Sovereignty.* Oxford: Praeger Security International, 2010.

Shorter, Alyward and Joseph N. Njiru. *New Religious Movements in Africa.* Nairobi, Kenya: Paulines Publications, 2001.

Shorter, Aylward. *African Christian Spirituality.* Maryknoll, NY: Orbis Books, 1978.

Stinton, B. Diane, editor. "African Theology on the Way: Current Conversations." *Society for Promoting Christian Knowledge,* Great Britain, 2010.

Strayer, W. Robert. *The Making of the Mission Communities in East Africa.* Heinemann, State Albany, New York: University of New York Press, 1978.

The Independent Churches of Ghana. Asempa Publishers Christian Council of Ghana, 1990.

Tienou, Tite. *The Theological Task of the Church in Africa.* Nairobi: Achimota, Ghana: Africa Christian Press, 1982.

Turaki, Yusufu. *Christianity and African Gods: A Theological Method.* Portchefstroomse University Vir: Christianlike Hoar Onderwys, 1999.

_____. *Christianity and African Traditional Religion: A Systematic Examination of the Interactions of Religions.* Portchefstroomse University Vir: Christianlike Hoar Onderwys, 1999.

_____. *The Foundations of African Traditional Religion and Worldview.* Nairobi, Kenya: Word Alive Publishers, 2006.

Vahakangas, Mika. *In Search of Foundations for African Catholicism: Charles Nyamiti's Theological Methodology.* Leiden, The Netherlands: Brill, 1999.

Waigwa, Solomon Wachira. "Pentecost Without Azusa: An Historical and Theological Analysis of the Akorino Church in Kenya." Doctoral Dissertation. Baylor University, 2007.

Walls, F. Andrew. *The Missionary Movement in Christian History.* New York: Orbis Books, 1996.

Wargo. G. William. *Identifying Assumptions and Limitations for Your Book.* 2015. Accessed on 7 April. 2017. http://www.academicinfocenter.com/identifying-assumptions-and-limitations-for-your-book.html.

Welbourn F.B. and Ogot B.A. *A Place to Feel at Home.* London: Oxford University Press, 1966.

Willie, Jennings James. *The Christian Imagination: Theology and the Origins of Race.* New Haven: Yale University Press, 2009.

Willis, Colin. *Who killed Kenya?* London: Dennis Dobson Limited, 1945.

Wilmore S. Gayraud and James H. Cone, editors. *Black Theology: A Documentary History, 1966 -1979.* Maryknoll, New York: Orbis Books, 1979.

Wiseman, E.M. *Kikuyu Martyrs.* London: The Highway Press, 1958.

Oral Sources

Gachanga, Joshua. An *Akũrinũ* lay leader and a lecturer (Candidate PhD) at Tangaza University.

Kamau, Timothy (Rev.). A theologian and a pastor of *Akũrinũ* Reformation and Worship Center (An *Akũrinũ* Contemporary Church) and the first Youth Coordinator of the Secretariat of the *General Conference of the Akũrinũ Churches Assembly*.

Macharia, Abraham Prince. A practicing lawyer, author of, *In Search of Identity: Akũrinũ Community Demystified*, a past youth leader in African Holy Ghost Christian Church (AHGCC) and the Current first and Secretary General of Secretariat of the *General Conference of the Akũrinũ Churches Assembly*.

Mburu, Mburu (PhD), a lay leader in *Akùrinù* Reformation and Worship Center (An *Akũrinũ* Contemporary Church) and also lecturer at Jomo Kenya University of Agriculture and Technology (JKUAT)

Mwangi, Moses Nga'ang'a, Archbishop of the Kenya Foundation of the Prophets Church.

Njũgũna Jesse. A Youth leader in African Mission Church and A student in Catholic University of East Africa (CUEA)

Ndũng'ũ, Stephen. A Youth leader in African Mission Church and a student in Catholic University of East Africa (CUEA)

Owuoche, Monica, an accountable professional and formerly a member of Roho Musalaba, a *roho* Church with similar practices with *Akũrinũ*, from Nyanza (western Kenya).

Index

A

African Christian consciousness 45

African Christian identity xvii, 34

African Christian scholarship xviii, 32

African Christian theology xv, 189

African Church xxv, 46, 89, 91, 251, 252

African communal values 164

African cultural institutions 24

African cultural values 69

African cultural wisdom xix

African founded schools 103

African idiom 30

African institutions 61, 101

African personality xxiv

African primal imagination 27

African religiosity 95

African religious 26, 28, 30, 34, 37, 46, 77, 128

African religious consciousness 28

African religious quest 46

African religious values 26

African self-rule 108

African sensibilities 54

African social imagination 13

African societies 4, 185, 212

African spirituality 69, 128, 143, 149, 157, 187, 203, 204, 205, 206

African theologians 27, 40, 41, 45, 145

African theological methods 35

African theology xiii, xv, xx, xxi, xxiii, 27, 30, 34, 36, 42, 44, 187

African traditional culture(s) xxiv, xxv, 20, 128

African traditions 79, 113, 139, 140, 152, 158, 185

African worldview xxi, 23, 25, 30, 103, 150

African writers 189

Ancestors 180

Apostolic 68, 146

Archbishop 21, 97, 130, 137, 147, 154, 171, 182, 209, 254

Authentic iv, 219

B

Baptism iii, 161

baptize 119

Bible iii, xxiv, 25, 30, 35, 40, 41, 44, 51, 52, 54, 60, 63, 64, 74, 77, 85, 89, 101, 107, 109, 115, 118, 119, 121, 124, 128, 130, 131, 133, 138, 140, 141, 142, 143, 144, 145, 146, 148, 155, 156, 160, 162, 183, 187, 188, 191, 192, 193, 194, 195, 197, 199, 200, 201, 209, 213, 250

Bible commentaries 144

biblical Christianity 128, 203

Birth ii, iii, 103, 128

Bishop viii, 3, 4, 5, 11, 52, 105, 123, 147, 154, 171, 199, 209

Book i, xiii, 68, 195, 247, 253

Brotherhood xii, 68

C

Capitalism 8, 9, 252

Charismatic 17

Christian cultures xxiv, 55

Christianity ii, xv, xvii, xviii, xix, xx, xxi, xxii, xxiii, xxv, 2, 11, 13, 16, 17, 23, 25, 26, 27, 28, 29, 30, 31, 32, 33, 34, 35, 36, 37, 38, 39, 40, 41, 42, 43, 44, 45, 46, 47, 51, 53, 54, 55, 59, 61, 65, 66, 67, 69, 70, 77, 83, 85, 92, 94, 103, 112, 113, 119, 123, 124, 128, 129, 141, 142, 145, 146, 147, 155, 162, 187, 190, 192, 197, 203, 206, 212, 247, 248, 249, 250, 251, 253

Christian theology xv, 43, 53, 189

Circumcision iii, 67, 174, 176

Colonial 112, 178, 249

Colonialism xviii, 10

Community iii, 104, 163, 165, 250, 254

Contextualization xxiv, 37

Conversion 74, 77, 206, 252

Cosmology ii, 72, 74

Courtship iii, 171

Creation 48

cultural understanding 77, 85

Culture ii, iii, xxv, 47, 48, 74, 80, 163, 212, 248, 249, 252

D

Dance 75

Dialogue i, xv, 33

E

East coast of Africa 59, 96

ecclesial groups 36

Ecclesiologies iv, 219

Ecclesiology ii, 117

Ecumenical 36

Enlightenment xxii, 38, 39

Environment xi

Eschatology 148, 250

European culture 3, 124

F

Father 42, 73, 88, 111, 135, 144, 212, 218

Fig tree 177

Folklore 4, 248

G

Global 134, 250, 252

Globalization 9, 249

H

Herbs 75

HIV 14, 122, 219

Holy Communion 162

Holy Spirit 54, 57, 68, 93, 107, 108, 109, 112, 114, 119, 130, 131, 132, 133, 134, 135, 136, 137, 138, 141, 142, 144, 146, 149, 154, 160, 161, 162, 164, 165, 173, 186, 187, 188, 195, 196, 198, 199, 207, 209, 210, 213, 216, 218, 220, 221, 249, 250, 252

Host 48

I

Identity i, 25, 32, 104, 105, 114, 116, 120, 123, 153, 166, 176, 193, 195, 196, 198, 199, 250, 251, 254

Inculturation 250

Indigenization xxv, 251

Indigenous Christianity ii, 65, 66

Initiation 100

Intimacy 47, 52, 62

Islam xxv, 26, 41, 43, 44, 57, 70, 123

J

Justice 9, 249

K

Kenya ii, xi, xxv, 1, 4, 14, 16, 20, 23, 34, 35, 47, 57, 60, 63, 64, 65, 66, 68, 69, 71, 72, 73, 75, 76, 78, 80, 81, 83, 84, 86, 87, 88, 89, 91, 92, 97, 99, 100, 101, 102, 104, 105, 111, 113, 114, 115, 119, 122, 127, 129, 137, 141, 142, 146, 147, 150, 151, 153, 154, 155, 156, 164, 171, 177, 178, 180, 184, 187, 188, 189, 194, 195, 198, 199, 201, 204, 207, 212, 214, 219, 247, 248, 249, 250, 251, 252, 253, 254

Kingdom of God 11, 111

Kiswahili dictionary 60

L

Liberation 8, 36, 249

Literal iii, 141

Liturgy iii, 137

M

Majority-World church xiv
Marriage iii, 171
Millennial 146
Missionaries ii, iii, 98, 190
Missionary Christianity 33
Morality iv, 7, 25, 211, 214, 249
Music iii, 137
Muslims 58

N

Neo-colonialism 18
NGOs 8, 22

O

Oral 121, 122, 123, 131, 132, 138, 142, 147, 148, 149, 154, 159, 160, 162, 167, 171, 172, 173, 174, 175, 176, 177, 185, 188, 191, 199, 209, 252, 254

P

Pentecost 43, 81, 82, 106, 109, 111, 122, 124, 132, 133, 253
Philosophy xviii, 150, 185, 250
Pneumatology iii, 131, 136
Poverty 146, 214
Power 52, 248
Prayer 133
Preaching 146
Priesthood ii, 80
Primal religions 43
Prophetic 250
Prophets 68, 114, 142, 254

R

Race 3, 94, 249, 253
Religion ii, xi, xvii, xviii, xxi, xxv, 2, 29, 47, 51, 65, 70, 74, 75, 78, 83, 133, 150, 153, 185, 189, 204, 206, 247, 249, 250, 251, 253
Religious culture 47, 48
Renaissance 54

S

Salvation 64
Scriptures 32, 44, 46, 68, 121, 133, 136, 142, 143, 145, 192, 193, 195
Sex 92
Study xxi, 129, 148, 252
Supreme Ancestor 216
Supreme Being 204, 214

T

Taboos 177, 185, 186
Theological ii, iv, 47, 81, 113, 206, 249, 250, 253
Traditional culture 65
Transcendent 42, 43
Translatability ii, 43
Translation 52
Turban 68

U
Uganda Railway 63

V
Vernacular iii, xiv, 163, 186, 248

Vernacular Theology iii, 163, 186

W
Wedding iii, 173

Western Christianity xviii, 11

Western education 27

Western legacy 118

Western worldview 42

White paternalism 4

Wife 92

Wife sharing 92

Wisdom 248

Women 170, 176

Worldview 253

Y
Youth 254

www.ingramcontent.com/pod-product-compliance
Lightning Source LLC
Chambersburg PA
CBHW030103170426
43198CB00009B/478